Communication: A Practical Guide to School and Community Relations

COMMUNICATION

A PRACTICAL GUIDE
TO SCHOOL AND
COMMUNITY RELATIONS

G. KEITH DOLAN

CALIFORNIA STATE UNIVERSITY AT SAN BERNARDINO

Wadsworth Publishing Company
I(T)P® An International Thomson Publishing Company

Belmont • Albany • Bonn • Boston • Cincinnati • Detroit • London • Madrid • Melbourne
Mexico City • New York • Paris • San Francisco • Singapore • Tokyo • Toronto • Washington

Education Editor: Sabra Horne
Assistant Editor: Claire Masson
Editorial Assistant: Louise Mendelson
Production Services Coordinator: Debby Kramer
Production Editor: Mary Douglas/Rogue Valley Publications
Print Buyer: Karen Hunt
Permissions Editor: Jeanne Bosschart
Designer: Randall Goodall/Seventeenth Street Studios
Copy Editor: Robin Kelly
Cover Designer: Ark Stein/The Visual Group
Compositor: Susan Benoit
Printer: Quebecor Printing Book Group/Fairfield Graphics
Cover Printer: Color Dot Litho

I(T)P The ITP logo is a registered trademark under license.

This book is printed on acid-free recycled paper.

Printed in the United States of America
1 2 3 4 5 6 7 8 9 10

For more information, contact Wadsworth Publishing Company:

Wadsworth Publishing Company
10 Davis Drive
Belmont, California 94002, USA

International Thomson Publishing Europe
Berkshire House 168–173
High Holborn
London, WClV 7AA, England

Thomas Nelson Australia
102 Dodds Street
South Melbourne 3205
Victoria, Australia

Nelson Canada
1120 Birchmount Road
Scarborough, Ontario
Canada M1K 5G4

International Thomson Editores
Campos Eliseos 385, Piso 7
Col. Polanco
11560 México D.F. México

International Thomson Publishing GmbH
Königswinterer Strasse 418
53227 Bonn, Germany

International Thomson Publishing Asia
221 Henderson Road
#05-10 Henderson Building
Singapore 0315

International Thomson Publishing Japan
Hirakawacho Kyowa Building, 3F
2-2-1 Hirakawacho
Chiyoda-ku, Tokyo 102, Japan

Library of Congress Cataloging-in-Publication Data

Dolan, G. Keith
    Communication: a practical guide to school and
community relations / G. Keith Dolan.
        p.   cm.
    Includes bibliographical references and index.
    ISBN: 0-534-25086-6 (text)
    1. Community and school—United States   2. Public
relations—Schools—United States.   3. Communication in
education—United States.   I. Title.
LC221.D65   1995   95-20975
370.19'31'0973—dc20

Contents

7

INTERACTING WITH PARENTS 169

INTERACTING WITH THE COMMUNITY 201

9

INTERACTING WITH THE DISTRICT ADMINISTRATION — 229

10

WORKING WITH THE MEDIA — 257

11

EVALUATING THE SCHOOL–COMMUNITY PROGRAM 280

Preface

COMMUNICATION: A PRACTICAL GUIDE TO SCHOOL AND
COMMUNITY RELATIONS is designed for educators who are seeking
certificates, credentials, or degrees that allow them to be part of the
administrative structure of school districts. It is intended for courses
that include school–community relations as a topic or for courses
that deal solely with this aspect of administration.

School–community relations are complex and are not easy to
conduct. Inherent dangers lie in the process. Poor handling of
school–community relations can fragment the groups that comprise
the school or its district. Educators therefore need to become aware
of the political, social, and cultural realities within their communities.
They also must be prepared to meet the challenges that emerge from
the vast number of changes that take place in our society as a whole.
Educational leaders who are adept at communicating can effectively
establish and maintain dialogue and can listen well to different groups
and individuals expressing their concerns and wanting their demands
met within the school structure.

Educators help forge and maintain a vision of the role and function of the school or district within the communities they serve.
Educational leaders communicate that vision in a variety of ways.
However, they also must understand that communication is two-way.
Encouraging cooperative efforts among various constituencies and
handling conflicts when they arise are essential skills for today's
educational leaders.

Communication: A Practical Guide to School and Community Relations consists of eleven chapters that explore communication skills with a variety of groups. The first chapter gives an overview of ideal school–community relations. Chapters 2 and 3 explore politics and power and some of the demographic changes found in most communities.

Chapters 4 through 10 focus on groups or agencies that are part of the community structure, both internal and external. Chapter 11 describes briefly how to evaluate a school–community program. Although the text focuses on site-level problems that occur in a school district, the underlying principles of the text apply in other situations also. Any educator who seeks improved school–community relations may find these principles applicable.

SPECIAL FEATURES

Each chapter of this text includes the following sections to enhance the instructor's presentation and the student's learning.

- The **Chapter Objectives** lists major ideas or concepts, in sequence, for the student to think about.

- The **Chapter Outline** lists the chapter's major headings to give both the student and the teacher a preview of the organization of the chapter.

- **References** appear at the close of the chapter.

- A brief **Summary** lists the ten major concepts discussed within the chapter.

- Following the summary are five **Discussion Questions** that can be used for either oral or written class activities.

- Following the questions are five **Activities** that can be assigned to students as field work projects. Students may use the results collectively for in-depth class discussions.

- The **Case Example** can be used for small-group study, class discussion, role-play, or as a written application challenge.

Appendix A features sample letters that administrators may use in various ways to improve or maintain good relations with teachers, parents, and others. Appendix B contains lists of items commonly included in handbooks for students, teachers, and parents.

ACKNOWLEDGMENTS

I am indebted to the following manuscript reviewers for their very helpful comments and suggestions: Charles Araki, University of Hawaii; Michael J. Garanzini, S.J., St. Louis University; Mark B. Kinney, University of Toledo; Dr. Charles W. Leftwich, Fort Hays State University; Larry L. Smiley, Central Michigan University; and Dr. Marilyn Wilkes Granger, Alabama State University.

G. KEITH DOLAN

Communication: A Practical Guide to School and Community Relations

INTRODUCTION

Leadership Qualities

One current, major topic in school administration is leadership ability because it is the leader who gets things done or gets others to get things done. Leadership is particularly important when states and school districts embrace the concept of decentralization.

Historically, schools have constantly been in a state of flux, and that has continued to be true during the last decade. Dramatic demographic changes are taking place in our country, many more groups seek equal participation in school operation, the public demands stronger and better schools, and we place greater emphasis on developing a school mission based on understanding its culture.

The principal is the primary person to give leadership to an individual school, although he or she has many tasks to perform and a variety of issues to deal with. This textbook specifically focuses on a number of leadership challenges that fall into the broad category of school–community relations.

A number of leadership models and theories are discussed in the literature other than trait theory, but as Hughes[1] quoted Bennis, five characteristics comprise a leader:

1. Leaders have a strong vision of where an organization needs to go and strong orientation to established outcomes.

2. Leaders can communicate this vision to others, often using metaphors as the communication device.

3. Leaders are persistent. Because failure is viewed as an opportunity to learn, leaders can stay the course when sudden setbacks occur.

4. Leaders know their organization and find ways and means to overcome obstacles.

5. Leaders empower others and develop an environment in which workers strive for excellence. Workers are given a clear sense that they are essential to progress and goal accomplishment.

Perhaps more important than the organizational structure a leader subscribes to may be his view of his ability to lead and the perceptions those who work closely with him have of his ability to lead. Leadership is a difficult characteristic to pin down. We all know of dynamic, powerful leaders whose personality types are all different but who can lead well despite these differences. Whatever the theoretical underpinnings of the particular leader, she has a vision and plan and seems able to get the job done.

Strong leadership is required in the area of school–community relations. Successful management of the never-ending list of contacts among the site administrator, his staff, and the varied community groups, which the school serves, requires vision and plans. All contacts must be handled skillfully and professionally, which requires leadership ability.

The most positive school–community relations begin in a school's classrooms. Students who like their teachers, enjoy their daily school experiences, and feel safe at their schools naturally relay their enthusiasm to their parents who radiate positive feelings about the schools their offspring attend. Problems that negatively affect this idealized scenario, however, often arise. Students do not always succeed in school; they do not always complete homework assignments; they sometimes become behavior problems at school. Some have difficulty relating effectively with their peer group, and others do not feel protected going to, or even attending, school.

Although classroom teachers try to alleviate these potential student problems, their main task is the daily teaching act itself; thus, principals must intercede with these student concerns. This places them immediately in the center of school–community relationships, which include interacting with students, teachers, and parents as well as many other individuals and groups. The leadership of school principals is a necessary ingredient if effective schools are to be developed and maintained; it is no different with school–community relations.

Although it is not exclusively the site-level administrator's task to carry out a strong school–community relations program, she must recognize that it is an important goal of effective leadership. This administrative task, like most of the others discussed in the following pages, is not something scheduled "for the third Tuesday of each school month" or when the community is asked for funds. It is the thread, or more accurately a series of threads, that runs through the fabric of all tasks and responsibilities of the site-level administrator. Successfully interpreting a school and its programs to the diverse groups who are a part of the school and community requires serious planning for the countless contacts that will take place with these individuals and groups.

Site-Level Administrative Tasks

he principal should be able to recognize the components needed to develop a successful school–community relations program. Developing such a program cannot be left to chance. It requires planning, beginning at the site level.

The school administrator should work carefully with teachers, parents, and community organizations. He or she must be available for each of these groups. The school administrator should have good listening skills and should be able to concentrate on careful planning of routine school events, which are part of the public relations process.

WORKING WITH TEACHERS

An effective leader in the area of school–community relations develops a dedication to a workable relationship program that seeks to include all members of the school community. One primary group is, of course, the teaching staff.

Most classroom teachers are skilled in establishing and maintaining rapport with their students, but not all are as adept at working with parents, volunteers, or even their colleagues. Some teachers tend to be critical of those who challenge what is done in our schools' classrooms and are particularly sensitive to the demands and criticisms of parents.

■ TEACHER–PARENT COMMUNICATION

Most colleges and universities do an excellent job of developing in teachers the skills they need to work academically, socially, and psychologically with their students, but they do not often stress the challenges, nor the skills required, when facing a parent who is irate, who demands too much, who does not place a high value on positive group behavior, or who does not value education highly. Because the vast majority of teachers are themselves products of a middle-class environment, they may have no experience working with families who are underprivileged, who are on welfare, where the parents themselves are uneducated, or who do not value teachers and public schools.

Teachers need help in conferencing with a variety of parents—those who are upset, those who do not understand the operation of a large-sized classroom, or those who do not understand the value of their child's completion of homework on a regular basis. Teachers need to learn the skills of reaching a solution that will be beneficial to all concerned; they need to learn how to calm angry parents, and they need to learn to avoid speaking educational jargon with nonprofessionals.

Obviously, this is where skillful school leaders can contribute to the knowledge of their staffs. In-service programs focusing on telephone contacts, parent conferences, and communication strategies can be extremely helpful to teachers, particularly those who are just beginning their teaching careers or those who do not relate to other adults easily. (The selling point is, of course, that all of us are evaluated individually by parents, students, and others on a daily basis and ultimately that is how the school is judged.) For example, a fifth-grade teacher met with the parents of one of her students who was not remaining on task in the classroom and was disrupting the others. Rather than concentrating on the student's classroom issues, the teacher became emotional and said to the mother, "Your child is being rude, and his behavior is totally unacceptable. He never does his homework." The parent became defensive;

the teacher also became defensive with inappropriate body language as well. Rather than mutually attempting to solve the specifics of the situation, both became emotional, and the parent walked out of the conference. Only by the efforts of the school principal were the two able to again meet and concentrate on the student's problem rather than the overgeneralizations of the teacher.

Helping teachers with the communications they send home to parents is another task for school administrators. Although teachers possess strong academic backgrounds, not all of them have writing skills of the same quality, and some may be too blunt in what they say to parents about their children. Some excellent teachers are not as careful (or accurate) as they might be in terms of spelling and grammar, and a single error can be interpreted by the receiving parent as a sign of the quality of a school system.

Although the principal does not need to read every item sent home by every teacher during the school year, monitoring written communications, particularly those of the beginning teacher, may be wise. If the administrator has the skill to edit materials easily and accurately, this service should be offered to the teaching staff. Make clear, however, that these efforts have *nothing* to do with the job-evaluation process; teachers must feel comfortable in asking the administrator to look at some written message they are proposing to send home to the parents of their students.

As an illustration of this kind of help, consider the following example. A third-grade teacher planned a field trip to the zoo. Three of her students misbehaved during class for two or three days prior to the trip. In a written note the teacher sent home to the parents, she stated, "Your child will not be going on the field trip because he doesn't know how to behave." No explanation of what had happened accompanied the notes, so all three parents were bewildered and angry because they had not been notified of the behavior when it occurred.

The parents contacted the school principal, who then talked with the teacher. At this meeting, it was ascertained that the teacher had not contacted any of these families earlier to discuss an intervention program to help the students with their behavior patterns. It was then mutually decided that the students would be allowed to go on the trip if their mothers would also be their children's chaperons. The students were then contacted to discuss their past behaviors and what was expected of them on the trip and in the classroom in the future. Further work with the teacher resulted in earlier notification of the parents when problems arose, as well as improved accuracy and tone in her written messages.

■ TEACHER–TEACHER COMMUNICATION

Teaching has been, and still is to a great extent, an isolated profession. Teachers can shut the doors of their classrooms and work alone with the group of students assigned to that grade level or subject area. They have become masters of their own little kingdoms and, except for an occasional visit by the principal, have remained undisturbed.

However, at times teachers are called upon to work with others in curriculum development; in planning grade-level activities, or on school committees. With the advent of classroom aides, and more recently the resurgence of cooperative learning (or team teaching), teachers are required to work with others in more situations. Many teachers have made this transition from a solo act to being a member of a team with little difficulty, but professional jealousy, disagreements about assignments, misunderstandings about roles, and other conflicts have caused strained relations between teachers. Every faculty possesses a "prima donna" or two (who may indeed deserve that title), who is easily provoked, angered, or insulted. Each school may also find a few mediocre teachers (who may also deserve that designation), who are easily provoked, angered, or insulted.

There are no easy answers to working with those who have difficulty with one another. It's a natural reaction for principals to want to help the prima donnas and ignore those who are mediocre, but members of *both* categories need their attention and the very best of their problem-solving skills.

When teachers have difficulties working together, the site-level administrator must help moderate the situation. Most problems are caused by not knowing the whole story, so one of the first strategies is conveying the facts to all parties involved. At other times, it's making changes in the situation that helps both parties to be at least semisatisfied (the win–win philosophy). In still other instances, the strategy is for the administrator to absorb the criticism so that the blame is redirected from a colleague to the principal. Sometimes a step just short of martyr-dom is a useful administrative tool when a teacher's pride can be saved.

Whatever the strategy used, the principal's job is to create positive relations within as well as outside the school. Morale is an important aspect of any organization, and good relationships between working members of a staff is a major factor in maintaining positive morale. For example, two high school teachers of Spanish, both native speakers, were jealous of one another and were frequently making sarcastic remarks about the other's teaching. Much of this began with the formation of a third honors class; previously, there had been only two, and each teacher was assigned one to teach. The verbal bashing accelerated around the time of the development of the master schedule. Knowing that one of the teachers would have to be assigned two of the classes, the principal called both teachers into his office. At the meeting, he praised the contributions of both instructors, shared the problem with them, and gave them two tasks to accomplish. The first was to coopera-tively develop the curriculum for the new class, and the second was to decide between themselves who would teach the class the first time with the understanding they would alternate years. They became better acquainted during the subsequent weeks of team work, and the back stabbing ceased.

PLANNING SCHOOLWIDE PUBLIC RELATIONS

An educational leader is one who helps formulate a schoolwide action plan for school–community relations, one that will include as many community and school groups as possible. This plan needs to be flexible because it will be evaluated continuously and updated as community changes take place.

As curriculum guides require goals and objectives, so do the plans for school–community relations efforts. Ideally, such a program will involve and reach everyone, but that is somewhat unrealistic. The leader must assess what has been done in the past, determine what has been success-ful and what has not, develop plans to continue the positive compo-nents, and concentrate on the areas that need additional effort.

School–community relations, as has been suggested, is everyone's job. A major goal of all those who are involved at a school site is to raise the level of community awareness of what the school is doing and why it is doing it. Many site-level employees (teachers, aides, counselors, and administrators) will have important roles to play in this regard. In addition, outside help will be required. One often-overlooked approach in developing a plan of action is to look at the site's efforts in relationship to other district schools of the same level. These schools will have a gold mine of successful ideas, which you can use; however, keep in mind that, when developing a plan, school–community efforts do not have to be identical but should be compatible. Finally, a school principal will probably also want to develop a cadre of supportive opinion leaders who have direct access to the community groups that most need information about the school's purpose and programs.

The goals and objectives of the plan help determine the methods of communicating with the people who need to be reached. As will be discussed later, the media, newsletters, school-sponsored meetings, special events, and individual conferences are but a few of the sources that can be appropriately used.

Suppose, for example, parental contact needs to be improved; then the kinds and the nature of contact methods need to be discussed. Perhaps more individual letters can be sent or newsletters published more frequently, but these plans have to be tempered by the resources available. In times of financial limitations (and it is rare when these conditions do not exist), budgets may restrict the paper and postage available for producing and mailing newsletters. The resourceful administrator may find ways to overcome the financial barriers (donations, for example), but needed resources should be included in the developed plans.

Every school operates within the parameters of a district calendar. Carefully scrutinize this calendar for school–community relations opportunities as well as realistic deadlines. A school holiday or scheduled event can be the vehicle for a media release or parental activity, whereas anticipating key dates well in advance can upgrade the quality of the planning and the opportunities for public notification.

After the plan has been developed and at least tentatively finalized, present it to the school's employees. As indicated, all have a role in supporting these planned efforts, and they, too, need to plan. You may have to consider staff development if new techniques or approaches are to be used to support the program. Finally, discuss the responsibilities of each person so that the plan has the best chance of success.

A school leader is one who seeks creative ways to communicate with various populations, knowing that language and dialogue have to be tailored to those populations and their unique needs. This understanding of the divergent groups within the community will make the plan work.

We will discuss the standard and proven methods of communicating with parents at the school-site level in Chapter 7. But how do administrators contact those parents (or community groups), who, for whatever reasons, do not attend school functions? Answers to this broad question are unlimited if you sincerely wish to develop a communication program for all citizens.

A number of recognizable factors explain low rates of contact between schools and the home. According to Chavkin[2], these fall into three broad categories:

- Limited skills and knowledge on which to build collaboration, such as parents' lack of English fluency, lack of information on children's progress, and lack of understanding of course content; school's lack of knowledge of children's home life and lack of any efforts to reach out to these families

- Restricted opportunities for interaction, including other demands on time, obstructive organizational policies or practices, or a lack of communication skills

- Psychological and cultural barriers that might be influenced by misperceptions, intimidation, and distrust; differences in language, values, and methods of education

It is recognized at the very beginning, however, that no matter what steps school administrators take, they will not truly be in contact with every parent, but the efforts will be worthwhile because each parent that is contacted will increase overall numbers. *Making an effort is the important action in a strong school–community relations program.*

The first step is to meet with either the entire faculty, representative members of that group, the administrative team, or an ad hoc committee to collectively determine the changes that have taken place in your community. Examples might include more new homes with young parents, more foreign-born families in which English is not the primary language, more parents who have sought cheaper housing and actually work many miles from their residence (and school), or a major change in the ethnic makeup of the community.

Whatever the observed community changes, include these groups as part of the school family. Establish a program of two-way communication so that newcomers will feel free to share their concerns about the educational program for their children, volunteer to be a part of the school program, or take part in the traditional school programs.

Teachers and others who have helped delineate the community changes will also be able to offer suggestions concerning how to involve these parents. Such creative ideas will help pave the way for future communication by those who make up a particular school. Here are five suggestions that may help the school staff in developing such a plan:

1. *Meet with parents in their homes.* Organize the meetings by geographic areas where different configurations exist, such as immigrants and ethnic groups. Hold these meetings in the evening or on weekends and include an interpreter if one is needed.

2. *Use community churches.* A local minister will know, for example, whether a group of parents, who always attends the same Sunday school class or participates in other church functions, might want to spend time sharing ideas with the principal of their children's school.

3. *Hold Saturday workshops.* Give parents opportunities to ask general questions about the operation of the school (for example, the district's curriculum) or specific questions about their children's education. Such efforts could even develop into a series of meetings.

4. *Organize a speaker's bureau.* Have volunteer faculty, members of the administrative team, and students visit various community groups to talk about what's taking place at the school. A particular focus could be the new organizations of the changing community.

5. *Publish bilingual newsletters.* Provide to families from other nations where English is not the primary language an effective means of communication in the native language. For example, ask the people whether they want a native-language newsletter or a bilingual newsletter.

Leadership requires an educator to not only be available to teachers, parents, and other groups but also be willing and able to communicate with all of them. Communication cannot take place unless an obvious willingness to meet is evident.

No principal can be available 24 hours a day; however, carrying out the leadership required for a strong school–community relations atmosphere occasionally demands time other than the traditional eight-to-five workday. Some parents work hours beyond the school's closing and sometimes many miles away from the city where they reside; meeting with those parents to solve a complex school problem might be well worth the principal's inconvenience.

Do not construe this approach as nightly attendance at the school site, but some schools in a number of states designate one night a month for call-ins from interested parents and others. Other school districts allocate evening hours for parent–teacher conferences, as well as the traditional afternoon sessions. Inaugurating such a program requires faculty agreement, as well as some negotiations with teachers' unions.

This same operational belief undergirds my feeling about maintaining a listed phone number. During my years as a site-level administrator, parents could always reach me. For all the years I was a middle and high school principal, there was no noticeable abuse of my availability, and those who did call usually had questions or information that was invaluable to school operation.

In at least one instance, however, the call seemed somewhat irrelevant: At 2 A.M. one Saturday morning, I received a call from a frantic parent. The caller's daughter had returned from a date and had confessed that she had sex with her boyfriend during the evening. The girl's father, who was also a neighbor, wanted to know what I was going to do about the situation. At that time of the morning, it was difficult to think of a logical answer for a rather disturbed parent, but it wouldn't have been any easier if the call had taken place 12 hours earlier! With some assurances that I would come over to see him the next morning (which I fortunately remembered to do), the call was completed, and I returned to bed. Rather an odd call but, under the circumstances, perhaps understandable.

Everyone wants to be heard, and as the appointed leader of a school, the principal is on the "most wanted" list for hearing about old problems, new problems, and the perhaps possible future problems. The best strategy? Listen, take notes of relevant data, lead these individuals toward formulating their own solutions or plans of action, and as a last resort, promise to get back to them at a later time. This time lapse lets you gather additional information, seek advice from others, and think about the problem. *It is important, however, to keep your promise and get back to the individual or group who sought your advice in the first place.*

These demands for an educator's time by others will often interrupt what was a well-developed agenda of scheduled activities. These demands on a leader's time, however, are all part of the positive school–community relations you are trying to establish at the school. A satisfied parent, teacher, or student is one of the best public relations ambassadors a school can have. Each will tell others about how skillfully his or her problems or requests were handled (at least that's the theory!).

Some activities, of course, will take precedence over these requests. Working on a master schedule, interviewing a prospective teacher candidate, meeting with a grade level or department, or conducting a classroom observation are all scheduled events that shouldn't be interrupted except under the greatest of emergencies. Most people will understand and accept the explanation (or that of the principal's secretary) about why the principal is not available at that exact moment, particularly if he has a reputation for being willing to talk with people and make efforts to schedule a meeting for another time.

WORKING WITH ORGANIZATIONS

Educational leaders need to work cooperatively with a variety of organizations, which include the board of education, the district office, teachers' unions, and community special-interest groups, along with many others. The list is endless, but these four groups are representative. Perhaps the most obvious strategy is to work carefully with the first three groups (because community special-interest groups are discussed in more detail in Chapter 3, we cover them only briefly here).

■ THE BOARD OF EDUCATION

Members of the board and site-level administrators usually do not meet often unless their children attend their schools. Those elected or appointed individuals, however, have legal control over the policies and operating procedures of the district. As custodians of the public trust, they need to know the operating status of all schools within the district.

Board members are the collective "boss" of the entire organization. Principals do not usually directly report to the board, but the policies they must follow stem from the philosophy of that group. Principals are therefore expected to carry out the directions and policies of the school board. Most boards understand the need for flexibility: Site-level administrators should operate schools as conditions might warrant, but they also should be consistent in the handling of situations embodied in those policies.

At times, principals see their schools as being unique and feel some adopted policies do not apply to their schools. This is dangerous ground indeed! When policies have been decided by the district or the board, a principal should avoid developing her own separate set of rules. The conflicts that have arisen in these matters, however, have helped bring about site-based management. This approach allows more decisions to be made at the individual building level, but it does not rule out the legal role of the board in such matters.

■ THE DISTRICT OFFICE

The district office can create a wealth of demands, as well as being a major resource for help. For the most part, those who have been selected to be part of the central staff have also served as site-level administrators and understand the problems faced at schools. When an unreasonable request or too short a deadline for a response is given, talk with your immediate supervisor and seek a clarification or another deadline. Chances are you will be given good advice and a time extension. This helps create the image of a team player rather than simply a "loose cannon."

Obviously, the goal of any school principal is to work cooperatively with district-level personnel. Cooperation sometimes involves interpretation of new policies or the reasons that something must be done a particular way. Teachers and others are sometimes suspicious of those who work at the district level because those people are, in their eyes, far removed from the classroom. Rumors often abound about what "they" (district personnel) are doing or why "they" are doing it.

The principal's role is thus one of clarifying the situation for the teaching staff, support personnel, and parents. These efforts will often negate overreactions to issues and help stabilize morale. If the district office develops a new policy that needs clarification, rather than interpreting the policy to those who need to know, the principal could invite the author(s) to attend a faculty meeting (or other appropriate gathering) to explain the policy and its possible ramifications.

Get involved with as many district planning committees as your time allows. These committees often make changes that directly affect your students, faculty, and programs; the closer you are to reliable information, the fewer problems you will confront later. You will become better acquainted with the districtwide staff and expand your understanding of the decisions made at that level.

Sometimes a principal will encounter an unreasonable stance on the part of a district-level administrator. Be clever instead of facing the person head-on. (You may win the battle but not the war!) For example, once I had a request from my faculty to replace a set of 26-hole folders, which had been issued to all district teachers, with a set of three-ring binders, which would ease the process of inserting and removing the monthly attendance sheets. Because it seemed like a reasonable request, an order for 150 replacement folders was submitted to the district office on the regular supply form. For some reason, the assistant superintendent red-inked the order and after subsequent discussion refused to change his decision even though ample supply funds were available.

It did not seem to be an event to argue further about and certainly not one to go over the assistant superintendent's head. Because one of my vice-principals was to be the summer school principal that year, it was far simpler to have him order the 150 three-ring folders for the summer session; the transaction was thus completed. The assistant superintendent never discovered this strategy. It was somewhat underhanded, perhaps, but no one was hurt by the charade. No negative feelings developed between the two of us, and the entire teaching staff had their request honored.

Teachers' unions have gotten stronger and have made great inroads on what was exclusively the turf of the site-level administrator in the past. So what? Representatives of these groups can be as obstinate and unrealistic as the mythical (or perhaps real-life) administrators they often attack in their professional newsletters, but the purposes of these organizations are defensible: They seek better salaries, better fringe benefits, and better working conditions for their members, as well as higher-quality teaching for the students. Who can disagree with these worthy goals?

School administrators *are* in a different position than teachers and may not always remember how difficult it is to face a group of students (or in secondary schools, several such groups) for more than 180 days a year. The events occurring in a school, which are seen differently by diverse participants, can be compared to the plot in the outstanding Japanese film *Rashomon*. This award-winning production depicted a single event from the divergent views of the three major characters. Although the event was the same for each individual, each interpreted it based on his or her own desires, beliefs, and needs.

Avoid confrontations with representatives of the unions. They have rights, which are spelled out by state mandates or district contracts, and responsible principals should aid them in their exercising of those rights. Teachers have the right to ask for help from their union representatives for a variety of grievances, and school principals must accept this as a fact of academic life.

A final word for the school-site administrator: Unions are not the "enemy." Unions may have weak leadership at times; if it is obvious to the principal, however, it will also be obvious to the teachers electing or hiring that leadership, which can be replaced. Although a principal might tend to take advantage or ignore the organization while it is weak, it will be strong at another time in the future, and the "temporary advantage" may be a liability because the principal's attitude is not forgotten.

Unions also represent *all* teachers on the faculty and the entire district—the weak as well as the strong. Most principals know who their best teachers are and are appreciative of the work done by them over the years. Deliberately referring to their organization in a negative manner will harm relationships with those faculty members. Being open, honest, willing to deal with issues with union representatives are the appropriate tactics of dealing with teachers and their union.

■ COMMUNITY SPECIAL-INTEREST GROUPS

Community special-interest (pressure) groups come and go, and all can cause one's temperature to rise, even when their goals are completely in line with those of the school site or district. *All* pressure groups require a site-level administrator's undivided attention. Some are fleeting groups of individuals who have only a one-item agenda; others are fixtures of a community and will still be making their dislikes known long after the current students, faculty, and administration have graduated or retired.

A site-level administrator cannot afford to ignore these groups, because educational history reports cases in which such groups have caused major disruptions to the public schools. Sincere groups of citizens have attacked individual schools and districts about books used in the classroom, sex education, and "Godless education." These emotional crusades have generally reaped more headlines than substantive changes in programs, but they have cost school districts and personnel thousands of hours of time, thus money. As reported in *Time* magazine,

> *Teachers in districts where the religious right has gained a strong voice complain that politicking and endless debates over curriculum impede their work. In Xenia, Ohio, two religious conservatives on the five-member school board tie up meetings with arguments against self-esteem programs (Weaken respect for parents!) and sex education (Undermines abstinence!).*[3]

On the other hand, groups of parents and other citizens have fought hard to improve schools by adding important programs or challenging undesirable school conditions. Some of these groups have focused on a single issue but others, like the PTA, have sought to improve school programs every year of their existence. Not as outspoken or as militant as other organizations, they have nevertheless quietly influenced legislatures to adopt hundreds of bills that have had impact on the nation's public schools.

School leaders must be willing to listen carefully to parents' point of view and make every effort to understand and accept those views; however, they must stand firm if the school is basing decisions on logical and realistic decisions. This is where the skills of conflict management (see Chapter 5) will be of immense value.

Most experienced administrators understand that many parents are uninformed, or at least only partially informed, when they confront teachers and/or the principal about something regarding their children or a group of children they represent. Parents have the right, however, to ask questions; at times, they have reasonable concerns and recommendations. For example, parents of elementary school children often misunderstand the reasons for their children's placement in a combination class and will call the superintendent (even board members) before the principal can explain the reasons. Middle school and high school parents will demand that their children be placed in second-period algebra (so the child can be with his closest friend) without the understanding of what a *single* change can do to a master schedule.

The site administrator must handle all of these verbal misgivings professionally. Most often, parents will not have all the facts and must be tactfully informed about what took place or what the school program is attempting to do; at other times, parents may be partially correct in their feelings, and a compromise needs to be reached. Although districts, schools, and teachers develop policies that seem logical in the abstract, they may not always seem as defensible when viewed in the light of a single case. *It is important that parents understand that something is being done to help their child before scheduling a conference.*

Some parents try to overwhelm, some try to threaten, and some seek to cast blame; all are frustrated because their offspring are not measuring up to what they (and the school) think the children ought to be— academically, socially, or psychologically. Principals, their only hope at that moment, need to help parents agree on a set of strategies that may improve the problem.

It is indeed rare when a single parental conference will create a "born-again" student, but these efforts can start to make a difference. At least the partnership has been forged and the door opened to further collaboration. What you must not do is develop a tendency to placate parents because they are who they are. Generally, teachers are right in what they have said or done, and students do things at school differently than they do when at home. Surrendering to a parent, based on fear of what the parent might do ("I'm going to the superintendent or to the board" are two favorite threats), is not being realistic or helpful to the child. What's more, it will soon develop into a major morale problem for the staff. Obviously, when parents are correct about their concerns, something must be done to remedy the situation. This can be done quietly, behind the scenes, so that the teacher does not look bad publicly. However, the most important strategy for the principal to use is to consider what is best for the child in the long run.

PLANNING ROUTINE SCHOOL EVENTS

The school leader develops skills for herself and in others so that routine school events do not become burdensome for the faculty or boring for the parents and are of sufficient quality that they enhance the school's image in terms of its vision. All scheduled events need to be carefully planned so that there are as few "glitches" as possible.

Someone once said that great athletes make it look easy; that same description fits the successful administrator—by judicious planning, school activities can be made to look easy. New events or programs obviously take additional planning because you cannot always anticipate what to expect the first time around. Planning repeated school-sponsored activities, however, should improve each year they are held. Keeping a file on each event—which lists tasks and time lines before, during, and following the particular activity—is one way to ensure a successful undertaking. Each year as new ideas or problems are encountered, add notes to the folder for the next go-around.

The opening and closing of school are two events occurring each school year. How students and their parents are greeted and given help the first day they come to the school makes a lasting impression. Extra clerical personnel, either paid staff or volunteers, should be available if the school usually faces a large new enrollment. Brochures with answers to the most common parental questions—key school-year dates, times for the beginning and ending of the school day, bus schedules, and costs of school lunches, for example—can be distributed to parents as they bring their offspring to enroll or to the students themselves if they are on their own.

The date for the closing of school is usually known by everyone long before summertime, but schedules of summer school (if one is held), community recreational programs, and the beginning of the next school year is information that can be distributed to students and their parents. Teachers also need to know the step-by-step process of checking out, and they need schedules for the final days of the school year.

For some schools, graduation is another event of singular importance. Although all levels of schools may hold a culminating activity, graduation from high school is highly important to seniors. Some schools have experienced unacceptable behavior by the students at these ceremonies. If this has been, or is rumored to be, a problem in the community, a strong principal needs to talk with the graduating class long before the night in question to discuss appropriate behavior. He then must be prepared to act swiftly if inappropriate behavior occurs.

A materials list should be available for those planning the event. For example, some years ago at a high school graduation in Kansas, the senior class president had 5000 spectators stand for the flag salute, and there was no flag on the stage! Fortunately, he had the presence of mind to continue the pledge, and probably most of the audience did not even notice the missing flag. However, a checklist with the flag as one of its listed items would have avoided the problem.

Other annual activities—including open house, back-to-school night or grade-level/department meetings—need to be planned so every part of the gathering (invitations, programs, classrooms, and materials) are ready for the parents when they attend. Lists of ideas for teachers on how to prepare their rooms can help; in-service programs might be used if there are a number of neophyte teachers.

Before the storm arrives, develop alternative plans for inclement weather. Anticipate such mundane items as directing parents who don't know their children's room numbers, posting the location of lost and found, and covering empty classrooms where teacher presence is not required so that the school puts its best foot forward.

Finally, there are the publications created by a school to raise the level of understanding about its programs and activities. Schools do not often have their own printing facilities; whether they have it done at school or by a commercial printer, the quality of the product should not detract from the school's image. These communications can be in a variety of formats: monthly school bulletins, letters, news releases, or an annual newsletter for a particular grade level, program, or department. They must be accurate in both content and language; a misspelled word or grammatical error can be seized by critics as "typical" of the school or school system. A gifted proofreader is therefore a must!

Although an attractive logo and format may not say much about the school's academic program, it does say a great deal about how you and your staff feel about the school. No publication should be released without being thoroughly scrutinized for both errors and attractiveness.

Budget limitations may determine the kinds and quantity of publications, but make efforts to reach those who are your loyal school supporters—those who volunteer at the school or hold key positions in your community organizations and, of course, the parents of your students. Most parents are loyal to their communities and to the schools their children attend. Reminding them of the good things taking place at the school helps strengthen school–community relations.

CONCLUSION

These seven examples are only a sampling of the influence of a strong leader in shaping school–community relations. Though it still includes "selling" the school to the public, this approach involves a much broader concept than that. A continual, multifaceted approach, it involves all who are a part of a school's operation and includes working within the school as well as out. It includes the parents and other citizens in the community and affects relationships with board members, district personnel, and the various groups operating within the total school community. Above all else, it includes the students whom we teach.

Understanding is perhaps the key word in the process, and that implies understanding is a two-way street. The individuals and groups that we as school administrators come in contact with are entitled to know what we are doing and why. On the other hand, we need to understand their concerns, both individually and collectively. By concentrating on this two-way exchange, joint understanding can occur.

1. School-community relations is a never-ending list of contacts with a varied group, all of whom need to be handled skillfully and professionally. These contacts begin in the classrooms (the students) but include many other groups such as teachers, parents, and other community members.

2. It is not exclusively the principal's task to carry out a strong school–community relations program, but she must provide the leadership. It is cooperatively developing a school–community relations program that teachers and other school personnel can understand and embrace.

3. A master plan of goals and objectives must be developed for a school–community relations program to improve. Teachers, parents, and others can help identify the strengths of the past and the needs of the future.

4. All school-site members should be dedicated to a workable school–community relations program. Morale is usually higher when others feel positive about the school, so the goals should be accepted by the majority.

5. A skillful school administrator must help his teaching staff improve its communication skills. Not all teachers have the same ability to communicate with students, parents, or each other, so in-service programs may be helpful. To gain a win–win result, other techniques, such as individual counseling or "buddy" teachers, can solve communication problems.

6. A site-level administrator must be available to a variety of groups both within and outside the school. Leadership requires contacts with others, so make efforts to be available as often as possible.

7. A site-level administrator needs to work cooperatively with the board of education, the district office, teachers' unions, and community pressure groups. These and other groups are part of a principal's constituency, so make efforts to recognize their needs and aspirations.

8. Although parental opinions and reactions are important, the school principal must know when to stand firm on issues. Parents are not always right because they do not always have all facts about a situation. On the other hand, they are not always wrong, so investigation is a key technique for the principal to use.

9. Plan routine school activities carefully so that problems are avoided and the school presents a good image. Parents, students, and others may make generalized judgments based on only one poorly planned event or program.

10. Materials sent to the various publics need to be of the highest quality possible so that the school's image is not tarnished. Proofing for spelling, grammar, and tone of all materials released to the public is a must for a high-quality image.

DISCUSSION QUESTIONS

1. What are the strengths and weaknesses of the school–community relations program at your school? How do you think the weaknesses could be improved?

2. Think of an incident you have observed during your teaching career in which a teacher used poor judgment with a parent or a group of parents. Indicate how the situation was handled and how you would have dealt with it if you had been the principal.

3. What kinds of conflicts have you observed between teachers or a school staff? How have these conflicts affected faculty morale? Did the school administration successfully intercede in these problems? How?

4. Is your school principal available to various school and community groups? What evidence have you used to make these determinations?

5. Is your teachers' association or union strong? Does it work closely or at cross-purposes with site-level administrators? Why do you think these conditions exist?

1. Interview your site administrator. Determine his or her role in the school–community relations picture and the roles of others on the staff in his or her opinion. Share, compare, and discuss the results of all interviews.

2. Collectively make a list of educational terms that we use professionally but may not be understood by parents and others. Present this list to a group of your school parents to see if they do understand them.

3. Make a list of the strongest pressure groups affecting the schools in your

THIS SIDE OUT

The year had begun well at Elm School. Considering the fact that almost one-third of the attending students were new to the district, the first few days had been easy for everyone involved. Principal Bill Johnson had been to visit all of his new teachers' classrooms and had spent part of each day since the opening of school on the grounds, talking with students.

On the second Wednesday of September, Johnson received calls from two of the new parents voicing their concerns about the science curriculum, especially the chapters about boy and girl

sexual relationships. Noting their questions, he reviewed the two chapters in the textbook himself, talked with all teachers at that grade level, and even sought the advice of Dr. Ruth Brookhart, the district's newly appointed assistant superintendent of curriculum.

He returned the two parents' calls and reassured them about the text, the approaches the teachers were going to use in their handling of the two chapters, and the procedures followed when adopting the materials that were being questioned. After his calls, he was convinced community. Ask your principal to do the same. Compare the two lists. If there are some differences, explain.

4. Select a common school activity held at the schools of your fellow students (open house, for example). Ask each of your site-level administrators to see the "check-off" list for the event. Compare the lists and create a class list for future use.

5. Interview your site-level administrator concerning a demanding parent that he or she had to "stand up" to and ask what technique worked to make the parent at least accept the decision. Share the skill with your fellow students.

that the concerns had been alleviated and was pleased that everything had gone as smoothly as it apparently had.

This week has been another story! The teachers reached the chapters about sexual relationships, and the phone has not stopped ringing. Ten different parents have called voicing their concerns about the teaching of sexual topics in a public school. Some have even called him several times. Despite his defense of the program to the callers, a number of them have threatened to go over his head to the superintendent, the board of education, or even further. Johnson knows that something has to be done to quell the concerns of the parents; he also realizes that nothing less than the actual shelving of the books or dropping the unit study would satisfy them.

The assistant superintendent has been adamant in her defense of the textbook adoption and has voiced little sympathy about the school problem. The teachers, sensing that their professional integrity is being challenged, have contacted their local union. Eric Sanders, the chapter president, has called to indicate that he hopes Johnson "Will back his teaching staff." Then today, the president of the school board dropped by to share her concerns. It seems that a number of the critics have contacted her and she knows that Johnson "will do the right thing to avoid a major problem within the district."

Various community groups are taking sides about the issue, and Johnson is caught in the middle. He knows he cannot satisfy all those involved who hold such divergent views, but obviously something has to be done. Just what choice to make is his major concern.

REFERENCES

1. Larry W. Hughes, ed., *The Principal as Leader* (New York: Macmillan College Publishing, 1995), p. 15.

2. N. F. Chavkin, ed., *Families and Schools in a Pluralistic Society* (New York: State University of New York Press, 1993).

3. Jill Smolowe, "Crusade for the Classroom," *Time* 142, no. 18 (1 November 1993):35.

DISCUSSION ISSUES

Past

1. What additional steps should Johnson have taken after he received the initial two calls? Did he communicate properly with the two parents?

2. Evaluate the tactics Johnson used after getting additional calls. What additional ones might have been utilized?

3. How much is a principal expected to know about the textbooks and other materials used by classroom teachers? Did Johnson receive appropriate guidance from his teachers? The assistant superintendent?

4. How representative are the "ten different parents" of the entire school? Should that have made a difference in Johnson's thinking?

5. Is the suggestion to "not make waves" a realistic one from the board president? Should that be a factor in the ultimate decision?

Present

1. Where does Johnson's allegiance lie? With the parents, the district, the teachers? Does a principal have to decide on the basis of these pressure groups?

2. After a final decision is made, what should Johnson do about working with the board, the union, his teaching staff, and parents in the future?

3. Do other parents need to be informed of the controversy regarding the science materials? If so, how should this be handled?

4. There may be other teaching materials challenged by parents. How can these problems be anticipated? Avoided?

5. What steps should Johnson take for the following year to avoid repetition of this event? Explain.

EDUCATION, POLITICS, AND POWER

History of the Modern School System

Our founding fathers did not mention education in the Constitution of the United Sates, but politics has always been involved with the teaching of the nation's youth: "Education and politics are intertwined and political values are built into the rules and structures of schools. Decision making structures ensure that certain values will prevail."[1] Thomas Jefferson, an outspoken proponent of public education, believed a strong link existed between educating the masses and the survival of a democratic government. Convinced that education was "an effective handmaiden to effective citizenship," Jefferson also claimed that the vitality of the nation's spirit would not improve without the "refurbished commitment by educated people to public probity and to the public interest."[2]

The role of education in American society has been frequently scrutinized and debated. Following the American Revolution, many educational ideas were proposed about how schools were to be organized and what their content would be. Despite differences in approaches, all emphasized the use of education as a means of unifying a diverse population, which included an array of languages, cultures, and religions.

The structure of the modern American school system was laid during the 1830s and 1840s, the period known as the **common**

school movement: "What was different about the common school movement was the establishment and standardization of state systems of education designed to achieve specific public policies."[3] This concept of education was to serve distinct social and political goals:

> *Three distinctive aspects of the common school movement made it different from past educational developments. The first was an emphasis on educating all children in a common schoolhouse. The second important aspect of the common school movement was the idea of using schools as an instrument of government policies. The third distinctive feature of the common school movement was the creation of state agencies to control local schools.*[4]

This common school movement created the structure for the modern school system, which was born from the political and social concerns existing at that time:

> *Politically, the success of the common school movement represents the victory of one political philosophy over another. Most individuals who worked for a common school system believed that government should play an active role in assuring the success of the economic and social system and that this was best achieved by centralizing and standardizing governmental processes.*[5]

Because the goal was to create a system of common schooling, a method was needed to achieve it. Centralization, which ensures uniformity of practices, thus brought about a bureaucratic system for standardization. By the late nineteenth century, the bureaucratic organization of the typical school system was made up of the following elements:

1. A hierarchy with a superintendent at the top and orders flowing from the top to the bottom of the organization

2. Clearly defined differences in roles of superintendent, principals, assistant principals, and teachers

3. Schools in which students progressively moved from one grade to another

4. A graded course of study for the entire school system to ensure uniformity in teaching of all grades in the system

5. An emphasis on rational planning, order, regularity, and punctuality.[6]

Government Influence on the Educational System

FEDERAL AND STATE GOVERNMENTS

istorically, the federal government has not attempted to administer elementary or secondary schools, with the exception of the schools for children of military personnel stationed overseas. It has not focused on education's shortcomings during the past century except for specific legislative measures: "Federal opportunities to initiate and implement reforms are largely confined to appropriating funds with strings attached; the strings are doing whatever the federal government decides school districts must do to get the money. In this way, the federal funds can be used to achieve a desired reform."[7]

This involvement has achieved some specific objectives—for example, education of the disadvantaged and disabled, vocational education, and scientific education. These were particularly prevalent during the 1950s when extensive federal involvement in education came about after the launching of the Soviet satellite *Sputnik I* and the accompanying concern that our schools were inferior to those of the Soviet Union. Obviously, these measures have affected the curricula of the schools and student educational choices.

Based on the Tenth Amendment to the Constitution, the delivery of education is a state government responsibility. To accomplish this goal, a system of state boards of education headed by superintendents of education was established: "Every state has a state department of education, headed by a state superintendent of instruction. These departments vary enormously in structure, resources, authority, prestige and just about every other meaningful criterion that can be applied to a governmental agency."[8]

State government legislatures also have a major effect on the schools because they pass laws that state departments of education must enforce. Every state has educational codes, which include hundreds of prescriptions and prohibitions. More important, through taxing systems, state legislatures allocate the funds for the financing of schools. During America's educational history, local property taxes have been the main source of revenue for schools; starting in the 1980s, however, many states passed legislative measures to place caps on this form of taxation. This has rekindled the controversies over the need for fairness and efficient use of the funds collected for educational purposes.

State legislators are bombarded with bills concerning the educational process. Special-interest groups—including interested citizens, lobbyists, administrative organizations, teachers' unions, and others—initiate many of these bills. Unfortunately, legislators do not have time to study all proposals adequately: "In addition to staff deficiencies, the legislators themselves find it difficult to devote much time to education. A recent study revealed that a majority of legislators identified as educational leaders devoted less than 25% of their time to education."[9]

What is being taught, who is teaching it, who goes to school and for how long, what textbooks and materials will be used, and who will pay for the ever-increasing costs are all issues concerning education; all have been debated and formalized within the political arena. At the national level, for example, educational task forces have given direction to the requirement of compulsory education as well as the curricula of the schools. In addition, Congress has debated and passed specific requirements into laws. Some examples include the following:

- Saluting the flag at school

- Singing the national anthem

- Removing "un-American" books from school libraries

- Dismissing teachers who hold views incompatible with national beliefs (loyalty oaths)

- Issuing block grants

Although we will not examine all of the preceding examples, the first one illustrates the political movements that have taken place. Prior to World War II, one's arm was extended toward the flag following the words "I pledge allegiance to the flag . . . ," but that physical movement was eliminated because some people felt that it was too much like the Nazi salute. In 1954, despite the separation of church and state, the words "under God" were added to the pledge. This patriotic exercise may not be considered a major aspect of our total educational process, but it nevertheless serves as a reminder that politics has influenced the activities of the nation's classrooms.

Ample evidence indicates that politics has also dictated the curriculum. During both world wars, for example, a greater emphasis has been placed on physical education for students attending secondary schools. When young men (and women) began failing the physical tests for induction into the armed services, politicians pushed for greater attention to individual exercise and fitness programs. Although that emphasis is obviously still of value, there does not seem to be a "national need" during times of peace, and the political demands have all but disappeared.

Beyond these examples of specific requirements, landmark Supreme Court decisions have politically influenced, as well as changed, schools at all levels. *Brown vs. Topeka* (Fourteenth Amendment), *Tinker vs. Des Moines Independent Community School District* (First Amendment), *Goss vs. Lopez* (Fourteenth Amendment), and *Wood vs. Strickland* (Civil Rights Act of 1971) are but four of the major decisions of the past three decades. The rulings for three of these cases were based on the First and Fourteenth amendments to the U.S. Constitution. These amendments serve as both political and legal limitations of government power in favor of individual freedom. Therefore, not surprisingly, some Court decisions have evoked disagreement from different segments of the U.S. population.

States have exerted political influence as well and have passed laws for financial aid for students who are disadvantaged, disabled, non-English speaking, or gifted, beyond financing the programs for all other students. States have also had a major impact on the building of schools, the certification of their teachers, and the housing of the pupils, as well as many other lesser aspects of our educational systems.

Although federal and state political structures have obviously influenced education, no national program of education is in place. As Kirst points out,

> There is no single central control point, but rather a fragmented collection of policy makers beyond the local school board: Congress, state legislatures, and the courts; outside interest such as the Educational Testing Service, the Ford Foundation, the Council for Basic Education, or the Council for Exceptional

Children; local internal interests, such as vocational education coordinators; and local external agencies, such as the police and the health services. All of these have an impact upon education policy.[10]

With the criticisms of the past three decades came a variety of suggestions of how to improve the nation's schools, and innovation became a consistent theme in school reform:

Federal, state and district policy makers have tried an enormous variety of policy tactics to bring about school and classroom level change. Virtually every major sub-system—programs, curricula, assessment, governance, management, finance, facilities design—has been subjected to direct intervention. The results, restructuring advocates seem to insist, have been disruption and contradiction rather than improved productivity.[11]

The political environment of education has also undergone critical change in the last two decades. Three major trends are important to note as we move into the twenty-first century: the changing roles of the federal and state governments in education policy; the growing political and programmatic fragmentation of education; and the re-emergence of non-education interests, particularly business, into the educational policy arena.[12]

LOCAL GOVERNMENTS

Political movements and pressures at the national and state levels, however, are beyond the influence of the typical site-level administrator. These actions have had immeasurable effects on schools and school districts, and there will be others in the future. All educators must stay abreast of new political movements, as well as adhere to mandates. Therefore, because this chapter is primarily devoted to the politics of a local district, the remainder of it will focus on that aspect of our political society.

With more than 15,500 separate and distinct school districts in the nation, as many diverse sets of political influences exist as there are districts. Employees, particularly teachers and administrators, are generally hired because they are seen to support the educational beliefs of the local school board; they remain employed as long as they continue to implement board policies. Although the educational background and certification requirements are mandated by state laws, the criteria for a particular community may differ widely. Discrimination is illegal, but some biases creep into hiring practices. For example, having a college degree from a particular institution may be a deciding factor by a local district, and some districts may require an advanced degree for certain positions, even though the degree may not have a direct bearing on the position.

The site-level administrator, as well as his teaching staff, has a unique political role in the community. The board creates policies that teachers and the principal must carry out, but parents and other community members expect and often demand more. The site-level administrator is expected to observe and react to often conflicting public desires for the schools. An example of this is dress codes, particularly where they define gang-related apparel, which many district boards have adopted. At some elementary and secondary schools, parents argue that the jackets or shirts they have bought for their children are not gang-affiliated and their youngsters should be allowed to wear them. Conversely, some parents feel the dress code does not go far enough and further restrictions are needed. The principal must then defend the general policy in relation to specific instances, and solutions for one group of parents may not be accepted by another.

The Community Power Structure

The leadership structure of the community is not always obvious. Because a community is composed of many diverse groups, there are also many centers of power: "[The] analysis of the community power structures is the analysis of how power is exercised and under what conditions power is compatible with particular political and moral goals." [13]

Community power can be held by a variety of people. Land developers, businesspeople, elected officials, industrialists, neighborhood organizations, ethnic groups, and feminists are just a few of the groups who will have a say about community policy making. Although diverse models of community power can be evaluated, we will briefly discuss only three. The first is **orthodox pluralism,** a model in which one person may hold more than one position or office at the same time.

> *Most pluralists regard elected representatives—especially mayors—as the most powerful actors in community decision making. But Dahl (in* Who Governs?*) also recognized that, within their policy domains, economic notables and bureaucrats (such as school administrators and the directors of urban development agencies) have considerable power.* [14]

Elite theory, another view, posits a small group of economic and social notables—the wealthy or persons considered the most prestigious in the community—dominates community policy making. According to some authorities, however, even here there are two levels: the front-stage and backstage settings for social behavior. The front stage may reflect the financial power of local elites (buildings, holdings, positions), but back stage (country clubs, private clubs) is where the elite may propose and discuss different courses of action. [15]

Adherents of **institutional politics,** the third model of community power, believe that the processes already in place (Congress, schools, and boards of education) have the broadest effect on decision making and problem solving. Institutional politics is based on these institutions having a public mission and a hierarchically organized leadership.

To discover where the power lies and how it is used would require a close look at all groups (social, financial, and so on) and their members. In doing so, we would find that some leaders control the financial aspects of the community; others are the political movers; and others, referred to as the "old money" or the "old guard," may no longer be active in either of these two power areas but still may have influence behind the scenes. [16]

To discover who these people might be, a principal does not have to conduct a sociological study of her community. Making a series of observations (or asking the district's superintendent) of the organizations and informal groupings within the school district will indicate how people are organized for professional, business, social, political, educational, and civic pursuits. Within these categories, some individuals will hold formal or informal positions of leadership, with varying degrees of power. By completing such an informal survey, the site-level administrator will become acquainted with the people who, because of their training, knowledge, position, or wealth, hold positions of influence and therefore are valuable resources for the educational system in general and school programs in particular.

Power is not organizations, businesses, or professional groups; it is the people who lead these particular groups and exercise the power mandated by their memberships. Although we do not understand how a person derives leadership qualities, we know that he or she has it. Similarly, we know what power is, but we cannot measure it. *What we cannot do is ignore it.*

The site-level administrator need not concern himself with the hows and whys of these leaders' power but should be aware of these individuals' influence within the school district. The knowledge of the existing power structure is information that can be used as a guide for planning and support for possible changes.

Kaufman and Jones state the reason that knowing the power structure is important: "There are those who believe that the major scientific test for demonstrating the existence of power in leadership requires a negative demonstration—that the same policy results would *not* have been obtained if the alleged power-holders did not exist, took no action or took different action."[17] It therefore behooves the site-level administrator to involve those who hold power within the community, especially when community-affecting changes are being considered.

According to some sociology and political science studies, a relatively small group of citizens cause things to happen in most communities. Thus, in many towns, these individuals have the power to control key decisions within those communities. This "power elite" is composed of high-status community members and, through a variety of methods, causes others to think or act along the same lines. Generally, the influence of the power elite is within a single area, so different individuals are found to influence different groups. Communities and their leaders, however, are under direct influence of organizations and institutions that have more power or influence than the local city or town, so they may not be as threatening as first assumed. In addition, those in positions of power belong to numerous agencies and interest groups that compete for both their time and influence. However, although a common focus does not exist and these individuals may not directly influence the operation and functioning of schools, they usually know each other and thereby have the potential of influencing one another and possibly the schools.

A school principal, however, cannot align herself with all of the power groups about school issues; not only would that be impossible to do, but it could also force a weak administrative style upon the site administrator. Principals should know which leaders are potential political advocates for strong schools and perhaps include them in the decision-making process. They can be not only critical but also supportive of schools. If educational controversies involving the community arise, these leaders might be valuable members of discussions of possible, early solutions.

These leaders may not necessarily take an active part in the functioning of schools except for their children's progress. Their collective interests may be in city development, urban renewal, or crime prevention. Even if this scenario is true, though, they are not individuals to ignore. Get to know them, include them (when appropriate) on planning groups, and listen to them when they voice the feelings of others about your school's programs.

Finally, these leaders always have a following, which may be a small group of dedicated followers or a large cadre of disciples who support the views of the leader. Individual members of these groups may also be given special consideration because of their group affiliation. Two examples come to mind:

- Rather than approaching schools as individuals, members of patriotic or religious groups may contact schools or school districts, with flags or Bibles prominently displayed. They expect their organization will gain them additional leverage, and this often works.

- Individual board members have no legal power when they leave the confines of the board room but are given special consideration because of their elected position.

The specific rights or demands that individuals may lay claim to will depend on the type of group of which they are members and the power of the leaders of that same group.

Community Power Organizations

All community organizations potentially have power, particularly if they possess strong leadership. In any community, dozens of groups may make demands on a school and its principal from time to time. These groups generally focus on a single issue; if the problem is satisfactorily resolved, they are not heard from again. However, you will have to deal with a few groups on a regular basis. We will select three groups—teacher unions, ethnic groups, and censors—for discussion. The methods these groups use vary from subtle influence to active demonstration.

TEACHER UNIONS

Teachers, under the First and Fourteenth amendments of the U.S. Constitution, have the right to organize and to be represented by their selected unions. Despite efforts to unify in the 1970s, the two major organizations—the National Education Association (NEA) and the American Federation of Teachers (AFT)—operate two separate teacher agencies.

The major tool for teachers is the negotiating process, which brings about the collective bargaining contract. Bargaining generally focuses on new rights or new economic benefits, and ". . . rules exist that define the rights and duties of teachers to a particular assignment; govern the compensation of teachers; establish disciplinary sanctions for failure of teachers to achieve certain standards; and provide for teacher participation in structuring the workplace."[18] Generally, the bargaining process does not involve the site-level administrator because the superintendent or other members of the district office conduct the negotiations. The principal must know the negotiated contract thoroughly, however, and must abide by its provisions. Regardless of the values and improvements that have come about since the negotiation process has been in effect, these "work rules place constraints upon both the administrative discretion and the educational policy prerogatives of principals, superintendents, and school boards."[19]

Unions have won the right to call meetings, defend members of its organization, and represent teacher concerns with the site-level administrator. Grievance procedures, specifically spelled out in these negotiated contracts, allow teachers to challenge administrative actions. At one time, principals had almost absolute authority at their schools, but now teachers can go directly to the superintendent of schools or to the board itself. However, if the principal understands the contract, complies with its stated rules, and communicates with her staff members regularly and with understanding, there should be no need to take such actions.

If negotiations do not go well, teacher unions in most states also have the right to hold demonstrations, picket, and ultimately strike. These activities may be based on demands that the site-level administrator completely agrees with; nevertheless, he is placed in an awkward position. Whatever his personal feelings, the school must continue to remain open, and it may place him in an adversarial position with the members of the teaching staff. Fortunately, most teacher strikes are short-lived, lasting less than two weeks, so the awkwardness of such a situation is generally not prolonged.

If not all teachers choose to strike and thereby cause two factions to exist on the same faculty, the administration may have difficulty in getting the two groups to work together in harmony after the walkout is over. This task, however, must be undertaken despite deep emotional feelings that may exist between the two groups.

ETHNIC GROUPS

As indicated in Chapter 3, many communities are seeing major changes in the ethnic makeup of their school districts. The term *minority group*, if not entirely obsolete, is at least gaining new meaning. James E. Allen, Jr., former U.S. Commissioner of Education, wrote,

> *The day of the melting pot is over. No longer is it the ideal of each minority to become an indistinguishable part of the majority. Today, each strives to maintain its identity while seeking its rightful share of the social, economic, and political fruits of our system. Self-help and self-determination have become the rallying cries of all minorities.*[20]

These groups, at one time or another, may make demands on the school. Blacks, Hispanics, Puerto Ricans, Asian immigrants, and Native Americans are but a few of the ethnic groups who have raised and will continue to raise educational issues.

The demands may have started with the segregation issue prior to 1954 and de facto segregation that was a major concern in the 1960s. Other issues have been brought forth, including testing procedures, the number of minorities assigned to special classes, the high dropout rates, and the lack of teachers representing a particular ethnic group.

Questions about these issues as well as others will be brought forth as our communities change and educational problems present themselves. The skilled site-level administrator must focus on these concerns and defend programs and policies that seem to discriminate but that in actuality do not. For example, one high school principal was asked by one of his counselors what should be done about a black tenth grader who wanted to enter the honors program but did not have the designated test scores. It was fortunate that his reply was "let him try it, and if he does not do well, we can always move him out of it." At the young man's twelfth-grade graduation, he was ranked third in a class of over 1000 students.

Most of the problems falling into this category are usually like the anecdote—a one-student or one-family demand or question. No ethnic group is monolithic; what has happened is the development of **cultural pluralism.** Leaders and members of all of these groups have ideas, values, and goals that range along a broad continuum. What they desire is the best education that can be obtained for their children, and the principal must see that they get it.

Although minority parents have not necessarily banned together on issues, unified groups of citizens have made demands at times of a school board, district, or school. For example, in March, 1991, a group of African-American parents, including representatives from the Nation of Islam, attended a board meeting of the Pomona (California) Unified School District. At that meeting, parents made specific demands of the district and "accused the district of smug indifference and callousness to African-American students and parents."[21] Some parents called for a boycott of the school and the resignations of the principal, vice-principal, and one teacher. Evidently, the problems between the Latino and African-American students had escalated when racist remarks and catcalls were made at an assembly in honor of Black History Month. The following were the major concerns: (1) nothing was done to end the racial remarks at the assembly; (2) not enough teachers attended the assembly with the students and some even refused to escort their students to it; and (3) campus security was inadequate.

We must always take care to guard against unfair treatment of any member or any group of our student population. By being diligent along these lines, we are sending a strong school–community message that we support democracy and expect it to be followed within our public schools. During the past few years, one problem resurging on school campuses is hate crimes. These kinds of crimes usually start out by the use of name calling, but as Troyna and Hatcher point out, "By far the most common expression of racism is through racist name calling . . . it is in general the most hurtful form of verbal aggression from other children."[22] Other forms of expression are symbols, caricatures, emblems, logos, and mascots that promote prejudice, but all of this has escalated into verbal and physical attacks against individuals or groups. The bulk of the incidents have been centered at the secondary level, but a growing number of situations has occurred at elementary schools: "The incidence of hate crimes is currently occurring at record-breaking rates nationwide, strong evidence that bigotry still plays a prominent role in contemporary America."[23]

The problem had become large enough for the NEA to include the topic as one of its 1993 resolutions. The organization said, in part, "The Association urges its affiliates, in conjunction with community groups, to create an awareness of hate-motivated, violent activities and to develop programs to oppose them."[24]

Although graffiti is the most visual example of biases against minorities and others, incidents of verbal comments, threats, and the actual physical abuse of individuals are ever-increasing. According to a number of research documents, the scope of incidents and the number of groups that have received both violence and harassment are of crisis proportions. Though many hate crimes have been racial in nature, they have also focused on ethnic groups, religious beliefs, and sexual orientation.

There are many causes of bigotry among students. Sometimes it is caused by what they have been taught by their parents; sometimes it is caused by too little contact with other groups; sometimes bigotry has an economic source such as foreign-market practices (the 1990–1995 concerns about the Japanese, for example); at other times, it may grow out of a particular school incident thought to have occurred along racial or other stereotypical lines. Whatever the reasons or causes, teachers and administrators should remain alert to potential problems. Furthermore, "schools need to adopt policies, develop curriculum, and implement programs designed to prevent and curtail hate crimes. The efforts of high schools and even elementary schools are critical to this effort as younger and younger students are involved in hate crime." [25]

CENSORS

Although not necessarily a group in the same sense of the other two, some organizations and individuals have a strong dedication to censoring programs, textbooks, library materials, or teaching methods. Some groups are affiliated with organized religion, some are members of obscure, conservative organizations, and others exist independent of any group or organization. Whatever the affiliation, there has recently been a strong push by conservative and reactionary social movements, which include antiabortion, pro-family, and antibusing groups. Out of this came the "Moral Majority," as an example of the right-wing movement. Members of this faction have made a number of strong educational demands and have used tactics such as direct confrontation with school boards and administrators, community rhetoric, and the lobbying of political representatives.

Some groups represent a definite political view and are supported by solid citizens, whereas others may be completely dismissed as examples of the "crackpot" variety. Although the school principal may think that these individuals are "off the wall," she must also remember to take these groups or individuals seriously. This stance requires an inordinate amount of administrative time; however, if these people are ignored, they may well gather converts on the basis of the school or district trying to "cover up."

These groups may attack any aspect of the school's program, or any material used by the district or a particular teacher. For example, one high school principal had calls from a number of parents who protested one of his teacher's using *The Daily Worker* in his social studies class. That same teacher used printed materials from all of the other "isms" of the political spectrum, and the parents were advised of the fact. As a follow-up, the teacher was asked to send a letter at the beginning of the next school year advising parents of all materials used in his classes. The phone contacts ceased.

Even textbook committees and boards can be "watch dogs" of American values, as was the case in Indiana:

> *A member of the Indiana state text book commission a few years ago proposed to forbid any books mentioning Robin Hood or the Quakers, on the grounds that Robin was a Communist (in that he stole from the rich and gave to the poor) and that the Quakers were un-American in their pacifism. Another board in 1962 restored the McGuffy readers in the elementary schools of their district."* [26]

Concerned parents have even attempted to entrap teachers by recording classroom discussions. Adversaries of one teacher sent a student to the classroom with a tape recorder hidden in a book carved out to conceal it:

> *In 1963, Mrs. Virginia Franklin, a teacher in Paradise, California, who had recently won the Freedom's Foundation award as an outstanding teacher of the "American Credo" was attacked by the American Legion post, some John Birch Society members. The charge was that she subverted the patriotism of her students by exposing them to leftist ideas.* [27]

In the early 1970s, religious groups (the Moral Majority, for example) started to challenge the curriculum by use of the Bible and absolute religious values. Evolution is still under attack, along with sex education, abortion, and other controversial topics discussed in the classroom. The principal can take a number of steps when attacks by religious groups begin to surface. First, talk over the board policies with the superintendent. A strong board that has anticipated these attacks should have a policy or set of policies that protect the full range of student values; these policies can be used effectively to thwart these groups. Next, have the group or individual parent put the concern in writing. This written complaint can then be reviewed by an appropriate committee composed of teachers and parents. The complaint, along with a recommendation from the committee, can be sent up the administrative ladder. Finally, share the verbalized or written concerns with the entire staff so they too can be aware of the criticism. This assures teachers that they are not doing anything illegal or contrary to either board policy or district guidelines.

The principal should never capitulate to unwarranted individual or group attacks. Teachers are not always right in how they relate to students, but neither are the parents in interpreting the actions. School principals need to listen to the demands of parents, take careful notes, investigate the situation, and then get back to the parent or group.

Sometimes a teacher or other school employee makes an error in judgment that most likely will not occur again, once the principal points out the error. An individual or group may overreact and demand that the principal "fire the teacher." An example of this is the following: A high school teacher of U.S. history was once challenged by the local American Legion because he had displayed the Nazi flag above the American flag in his classroom. The cause of his "un-American" action? Students had been removing the Nazi flags, when they were placed lower on the bulletin boards, for their own personal use, which necessitated his placing of the flag as high on the wall as possible. The teacher understood the stand of the Legion and removed the flag, but the teacher was not "released from his contract" as originally demanded.

Principals will receive many requests from parents about their own children, and parents certainly have the right to challenge policies, programs, or teaching methods. All must be heard, but the voice of an individual parent, or even a group of parents, does not necessarily reflect the feelings of all parents. Wholesale curricular changes should not be put into effect because one parent objects to what is being taught.

Teacher Empowerment

nother emerging aspect of power in education is the concept of **teacher empowerment.** This is not exclusively a movement in educational circles, however. Throughout the world, particularly in emerging nations, there is an ever-growing demand for worker participation in the labor force: "This idea . . . [self-management] . . . allows that ordinary members of the organization should have a certain degree of influence on decisions concerning the objectives and the actual operation of the affairs of the organization." [28]

The powerful and established teacher unions have strongly advocated teacher empowerment for many years. Twenty years ago, Albert Shanker, as leader of the AFT, was quoted as saying, "Power is never given to anyone. Power is taken, and it is taken from someone. Teachers, as one of society's powerless groups, are now starting to take power from supervisors and school boards. This is causing and will continue to cause a realignment of power relationships." [29]

During the two decades since Shanker's statement, educational critics, teachers, and the AFT and NEA have attempted to define and operationalize the idea of empowerment for teachers. Although a number of complex definitions of the process has been offered, the definition is rather simple: "To empower teachers means involving teachers in the important decisions that affect their students, classrooms, and schools." [30]

Many forces are behind this empowerment, but two causes come to the forefront. First, our schools are not doing as well as they might, and several national organizations have published papers strongly criticizing the state of education in America. These organizations include the National Commission on Excellence in Education, the Carnegie Forum on Education and the Economy, and the Carnegie Foundation for the Advancement of Teaching. Second, because we live in a democratic nation, the involvement of the worker in any form of endeavor is considered just and beneficial: "The second general basis on which worker's participation has been advocated, the sociopolitical argument, treats worker's participation as a means by which democracy is extended to the sphere of industry, which, it is agreed, operates autocratically even under liberal democratic political systems."[31] Most U.S. citizens have encountered the bureaucratic problems of public- and private-sector agencies. These bureaucratic roadblocks also exist in our schools, and teacher organizations have gathered much support as they have exploited them.

Perhaps educators, as well as others, are looking for a quick fix when the problems of our schools seem to be much larger; however, for whatever reasons, teacher unions have seen teacher empowerment as being one of the cures. There are, of course, strong reasons for expanding the roles of the teachers in the educational decision-making process, particularly when ample evidence shows that by so doing the bureaucracy of the school district is bypassed. However, no known data show that teachers will be more adept at improving the schools than the existing school administrators and boards. As Glickman states, "Although there is little doubt that 'empowered schools' provide better educational environments than they did before they began the empowerment process, such evidence still does not amount to what my friendly critic refers to as 'substantial change'!"[32]

Some data show that empowered schools are better because of the way the teachers, administrators, and students treat one another, but little evidence exists of improved student learning. Perhaps in the long run, studies will show this to be true; at the present, it seems to be a movement in the power sector rather than an academic one.

Teachers, as the direct deliverers of the educational program to students, need to increase their contributions to the total school program. They must work closely and cooperatively with site administrators and others to create a vision for instructional excellence. They obviously need to have a voice in the organization of the school day; the development of the school curriculum; the ordering and the use of school supplies, support materials, and equipment; and other tasks directly related to their roles as teachers. The managing of schools, however, may not be what is needed. The transferring of these tasks from the shoulders of existing administrators to the shoulders of others may not necessarily improve the situation. More time and more studies of the results need to be made.

Future administrators will face greater demands from teacher groups, and the future principal needs to be comfortable with sharing the decision-making process. Teacher empowerment is not going to go away. Lieberman said in 1990, "If there is to be a community of leaders in a school, teachers must have opportunities to take on more responsibilities, more decision-making power, and more accountability for the results."[33] The last part of this statement must be implemented and tested. In actuality, who is held accountable—the appointed leader, the group as a whole, or the teacher who assumes this new role? This raises the issue of responsibility. Teachers are not officially or legally responsible to the public in the same way that school administrators, districts, or boards are at the present time. However, as the ones responsible for student learning, they are responsible for the development and execution of a meaningful educational program.

School Decentralization

uring the past 25 years, the participation of citizen groups similar to those summarized above has influenced many aspects of political life. Some groups have sought to change social services, the structure of health service, and even the operation of city development. Thus, it is not surprising that efforts to decentralize schools into more workable and responsible units have occurred.

Swiss defined **decentralization** as "the location of organizational power at a number of points rather than one central location. The term is used both when organizational power is moved from a central headquarters to field offices and when it is moved from top- to lower-level managers."[34] Much of the unrest and subsequent efforts to decentralize have developed because school districts and their bureaucratic structures have become insulated and have failed to respond to the needs of some segments of the communities served.

It's probably not coincidental that large urban districts were the first to face these demands.[35] The groups making the demands for smaller operating units sought to increase the participation of parents and community residents while measurably reducing the power of the board of education, the district bureaucracy, teachers, and administrators. Though not exclusively an effort by racial groups, large districts were more likely to move toward decentralization, and the size of the non-white population was significantly correlated with decentralization.[36]

The major decentralization efforts of Ocean Hill–Brownsville in New York, Morgan in Washington, D.C., and those of Detroit and Los Angeles have been studied and analyzed for the past two decades. There are conflicting reports about the results of these experiments when measuring student progress is concerned. Ravitch in her article "Community Control Revisited," which focused on the Ocean Hill–Brownsville efforts, stated that "no one gained educationally."[37] On the other hand, those adults actually involved in the decentralizing process in New York City reported that the effects on the school governing board members were increased knowledge of school matters, greater militancy in seeking reforms, and a stronger sense of efficacy and self-esteem. These two separate studies indicate that adults achieved positive results but that students gained little in measured educational achievement.

Perhaps the most dramatic case for decentralization occurred in 1988 when a law was passed that transferred the authority for Chicago's 540 public schools to elected councils of citizens and site-level administrators. These councils dealt with the issues of personnel, budget, and curriculum at the school level. As in other studies, the Chicago initiative was evaluated and found to have mixed results. Parent participation improved, as did communication between the schools and the communities, "but the councils have made little headway in addressing the poor academic performance of Chicago's students. For one thing, the teachers' panels that were supposed to advise the councils on academics have performed poorly, leading many councils to make bad instructional decisions."[38] For example, one elementary school invested $70,000 in computer software that was never used by the teaching staff.

Perhaps more than anything else, as will be repeatedly emphasized in this text, *how* something is done is more important than *what* is done. In other words, the *process* of these decentralization efforts may be the major payoff. Some writers believe that the schools of our largest cities can only survive by breaking the hold of the professional bureaucracy and allowing parents and other community people to share in educational decision making. Other researchers conclude that these decentralization efforts lack grassroots participation, and they are pessimistic about the movement's effectiveness.

In 1979, Barbara Hatton at Stanford University stated,

> *Decentralization of school districts with the accompanying community participation in the form of parent advisory boards, school–community councils, and the like has not effected the basic restructuring of school districts it purported to accomplish. The decentralization which has occurred has in fact occurred without significant changes in the organizational power structure of schools, despite the attempts of concerned academics or social science professionals to accomplish this goal.*[39]

However, Herbert Walberg, a University of Chicago researcher who has studied district size and academic achievement, stated, "When it comes to reform, the popular thing is to decentralize. But it does not seem to have worked. . . . It just means another layer of bureaucracy."[40]

Although only time and longitudinal studies will help determine if either group of researchers is correct, the site-level administrator must be prepared for a variety of demands from a number of interested groups. For those employed in a large district, pressures may arise to break the district into smaller units.

At the School Site

The conflicts raised between pressure groups and members of any bureaucratic organization are some of the most basic aspects of decision making. On one hand is an institution of government—in our case, a school—and on the other hand are groups of people who represent a limited interest and who want (and sometimes demand) special treatment.

In our democratic form of government, we expect these demands to take place, and that's one reason that school administrators are employed: They must handle these requests and grievances so teachers can do what *they* are hired to do best—teach. Fortunately for the school principal, many of these demands and much of the rhetoric of these groups are done at the district level and will not be a common site problem.

Some demands, however, will be initiated at the school level and are best handled by the principal and his staff. There may be some groups (or individuals) that want a change in school policy and want to know why the existing policy exists. In cases of this type, knowing how and why some policies were ever adopted is sometimes challenging. One high school principal was confronted by an irate parent with a support group who demanded that the student, who was a sophomore, be allowed to try out as head baton twirler. A previously adopted policy indicated that only juniors and seniors were eligible to seek that prestigious position; younger students were assumed to have inadequate experience. The student in question was currently a twirler for the Los Angeles Rams football team and had more than 100 major awards for her skills with a baton. At that moment, defending the policy seemed somewhat difficult. Negotiations with the sponsor of the pep groups obtained a reluctant willingness to give the student a "special tryout." The group agreed this was a fair compromise, and two days later the girl performed before a hastily assembled group of judges. It took only a few minutes for the sponsor to suggest that the old policy be altered.

Perhaps the best attitude to embrace when individuals or groups are making demands is that we need their input. Policies, programs, or standards are not changed if someone does not question what currently exists. Many schools probably support policies and rules, for example, that no one on the present staff can remember having adopted. The policies and rules are simply there. Some may be archaic and may no longer be essential (assuming they once were) to the smooth running of the school. A concerned parent or community group may be the very catalyst to cause a rethinking of that policy or rule. Schools, of themselves, do not possess all answers, so these individuals and groups can help us develop sound, logical policies to fit our changing communities and world.

There is, of course, what Black and English label as "the lunatic fringe."[41] Either as a group or as individual parents, members of this group make demands; you need to listen carefully, focus on what is best for the student, and defuse the hostility. The following are real-world situations that have occurred to site-level administrators across the United States:

- A group of members of the NAACP accompanied a mother to protect the "unfair" method of holding her son accountable for his attendance. The mother had not given all of the information to the group, which left after the facts were revealed.

- One father who attended every PTA meeting, every teacher conference, and every school–community meeting demanded to know why schools no longer taught spelling. His son was a wonderful young man, an outstanding student, but didn't spell well. The concern was just, but the methods of attacking all schools and all teachers were not.

- One child's parents planted a tape recorder in their son's hollowed-out textbook so that teachers could be taped and their "subversive activities" uncovered. Although the tapes showed nothing out of the ordinary, the parents "interpreted" them differently.

- A large segment of parents banned together after one parent's daughter had falsified a school incident and blamed it on one particular racial group. The parental group demanded that all members of that race be lectured to at a schoolwide assembly. When the request was denied, a torrent of phone calls and letters to the local newspaper began. After the girl's lies were exposed, not a single member of that group called or wrote apologizing for either their demands or their behavior.

With a strongly developed program of school–community relations, the site-level administrator, teachers, support groups, and others can develop strong relations with many of the leaders of the community. This will require a vision of the school, which has been developed by those who wish to be involved in that aspect of a school's focus.

Continued participation by parents and other community members in a variety of school activities and planning sessions will do much to defuse unwarranted attacks or demands on an individual school staff member, a school, or even an entire district. People generally support those ideas they understand, and they are particularly willing to offer support if they have had a hand in helping shape policies.

If concerns are voiced and have merit, then give them careful consideration and discuss possible changes to current policies. If the individuals or groups asking for changes see that the schools are willing to listen to their suggestions, discuss them at length and with appropriate modifications (if needed), and adopt them as part of the school's operation, the suggestions may even become a part of school's support group.

SUMMARY

1. The major emphasis for education following the American Revolution was to unify our diverse population. Education has never been separate from politics since that time, with the federal government continuing to play an influential role.

2. The various states have also influenced education through laws relating to finance, programs, and the certification of teachers. Although the principal does not directly influence these lawmakers or laws, they have an influence on the site administrator.

3. Because there are many groups in a school and community, there also may be many centers of power. The school principal should become aware of these power groups and the individuals who serve as their leaders.

4. Three of the most obvious community power organizations for administrators to note are teacher unions, changing ethnic groups within communities, and censors. All three may make demands or question the curriculum, and all should be taken seriously.

5. Teacher empowerment has increased extensively during the past 25 years and will continue to expand in the future. The two major teacher unions (AFT and NEA) are the strongest advocates of this movement.

6. Generally, the principal will not be involved in the teacher union's bargaining process, but she must know the negotiated contract thoroughly. This document will limit what a site administrator can or cannot do.

7. The right to strike is the right of teachers in some states. Although history has shown that most teacher strikes don't last very long, the division between groups takes its toll even years later.

8. Ethnic groups change as do communities. Because no ethnic group is monolithic, the leaders and members of all ethnic groups possess ideas, values, and goals that stretch across the entire spectrum of civilized thought.

9. Censors may simply be concerned parents whose values contrast with some part of the curriculum or a textbook or an organized group that has a definite "agenda" to push. Either way, the school principal is obligated to listen and try to absolve the conflict.

10. To increase participation of citizen groups, some districts have decentralized their schools (perhaps the greatest effort having been the Chicago school system). Mixed feelings exist about these efforts, and research shows few educational gains for the students in these districts.

DISCUSSION QUESTIONS

1. In what ways have recent political changes directly affected your school or district? In your opinion, have they helped or hindered education?

2. What community groups do you think have the greatest influence on the schools in your district? How does this group affect schools in your district?

3. Do you think teachers have gained power in your school district? (If you are a relatively new teacher, you may wish to discuss this with one of the "old timers.") Do you think that teachers should be empowered in other areas? Explain your answer.

4. Have you been aware of any examples of hate crimes in your immediate area? If so, list these examples and then discuss how to spot these problems before they become overt actions.

5. What do you think are the major strengths and weaknesses of the decentralization efforts within large school districts? Do you think this trend will continue or discontinue? Explain your answer.

1. List the five most powerful figures in your school district. Without necessarily revealing the names, compare their bases of power with those of other members of the class. Compare trends if there are any.

2. Divide the class into groups—the board, a challenging group of parents, and the administration—and role-play how a confrontation at a board meeting could be defused.

METHINKS YOU PROTEST TOO MUCH

Yesterday had been an unusual challenge for principal Bill Johnson, and, as he was driving to school, his thoughts were still reviewing what had occurred. He was in fact a few minutes behind his normal schedule because his mind had been preoccupied while getting ready this morning. Beyond the usual everyday problems at Elm School, six parents had made an appointment to see him early yesterday morning. Their collective concerns were about the new textbook that had been adopted for the English program this school year.

Specifically, the group objected to some of the language used by some of the contemporary authors and virtual exclusion of selections by minority writers.

Mrs. Ernest Garcia, leader of a number of community groups, had been the major spokesperson and voiced her concern that a book entitled *American Literature—A Historical Perspective* should represent the United States as it is today. The others who had accompanied her were in agreement, at least at the beginning of the conference.

Johnson had tried to defuse the group's obvious emotional state by carefully listening to their concerns, using his communication skills to reflect what they were saying, and then patiently going through the state textbook-adoption process. The meeting had been a long one, but Johnson had pointedly canceled his other obligations by instructing his

3. Talk with your principal to see if he or she or the district has confronted censors demanding changes at the school or district. Share the incidents and, if possible, the materials with members of the class.

4. Talk with your principal to discover if any groups or individual parents have been successful in obtaining changes, either at the school site or at the district level. Discuss with your classmates whether these changes were of value.

secretary that he was not to be disturbed.

To support the school's position on the matter, he had even twice called for reinforcements. He had asked his department chairperson to stop in to explain how the textbook was used in the classroom and to explain why the English staff felt the selection was, as the book title implied, representative of our nation's literary history. Johnson had been pleased with the way Mr. Shakespeare, the department leader, had handled the situation. There had been some question about the adoption procedures at the district level, so he had telephoned Dr. Ruth Brookhart, the assistant superintendent. Fortunately, he had caught her in her office, and

she was able to answer the group's questions.

After two and one-half hours, the tide had turned as the group seemed to be running out of questions. Johnson felt that the expressed anger at the beginning of the conference had mellowed and that the group now understood the processes involved in the adoption of state textbooks. He was confident that the last question, "When will be the next adoption?," was a sign that this group of parents, while perhaps still harboring some misgivings, would at least be able to wait for the next adoption, just four years down the road. These members of the group made a point of indicating their support for his position as they were leaving.

As Johnson pulled into the principal's parking spot, he noted a large group of adults in front of the school entrance. He also noted a sizable group of students on the lawn watching what was taking place. There were even a few teachers, some of whom were arriving as he was.

As he left his car and walked toward the school entrance, he could see that the adults were carrying placards. They were picketing the school! He could read some of the signs as the group strode around in a tight circle:

"Principal Supports Biased Textbooks"

"'No Change for Four Years,' Says Johnson"

"School Discriminates Against Minority Writers"

5. As a class, develop and write a policy to deal with the would-be censors of our schools. Discuss how this developed document fits into or comes in conflict with the U.S. Constitution.

Past

1. Could Johnson have dealt with the group of parents any differently on the previous day? What might he have done instead?

2. Johnson seemed to use appropriate communication skills when dealing with the group of parents, but what went wrong? How could he have helped avoid the situation this morning?

3. Both of Johnson's reinforcements were able to answer the questions that were asked, but what went wrong here? Is there anything that could have been changed?

4. What deeper concerns failed to surface in the parents' meeting with Johnson? Could he have sensed what they were?

5. Although half the parent group agreed with him yesterday, what assumptions did he make? Could he have done anything at that time to possibly avoid today's actions?

Present

1. What should Johnson do immediately about the pickets in front of the school? What options are open to him?

2. Who needs to be informed of the situation within the district? What kinds of communication methods should be used?

3. Assuming the local media want to cover the story, what should Johnson say to the reporters? Who else should be involved in making statements to the media?

4. The situation may eventually get to the school board. What should Johnson do before that occurs?

5. What kinds of demands does this group legitimately have? What can realistically be done about these concerns?

REFERENCES

1. Catherine Marshall, "Educational Policy Dilemmas: Can We Have Control and Quality and Choice and Democracy and Equity?" in *Contemporary Issues in U.S. Education,* edited by Kathryn M. Borman, Piyush Swani, and Lonnie P. Wagstaff (Norwood, N.J.: Ablex, 1991), p. 8.

2. S. K. Bailey, "Thomas Jefferson and the Purpose of Education," in *The Changing Politics of Education,* edited by E. K. Mosher and J. L. Wagner (Berkeley, Calif.: McCutchar, 1978).

3. Joel Spring, *The American School 1642–1985* (White Plains, N.Y.: Longman, 1986), p. 70.

4. Ibid., p. 71.

5. Ibid., p. 107.

6. Ibid., pp. 132–133.

7. Myron Lieberman, *Beyond Public Education* (New York: Praeger, 1986), p. 110.

8. Ibid., p. 112.

9. Douglas E. Mitchell and Margaret Goertz, eds., *Education Politics for the New Century* (London: Falmer Press. 1990), p. 4.

10. Ibid., p. 160.

11. Lieberman, *Beyond Public Education,* p. 115.

12. Michael W. Kirst, *Who Controls Our Schools? American Values in Conflict* (New York: Freeman, 1984), p. 13.

13. Morris Janowitz, *Community Political Systems* (Glencoe, N.Y.: Free Press, 1961), p. 15.

14. Paul Schumaker, "Estimating the First and (Some of the) Third Focus of Community Power," *Urban Affairs Quarterly* 28, no. 3 (March 1993):448.

15. Albert Hunter, "Local Knowledge and Local Powers: Notes on the Ethnography of Local Community Elites," *Journal of Contemporary Ethnography* 22, no. 1 (April 1993):38.

16. John A. Black and Fenwick W. English, *What They Don't Tell You in Schools of Education About School Administration* (Lancaster, Penn.: Technomic, 1986), pp. 54–60.

17. H. Kaufman and V. Jones, "The Mystery of Power," *Public Administration Review* 14 (1954):204–212.

18. Randall W. Eberts and Joe A. Stone, *Unions and Public Schools* (Lexington, Mass.: Heath, 1984), p. 13.

19. Ibid., p. 22.

20. Carl A. Grant, *Community Participation in Education* (Boston: Allyn and Bacon, 1979), p. 27.

21. David Fonder, *Inland Valley (California) Daily Bulletin* (4 March 1992).

22. Barry Troyna and Richard Hatcher, *Racism in Children's Lives* (London: Routledge, 1992), p. 195.

23. Christina Bodinger-deVriarte, *Annual Report on Political and Hate Violence,* Anti-Discrimination Committee, Washington, D.C., 1991, p. 1.

24. *NEA Today,* "1993 Resolutions," September 1993, p. 16.

25. Bodinger-deVriarte, p. 5.

26. William M. French, *America's Educational Tradition—An Interpretive History* (Boston: Heath, 1964), p. 325.

27. Ibid., pp. 360–361.

28. Assef Bayat, "Work Politics and Power," *Monthly Review Press,* 1991, p. 37.

29. James W. Guthrie and Patricia A. Craig, "Teachers and Politics," *Phi Delta Kappa Fastback* 21 (Bloomington, Ind.: Phi Delta Kappa Educational Foundation, 1973), p. 25.

30. Marilees C. Rist, "What It Means to Empower Teachers," *The Executive Educator* 11 (August 1989):16–19, 29.

31. Bayat, "Work Politics," p. 40.

32. Carl D. Glickman, "Pushing School Reform to a New Edge: The Seven Ironies of School Empowerment," *Phi Delta Kappan* 72, no. 1 (September, 1990):68–75.

33. Ann Lieberman, "Teachers and Principals: Turf, Tension and New Tasks," *Phi Delta Kappan* 69, no. 9 (May, 1988):648–653.

34. James E. Swiss, *Public Management Systems: Monitoring and Managing Government Performances* (Englewood Cliffs, N.J.: Prentice-Hall, 1991), p. 288.

35. Mario Fantini, Marilyn Gittellard, and Richard Maget, *Community Control and the Urban School* (New York: Praeger, 1970).

36. John D. Hutcheson and Jann Shevin, *Citizen Groups in Local Politics: A Bibliographic Review* (Santa Barbara, Calif.: Clio Books, 1976), p. 135.

37. Ibid., p. 141.

38. Thomas Toch, "Parental Power in Question," *U.S. News and World Report* (24 December 1990), p. 54.

39. Carl A. Grant, *Community Participation in Education* (Boston: Allyn and Bacon, 1979).

40. *Los Angeles Times,* 19 May 1993, p. A-12.

41. Black and English, *What They Don't Tell,* pp. 241–249.

COMMUNITY CHANGES

Social Changes and Problems

Many smaller communities have remained relatively stable throughout the United States since World War II, but this is not true for the nation as a whole. The population is now centered in large urban areas, although there has also been a flight to the suburbs during the past four decades. Urban areas have mushroomed, and the more populated states have grown at a geometric rate: "Today, only one out of four Americans lives in a rural area."[1]

With the population migrating to metropolitan areas, social problems have developed that greatly affect life as well as the educational system. The inner city has become increasingly crowded, and housing has become more expensive and, more dilapidated despite major efforts by cities to support urban renewal. These conditions create special problems for ethnic minorities and the elderly, who are often housed in the inner city.

Crime is on the increase in most of the country, but it is a major urban problem: "Official statistics show that big cities have four times as much violent crime as their suburbs and over six times as much as rural communities."[2] However, no part of the nation has been spared, because crime rates are increasing in all parts of the country, including within the walls of the schools.

Besides these population shifts, there also seems to be a change in our value systems. Sociologist Robert Bellah suggests that Americans are increasingly emphasizing their own private lives and are gradually abandoning community and public concerns. His studies found the end result of this trend to be a damaged "social ecology."[3]

Many social psychologists feel that this deterioration of our value system is a direct result of the move toward urbanization. There has been a long-time American devotion to the values of small-town life, and these feelings may stem from that love affair. There certainly have been efforts (particularly by ethnic groups) to develop and maintain urban neighborhoods like those found in rural areas, but the subsequent community identification has not offset the problems present in urban areas. Many of these social concerns can be attributed to the fact that large cities have produced slums and many serious social ills, including alcoholism and drug addiction, which are much more common among people who live in those conditions.

Other social psychologists feel it isn't a rural–urban issue but a change in the nation's value system itself. Although writers and speakers have commented on these observed changes for many years, little has been accomplished to reverse the trend. One social movement, however, has risen: "Sick of liberal and conservative failures, sociologist Amitai Etzioni called together his friends a few years ago and came up with a big new idea: the Communitarian movement, a prescription for the we decade."[4] This group, not widely known, has had little effect on the thousands of small and large communities of the nation. Many people, however, would agree with their goals: political changes in our lifestyle that may curb what they consider the deterioration of America's values. Some of the Communitarian ideas may seem radical, but they are dealing with the voiced concerns of millions of American citizens. Many Americans are frustrated by the problems that the country faces and must solve. Many probably would concur with the Communitarian perspective, that "somewhere between individual rights and the power of the government lie the broad interests of the community. These interests—in public safety, the welfare of children, etc.— have been ignored too long."[5]

Schools need to develop strong links with the communities they serve to honestly deal with the problems. It will take more than a single town-hall meeting because the problems are immense and changing every day. Every school district has a responsibility to not only lead the youngsters attending its schools but also to help the parents band together to support their children and avoid some of the problems that will be enumerated in the remainder of this chapter.

The Changing Family Structure

hroughout most of the world families consist of the grandparents and their sons and their wives and their children. This **extended family** was also found to a great extent in the United States when it was an agricultural society. However, when America made the transition to that of an industrialized nation, the dominant household unit became what was termed the **nuclear family,** a married couple and their children only.

As the United States was in the process of becoming more industrialized, family life changed too because there no longer was an economic reason for all of the relatives to live in one place. The number of persons important to the raising of the crops was not a necessity when individuals had separate working roles. Jobs were farther away from the home itself, and workers were required to move from one place to another to seek employment. During these transition years, many families migrated to the cities.

During the last half of this century, family structures have been romanticized by such television shows as *Father Knows Best* or *The Bill Cosby Show.* Though many viewers may have accepted these portrayals as "typical" American families, these idealized versions were not true. The family long ago ceased serving the total needs of its members, and the school began expanding its function to fill the gaps. However, families are still an important part of our social structure and, as in the past, continue to provide a major portion of a child's education as far as socialization and social control are concerned. Attitudes and values were taught or modeled from generation to generation in the extended family so that they became part of our community culture of the past. There are those who believe, however, that these aspects are no longer being stressed.

Although the nuclear family continued the same process of

culturalization in the beginning, further breakdowns of the family structure have occurred during the past few decades. There seems to be less family unity and support than there was previously. Families continue to move from community to community, and in more families both adult members are becoming part of the nation's workforce. The women's financial contribution to the economic welfare of the family has been partially one of personal fulfillment, but it has also been one of necessity with the financial burdens of the present time.

According to most sociologists and psychologists, scientific evidence does not indicate that children are harmed when both parents work. It is estimated that by the year 2000 both partners in as many as 75% of the family units (married or unmarried) nationwide will work.[6] One could even argue that the accrued financial benefits improve the living conditions for youngsters as they are growing up. There could be other benefits, too: The father may assume more responsibilities in the rearing of the children, and the mother may well serve as a stronger role model.

Along with these continuing changes in the nuclear family structure, there has also been a dramatic increase in **single-parent families:**

As recently as 1970, single-parent families made up less than 13 percent of all the American families with children, but by 1990 there [were] 15 million children being reared by single parents whose family income averages about $16,124. . . . Almost 60 percent of all Black families with children have only one parent living in the home.[7]

Let's put these demographic changes in another perspective: In 1955, for example, 60% of the households in the United States consisted of a working father, a mother who was a homemaker, and two or more school-age children. During the 1990s, 50% of America's young people will spend some years before they reach age 18 being raised by a single parent, most of whom are women. Of every 1000 children who were born in the 1980s, only 41% will reach age 18 in a home with the 1955 configuration.[8]

For educators, however, there are to be disadvantages to this family organization. For many families, no one is at home to greet children when they return from school. Estimates indicate that more than 2 million school-age children live in households where this is the case, and this phenomenon of latchkey children is continually growing.

Patricia Fosarelli, a physician at Johns Hopkins Children's Center, ran a survey in the *Weekly Reader,* sixth-grade edition, and found that "almost half of the nation's sixth graders—49 percent—go home to no one after school."[9] Many young people have been taught to take care of themselves, or they stay with a sitter or neighbor. But some students are "in the streets" more and have little opportunity for the supervised completion of homework assignments.

In addition, only so many things can be accomplished in a single day, so neither parent may be available for school conferences or for attendance at school functions. The opportunity to serve on parent organizations, attend school conferences, or volunteer to work at the school may be severely limited. If the child comes from a one-parent household or both parents work and are not available during the traditional school hours, how can they become part of the support system needed by the school and the child?

If these parents are to communicate with educators about their child's learning problems, other arrangements obviously must be considered. For example, hold meetings and programs in the evenings or on the weekends and use home visits to emphasize the importance of this personal contact between parent and school official.

Compromises can be reached; for example, parents may be willing to occasionally change their work schedules once they have become involved with the school and their child's learning. Parents need to understand that their personal situations (being a sole caregiver, having a busy work schedule, and so on) affect their children's success in school. Just getting the children to school each day, which in some cases is highly commendable, may not be enough. Working out schedules for checking homework, anticipating reporting periods so that the reports are read, and even adhering to an individualized contract for the student can be important contributions to the child's learning progress by involved parents.

All parents need to be a part of the education of their children. Some have the time to participate at the school itself by volunteering or serving on a parent support group; others do not. As site-level administrators, we cannot write off the offspring of those who have a different home configuration; instead, serious efforts need to be made to involve as much as possible those from both single-parent families and families in which both parents are employed outside the home.

Social Changes and Their Effects on Schools

one of the educational reform efforts in American education has been able to stem the tide of societal changes faced by our communities. Many are too large for our educational institutions to handle, but the schools must do everything they can to help children who are adversely affected by social circumstances. Teachers and administrators must be aware of these problems and develop strategies to overcome them.

POVERTY

A higher degree of poverty exists in the United States than ever before. Most poor people in the United States are white (in fact, about two-thirds). However, only 11% of the white population is poor, whereas 34% of all blacks are poor. Many of us may equate children of poverty with undeveloped countries, the rural areas of the South, or the inner cities, but that is not an accurate picture. According to a number of national studies, the incidence of poverty among children has steadily increased and in 1975 this group had become the poorest of *all* age categories. Reed and Sautter report that "by 1989 young people accounted for 39.5% of America's poor."[10]

There are close to 40 million people in our country with income levels below what is designated as the poverty line (that is, $14,335 a year for a family of four).[11] Working with poor people as part of our school population is in itself a challenge, but there are a number of accompanying problems as well—higher incidences of illness, malnutrition, and related family problems (psychological stress, for example)—that affect poor youngsters who attend school. Many of these same children are a part of families who change locations often, so the youngsters move from school to school and do not always acquire the basic skills needed to succeed in subsequent grades.

At the high school level, some of these students seek jobs to offset the lack of family income. Although we can praise their efforts, it encourages some of them to violate the child labor laws adopted to protect them. They may work more hours than is deemed legal. Work can curtail good study habits and school attendance and can eventually lead to school failure. Violation of child labor laws is not a condition of the past, as *NEA Today* reports:

> *Child labor law violations have increased dramatically in the 1980's and early 90's. Without looking very hard, the Department of Labor found more than 42,000 child labor violations in 1990—up 340 percent since 1983. More than 38,000 minors were illegally employed. Experts say these figures are just the tip of the iceberg.*[12]

Reed and Sautter also report that "the U.S. Department of Education estimates that 220,000 school age children are homeless and that 65,000 do not attend school."[13] If the magnitude of these numbers were not enough to cause alarm, a House committee, in its 1989 report, concluded that by 1995 nearly 1 million children no longer living with their parents will be a serious problem for the schools of our country.[14]

Some of the problems currently confronting our society—teenage pregnancy, substance abuse, neighborhood gangs, teenage crime— are not necessarily a direct result of poverty, but they correlate highly with people who grow up poor and thereby have little opportunity to reach their goals. Young people of school age need to learn the skills that will permit them to cope with their economic plight and/or escape from it. However, schools have not been able to develop these skills for a large portion of these youngsters for two reasons: (1) Many young persons are virtually illiterate because they have not attended school on a regular basis, and (2) they have a very limited exposure to what Hirsch refers to as "cultural literacy."[15]

Research about disadvantaged children has flourished during the past several decades, and some of these findings have influenced the passage of the landmark federal grant program, the Elementary and Secondary Education Act of 1965, Title I. That an extensive disparity existed between children of middle-class-income and lower-class-income families was known. To lessen these differences, this legislation provided additional funds to schools for special education, to help end the cycle of poverty. As technology increases, educational requirements increase for many types of occupations. Without special education, the poor are left even further behind, and poverty is passed from generation to generation. Because younger children were perhaps the most affected, the preschool program Head Start was established to provide for the special needs of educationally deprived children. Not all schools, however, are entitled to Title I (now Chapter 1) funds. Those schools that are not entitled to these funds do not have enough families receiving Aid to Families with Dependent Children (AFDC) or the school board has determined that other schools within the district are in greater need. And, as noted earlier, more and more young people are poor and are not necessarily from lower-income neighborhoods or families, so the need is exceeding the entitlements.

Although teachers, through their training and experience, may not react to poor children differently, as studies have indicated in the past, they still may not set high standards for those students who are poor, or they may not expect as much from them. Teachers who unknowingly categorize disadvantaged youth academically may need additional in-service training or discussions about students who are poor.

Nutrition programs in the form of school breakfast, snacks, and lunches have done much to offset the effect of hunger on academic achievement, but nothing has been developed yet to offset students' feelings about being poor and their social relations to other students. Free public education still requires students to have money in order to attend social events, participate in school activities, and even graduate from high school. Many schools have established funds to aid students who need financial help—either in the form of loans or outright gifts. Some students, however, are reluctant to apply for these monies even if available and ultimately may drop out of school. School officials need to monitor the young people who fall into this category to see what help can be offered to them. The following example illustrates why this is important.

At one high school, a rather sizable fund was established to help students with these kinds of problems. Most requests were for small amounts directly related to student educational costs, but one day a senior, who was about to drop out of school because she had been literally abandoned by her mother and stepfather, told her counselor she had no place to live. The school arranged to rent a small apartment for her for the remaining four months of the school year. When given the money, she stated she would pay it back; because of the amount required and her obvious financial condition, however, the fund committee felt that was an empty statement. The young woman graduated and 18 months later came to the office with the money and said: "Use this for someone else who may need it in the future." How can we not seek ways to help students who possess those attitudes?

EXCEPTIONAL CHILDREN

Since World War II, the National Association for Retarded Citizens' Council for Exceptional Children and other groups have been advocating better education for the disabled and for protection of their civil rights:

> A major victory for these groups came in 1973 with the passage of the Rehabilitation Act of 1973. Section 504 of this legislation was equivalent to Title VI of the 1964 Civil Rights Act in that it required the withholding of federal funds from schools that discriminated against the handicapped.[16]

Passed in 1975, the Education for All Handicapped Children Act (public law 94-142) prescribes that each disabled child receive an individualized education program (IEP). This law requires the school to place a child in an instructional setting in which he or she is capable of functioning but as close as possible to regular class placement. Although often referred to as **"mainstreaming"** by educators, the law actually reads as the *least restrictive environment*.

A disabled child must have an IEP developed each year, in which the parents, the principal or his designee, teachers, and appropriate district specialists are involved:

> Each IEP must contain certain minimum information: (1) a statement of the child's primary handicapping condition, (2) a description of the child's current level of functioning, (3) a description of the annual instructional goals for the child and short-term objectives that will be used to reach these goals, (4) a description of special and related services that will be provided, (5) dates and timelines when services will be provided, and (6) criteria by which success of the child's instructional program will be provided.[17]

The law requires that parents be involved in the total process regarding their child's education. This includes the IEP conferences; the school must make the times convenient for parents to participate and must document its efforts to do so. If English is not the native language of the parents, the meeting must be held in their language, with an interpreter's assistance.

With these guidelines, principals must take the time to organize, implement, and monitor programs for the disabled. As part of her supervisory role, the site-level administrator must be concerned with the efforts of all teachers and their commitment to carrying out programs. More and more schools are developing a collaborative consultation model whereby teachers cooperatively deliver services to students with disabilities.

ETHNIC MINORITIES

The nation's ethnic makeup is also changing:

> *The Immigration Act of 1965 modified the quota system that favored European immigrants and opened the door to more people from the Third World. In the last 25 years, about 40 percent of the legal immigrants to the United States have been from Latin America and the Caribbean, 30 percent from Asia, and only 22 percent from Europe.*[18]

In part because of this influx of people, predictions indicate that by the year 2000 America will be a nation in which one of three persons will be nonwhite. Of that number, two ethnic groups—blacks and Hispanics —will constitute a larger portion of the total population in the future because these two groups are currently showing higher birth rates than the general population.[19]

These ethnic changes will not be apparent in all states or in all communities, but the schools where these population shifts do occur need to be prepared for changes within and outside of the classrooms. Inner-city educators have seen massive changes take place. The laws excluding blacks, Hispanics, or other minorities from residing in some parts of town are no longer permitted, but hostility and fear have caused mass exoduses to the suburbs: "The percentage of Blacks in the population of America's central cities rose from about 7 percent in 1900 to 22.5 percent in 1980. . . . When minority group members move out of the city, they are likely to move into segregated suburbs."[20] Along with this de facto segregation, the quality of housing may be poor. Blacks, Hispanics, and Native Americans have often been isolated in areas of a community where poor housing is due to economic factors or the not-so-subtle form of ethnic discrimination.

Site-level administrators must also be aware that our schools have hidden biases built into both the curricula and the expectations of their teachers: "The cultural assumptions of the white middle class are built into today's schools, and ethnic minorities have behavioral as well as learning problems as a result. For example, success in school depends largely on the student's ability to meet middle-class standards of discipline and self control."[21] Many teachers, however, are aware of the cultural differences between ethnic groups and anticipate potential learning problems as they plan their lessons and work with individual students. Many districts, particularly those with large minority populations, have actively recruited black, Hispanic, and Asian teachers who are familiar with the cultures of their students and who can also serve as positive role models for them.

If schools are not located in the inner city and if there is not a large population of poor minority children, differences in learning styles or outcomes may not be noticeable. It is social class, not race, that seems to make a difference. The children of middle- and upper-class parents do better in school than do the children of the poor. The Coleman report indicated that social class was the single most effective predictor of achievement in school.[22] This is primarily because middle- and upper-class homes emphasize books, a large vocabulary, and achievement in school, and schools are primarily organized around these same components.

Many minority students encounter racism within the school system itself. Despite the civil rights push of the 1960s, numerous incidents of bigotry are documented yearly in the public schools. Site-level administrators must ask a number of questions about teacher training that involves our living in a pluralistic society and teaching students to accept others. Some of the questions that might be asked are: Do teachers secure the necessary training in their teacher training programs to recognize racism in the schools? Are teachers aware of the psychological harm that can befall a student who encounters racism (intentional or unintentional) on a regular basis at school? Are the teachers prepared to deal appropriately with racial issues that crop up? Are the teachers themselves serving as appropriate models to combat or lessen acts of racism or bigotry?

Del Stover, associate editor of *The American School Board Journal*, suggests six strategies for administrators to consider in developing a sound school–race relations program (at both site and district levels):

1. *Adopt a firm policy of zero tolerance for racism in any form (set penalties for prejudiced behavior)*

2. *Consider unintended messages (no minorities winning awards, for example)*

3. *Start early (lessons in tolerance for preschool and elementary children)*

4. *Expand social contacts between racial groups (integrated teams of all kinds)*

5. *Investigate in-service opportunities for teachers and administrators (instructional strategies)*

6. *Consider adding multicultural education programs to the curriculum (a method of cloistering minorities students' self esteem)* [23]

UNMARRIED MOTHERS

Like many other changes in the nation, the number of children born outside of marriage has risen sharply every year. Of these children, half are offspring of teenagers. On any given day, forty teenage girls give birth to their third child. These babies are often premature with low birth weights, a strong predictor of major learning difficulties.[24] Birth statistics also show substantial differences between various ethnic groups in the number of children born to single mothers: "In 1981, 56 percent of all Black babies were born to unmarried mothers, while 11.6 percent of white babies were."[25] However, the birth rates of unmarried women are growing rapidly among *all* ethnic groups, with blacks being the first group to face this trend.

Debating the reasons for the differences between the ethnic groups in such teenage births or condemning or condoning teenage sexual practices is not the purpose of schools, but principals will have to deal with these problems by addressing a number of issues. First, many young single mothers will have dropped out of school, will be working at much lower paying jobs, or may be unemployed altogether. Thus, their school-age children are apt to live in poverty. Second, as young mothers, they are not likely to be prepared for the responsibilities of motherhood. There is a lack of parental supervision and guidance and little time to support the school in its efforts to educate their offspring. The schools can offer courses about parenting through its PTA or other support groups. Child care can also be provided to increase the attendance at such programs. Pamphlets on parental support can be distributed to the parents of school-age children.

Third, the family physician seems nonexistent in the lives of many young mothers-to-be. Whether the failure to seek adequate medical care stems from being poor, not possessing health insurance, or simply a lack of health-care knowledge, a surprising number of women do not obtain it during pregnancy: "One-fourth of pregnant mothers receive no physical care of any sort during the crucial first trimester of pregnancy. About 20% of handicapped children would not be impaired had their mother had one physical exam during the first trimester, which could have indicated potential problems."[26] Obviously, many women need additional health-care guidance. Schools need to continue to seek ways to deliver this valuable information to school graduates and nongraduates alike. This may well be another example of eliciting the aid of those in the health professions who are not directly part of the school system. For example, volunteer dietitians could provide materials on nutrition to teenage mothers and mothers-to-be so that their children will not encounter learning disabilities when they start school. This emphasizes the importance of good nutrition during pregnancy and after birth.

Fourth, the nationwide problem of drugs is another major dilemma for schools. Schools for years have presented information to school-age young people about the use of drugs. Many outside agencies not only have supported these efforts but also have been invaluable resources to schools at all levels. Despite the time and money spent for these preventive programs, a startling fact remains: "Every year, about 350,000 children are born to mothers who were addicted to cocaine during pregnancy. Those who survive birth become children with a strikingly short attention span, poor coordination and much worse."[27] Schools need to emphasize parenthood in classes where drug use is a logical part of the curriculum.

Fifth, many schools have established nurseries on campus so that young mothers can continue their education and other students can gain experience in working directly with young children. If these kinds of arrangements are not possible, teachers, counselors, and school administrators need to know alternative educational choices for students. Dropping out of school is not the answer. Young parents need education in their lives more than ever before.

Finally, all students need education about sex and the responsibilities of parenthood. Many strong school programs and materials, which can be screened for relevance, have been developed to deal with these issues. Although no amount of education will do away with teenage pregnancy, perhaps some can be provided to limit this outcome. Educators, along with teens' parents, share the responsibility of helping teenagers through the years of adolescence, and part of this is being realistic about sexual relations, pregnancy, and the responsibilities of parenthood.

PEER GROUPS

As humans, individuals interact with other humans with whom they come in contact. Initially, this is generally the family unit; however, as these individuals grow older, other relationships are formed in terms of close friendships and interest groups.

During the school years, an important form is the **peer group** because schools are organized of boys and girls of the same age and approximately the same social status. The major aspect of the peer group is social interaction, and it is a major determiner of group-behavior patterns during the adolescent years. In the adolescent culture, the latest style of dress, knowledge of the current popular songs, and the expressed devotion to "accepted" movie stars, athletes, or singers is important. Good teachers and strong administrators are always aware of the latest fads and crazes and, although they don't always agree with the choices, understand the pressure on adolescents to adopt them.

Peer pressures are not always negative, but instances of delinquency, drug addiction, and other antisocial behaviors have been a direct result of wanting to be loved and respected by peers. One of the oddest of distorted peer pressure by inner-city students was reported in *Time*:

> *The pattern of abuse is a distinctive variation on nerd bashing that almost all bright, ambitious students—no matter what their color—face at some point in their young lives. The anti-achievement championed by some Black youngsters declares formal education useless; those who disagree and study hard face isolation, scorn and violence.*[28]

This value equates social success with academic failure so that, if a student desires to be accepted and perhaps avoid personal violence, he or she must reject self-improvement. This attitude toward educational success is not consistent with the progress that African-Americans have made. In 1990, for example, 33% of all black high school graduates went on to college, which is a 10% increase over 1976. Also since 1976, black Scholastic Aptitude Test scores have increased by a greater percentage than the scores of either whites or Asians. Thigpen explains this dichotomy: "Some education experts associate the rise of the culture of antiachievement with the advent of public school desegregation and the flight of the Black middle class to the suburbs. This left fewer role models where success reinforced the importance of education. . . ."[29]

Another peer group is the gang, which has often influenced the lives of adolescent boys in particular. Traditionally, this has been a delinquent subculture. Gangs differ noticeably from a common core of ideologies:

> *In the process they generate a unique set of understandings, behaviors and forms of their own. Members then come to loosen their commitment to the common core culture, permitting them to generate shared values that, in turn, allow them to violate, or intensify, significant aspects of it. In effect, a "consciousness of difference" rather than a "consciousness of kind" has emerged.*[30]

Most gangs in California, for example, are organized along ethnic lines. The major groupings are Asian, black, Hispanic, and white. Although other groups exist in other states, these gangs have received the greatest amount of attention during the past few years. Gang members include both sexes, and both can be equally violent.

Gangs have been part of American culture for many years, but now they are better armed and are more violent. The gangs of *West Side Story* are tame compared with the vicious groups of the 1990s. The major change has been the frequency of drive-by shootings, which take place for the purpose of revenge on a member or members of a rival gang but which often involve innocent bystanders, including small children. The weapons of today have changed from fists and knives to handguns, shotguns, and automatic weapons.

School authorities cannot possibly control the outside activities of students who are members of these gangs, but they can become aware of the dress and graffiti representative of them. Students often write on their school folders and clothing, and teachers and administrators need to be on the lookout for these symbols, particularly with younger children. Graffiti is often the first indication that gangs have entered a particular community. Although the typical age of gang members is 12–24 years, younger members are often recruited before age 12, and school personnel may be able to counsel younger children before they are influenced to join a gang.

Gangs often adopt colors and designated wearing apparel including jackets, caps, shoes, sweatshirts, and even shoelaces. Some hair styles are also means of identifying groups. However, because fashions change with gangs as they do with the rest of society, school administrators need to keep in close touch with law enforcement officials before concluding that certain colors or haircuts are representative of a particular group.

Groups of these types are not isolated pockets of young people:

> *Currently in Los Angeles County, there exist over 650 street gangs with an estimated membership of between 40,000 and 50,000. Approximately 280 of these are Black gangs with 15,000 members. All of these groups contribute to the crime problems within Los Angeles County and some are spreading to other communities throughout the country.*[31]

Though the defense of territory, or turf, is still an issue with gangs, many gangs have moved toward organized crime. Robbery and theft are often part of a gang's activities, along with narcotic trafficking: "At the present time there are approximately 25 major Black gangs from Los Angeles that are trafficking narcotics in other states. . . ."[32]

Many officials believe that this factor alone is the major reason for increased gang involvement in crime-related activities.

Because of their middle-class upbringing, in addition to their years in college, many teachers are completely unaware of the pressures brought about by gang members on younger students. We, as administrators, may be in the same boat. All of us are aware of their existence, but we do not fully understand their purposes, their symbols, or their behaviors. There are organizations that do understand them as well as any outsider can. Site-level administrators need to contact leaders of these groups. One such organization is the Gang Alternative Prevention Program (GAPP), a county probation program in California; other states promote similar efforts. Teachers, parents, and others in the community need to talk with the people from these programs to fully understand how to oppose the growth of the gangs and how to identify their members.

Community Needs

Although we could include more examples and supportive statistics, the preceding ones underscore the fact that diverse community needs exist in every school district and need to be addressed as an integral part of a school–community relations program. No organization, not even the best of schools, can cope with all of these existing sociological factors. Every site-level administrator needs to become aware that the problems are real and that many of her students and families live with them on a daily basis. She then needs to concentrate on those problems that affect the school to the greatest extent.

The National School Boards Association (NSBA) suggests a number of remedies that could be adopted by a total school district or an individual school:

1. *Establish a local policy to help all children learn—perhaps by means of counseling programs, tutoring or parent involvement;*

2. *Examine the needs of the community and determine whether parents need day-care service, health services, job skills, or the help of volunteers;*

3. *Develop a demographic profile of the school system—find out whether*

families are in poverty and whether they are single-parent families, migrant families, immigrant families—and communicate this information to all people in the school system;

4. *Define and identify all youth at risk—considering such factors as student absenteeism, poor grades, low test scores in math or reading, chemical dependency, boredom, and family mobility;*

5. *Follow student progress in school by keeping comprehensive records;*

6. *Evaluate programs that have already been implemented;*

7. *Give administrators and teachers flexibility in helping students at risk and make use of student mentors, faculty advisors, teaching teams, and tutoring;*

8. *Involve parents in children's schooling; and*

9. *Work with local businesses, agencies, and organizations to develop and fund programs.*[33]

No school principal or school staff can implement these practices alone. Actions to develop such comprehensive efforts will require board support, adopted district policies, and strong community commitment.

All too often, we embrace a single change for our school, either curricular or in teaching, and expect innovation to do away with all educational problems that exist at the site. Many of these new ideas have contributed to better education for youth, but a single change or recommendation has never been successful for everyone. In 1983, for example, the National Commission on Excellence in Education issued its landmark report entitled *A Nation at Risk,* which identified problems within the nations' schools and offered a series of recommendations to come to grips with the problems. Although the report had a major impact on people's beliefs that a "rising tide of mediocrity" was in our schools, it did little to develop strategies for dealing with these problems, particularly those suggested previously. The efforts of the states that heeded the concerns brought forth by this report, and similar ones, were instrumental in increasing teaching salaries, requiring more academic courses, developing higher graduation standards, and increasing the amount of time in school.[34] These efforts as well as other adopted changes, however, have had little effect on community problems or the demographics of individual school districts. What takes place daily on a school campus is the responsibility of the professional staff and the community as a whole.

Each community is unique, and higher graduation standards may do little for the at-risk student who lacks parental support, suffers from economic deprivation, or has little incentive to succeed at school. The professional staff of an individual school campus must devote all of its energies to seeking out youth with needs and attempting to remediate the problems. What takes place with students daily on a school campus will not be improved by the actions of a national task force, no matter what its good intentions are, but only by the commitment of a school faculty and the community as a whole.

If the NSBA recommendations are to be implemented, the community needs to support the schools, and such support is not as easy to secure as it once was because of the ever-changing faces of our communities. However, the needs and expectations of parents and their children must be determined so that appropriate programs can be developed.

Assuming that such data are available, the site-level administrator must be willing to take the leadership in disseminating information about how the school is doing. Information routinely accumulated within the regional accrediting documents may well be a place to start. These evaluations seek to emphasize the major strengths and weaknesses of a school and, if used appropriately, can be the beginning of the effort to implement the NSBA proposals or others that may present themselves.

The communities of the nation's school districts will vary to a great extent. None of them will fit a single mold, but all need the best schools possible for their children. If students are having difficulties learning, it's up to us, as professionals, to do something to overcome these road-blocks. We need to stop blaming the parents because, as one educator said, "They send us the best kids they have."

As Rutter found in his research, high-performing schools maintained high standards, required more homework, had clear and well-enforced standards of discipline, and yet still created a comfortable, supportive atmosphere for students.[35]

Although Rutter's research may sound easy to implement, it is not, as any school-site administrator knows. For starters, you must address a long list of questions centered on this research, including the following:

1. How can high standards be maintained with large classes and decreasing budgets? With students who are not motivated to learn?

2. How can more homework be required when some teachers balk at grading it? When some students do not complete what is currently being assigned?

3. How can we get all teachers to agree to the same standards of student behavior?

4. How do we communicate the established standards to all students and their parents?

5. What is a comfortable, supportive atmosphere for students?

6. Do all faculty and staff members know how to support such an atmosphere?

SUMMARY

1. The changes in the size of communities have also brought about a variety of social problems. These problems have included crowded conditions, high-priced housing, crime, and special concerns for ethnic minorities and the elderly.

2. The family structure of the American agricultural society has been all but replaced by a variety of configurations in today's industrialized society. The most dramatic change has been in the number of single-parent families. Evidence does not indicate that children are negatively affected by both parents working, but the phenomenon of latchkey children is more widespread. Left to fend for themselves, many of those children ignore homework assignments and are given little time to discuss school with their parents.

3. A higher degree of poverty exists in the United States than before, and almost 40% of young people are a part of low-income levels. Some 40 million people in our country are at income levels designated below the poverty line.

4. All disabled school children must be placed in an educational setting in which they can function. Students must be assigned to the least restrictive environment and must have an individualized education program (IEP), which requires the involvement of the school principal as well as others.

5. A higher percentage of Americans are ethnic minorities, and many schools are encountering ethnic changes in their classrooms because of this growth. School administrators need to be alert to hidden ethnic biases built into the curricula and the expectations of teachers.

6. The number of children born to unwed mothers has risen dramatically, and that fact can bring potential problems to our schools. Schools need to consider parenting classes or emphasize parenting skills in regular classes to deal with this trend.

7. Peer pressures continue to have influences on adolescents, which can affect their progress in school. Most notably, these pressures can lead to drug use and other antisocial behaviors.

8. Gangs are on the increase in America and are both better organized and more vicious than ever before. Principals need to contact outside agencies that deal with gangs so both principals and teachers can keep up to date with gang symbols.

9. If the problems confronted in our communities are to be changed, it will take the combined efforts of the schools and the communities they serve. Individuals and community agencies are vitally interested in the public school system and should be a part of solving existing problems.

10. Each site-level administrator of a school must work with his teaching staff and community to answer questions directly related to creating an outstanding school. These problems will not be the same for all levels of schooling or for all school districts, but all schools can improve.

DISCUSSION QUESTIONS

1. With the economic conditions the way they are in the United States, many parents feel they both must work. What suggestions as a teacher

or potential administrator would you make to parents regarding their school-age children?

2. As educators, we have no control over who is poor and who is not. In what ways do schools make poor children second-class citizens, and what can we do to prevent this from occurring?

3. Unmarried mothers are usually at the high school level, although not always. What educational options does your district offer for young unmarried mothers? How are these options conveyed to the pregnant teenager?

4. Does your community have gangs? What evidence have you observed or read about their activities? What community or school programs have been created as a result of their existence?

5. How does your school compare to the four criteria of Rutter's research? Where do you believe your school could improve for each of them?

ACTIVITIES

1. Talk with the seasoned members of the school where you work and ask them to list community changes they have observed in the district during their tenure. Share this list with your fellow students. Are there common listings, or is each community unique?

2. Without raising any political issue, gather statistics about the ethnic makeup of your student body and faculty. Does each sizable ethnic student group have role models with whom to identify? Discuss with your fellow students efforts that could be used fairly to offset any glaring discrepancies.

3. Take the NSBA list of recommendations to your principal or district administrator and evaluate each item as either "completely implemented," "partially implemented," or "not implemented." Discuss the results with your fellow students.

4. Interview a member of the local law enforcement agency (city police or county sheriff) and ascertain the problems caused in the community by youth or gangs. Share this information with your fellow students.

5. Do you think it's possible for schools and communities to face up to the challenges of our changing communities? Explain your answer.

PARENTS DEMAND THAT THE SCHOOL YEAR REMAIN A TRADITIONAL ONE

As Bill Johnson drove toward Elm School where he was the principal, he thought about the year that was winding down to a close. It had been an interesting and challenging eight months, with the new programs in science and social science, six new teachers, and the crowded conditions.

The overcrowding, at least, would be resolved with the year-round program starting in the fall. Both the district and the faculty of Elm School had been discussing the proposal for several months. With the increased number of housing developments within the school's attendance area and the inability of the district to pass a bond issue for a new school, there seemed no alternative but to adopt a plan that would accommodate 20%–25% more students at the existing sites.

The district had been cautious about the decision—visits had been made to other districts within the state where the plan was already in effect. Several teachers from his staff had been given release time to visit these schools and to talk to teachers who were on year-round schedules, to gain their perspectives. In addition, all published materials available about the system were distributed to teachers and administrators of the district to read before their in-service sessions.

Despite these investigations, heated arguments had risen among some of the teachers. During a number of meetings, staff members debated their concerns about sharing rooms, the packing and unpacking necessary to prepare for the teachers of the next track, and the loss of traditional holidays, which many teachers had thought of as part of the curriculum. Two teachers, Mr. Brown and Ms. Silver, had voiced particular antagonism about the supported plan and at times had actually been angry with other teachers who were slowly convinced that the year-round proposal was the correct one.

As the site administrator, Johnson felt that the in-service programs and the release time for the visits had been worth both the cost and the time involved. Just yesterday, the school superintendent had commented upon the work Johnson had done in this regard. In just two weeks, the proposal would be presented to the board, and both Johnson and the superintendent were convinced that it would be adopted with little or no opposition.

Johnson's thoughts were brought back to the present as he eased his car around the corner and into the parking lot of his school. He was instantly startled by the number of cars already there. The annual spring musical was usually limited to the parents of the performing students. If the parking lot was any indication, there would be an overflow crowd!

As he entered the auditorium, an unusual feeling was obviously in the air. Many voices echoed throughout the room, and parents were gathered in small groups rather than having taken seats for the evening's performance. As Johnson strode to the microphone, he caught snatches of conversations that were obviously not about the musical program. He thought he had better calm the group before things got out of hand!

He was able to say "good evening," and the first interruption came from Charlene White, one of the more vocal and critical parents: "Mr. Johnson, before we start tonight's program, we want you to tell us about the rumors we have heard about a year-round schedule for our children this coming fall."

Momentarily taken aback by the abruptness and tone of the question, Johnson realized he had to do something. He quickly pulled himself together and said, "We are here this evening, ladies and gentlemen, to honor those students in band and chorus who have waited all year for this evening's program, and I do not feel any of us wants other issues to supersede that purpose." There was a rather sizable round of applause from a good portion of the seated parents at this remark, but it did not quell Mrs. White, who continued: "But many of us here are concerned about how our schools are organized, and as parents we need to know what's going on."

"And you will be told, Mrs. White," Johnson responded, "but tonight's performance is neither the time nor the place. I'll set up a meeting for next week, and all of you will be notified."

Another voice came from the audience: "Mr. Brown and Ms. Silver told us you would try to put us off."

And yet another parent: "Our families want the schools run as they've always been, and we don't want to copy other districts who don't care."

DISCUSSION ISSUES

Past

1. What school-community techniques were overlooked during the planning for a possible switch to year-round schools?

2. Who was the one responsible for the breakdown of communication to the site-level administrator or superintendent? How could better planning have avoided blame?

3. How could the reactions of parents been anticipated? What measures of public opinion were overlooked?

4. Knowing that at least two outspoken teachers were against the proposed plan, how could Mr. Johnson have measured the degree or depth of concerns of his total staff?

5. What factors seem to be influencing the teachers and the parents about year-round schools? What steps could have been taken to anticipate what they would be?

Present

1. What should Johnson do at this moment? How can he avoid alienating either the parents who want to hear the music performance and those who want to discuss the year-round school issue?

2. Assuming that something is done temporarily to quiet the crowd at the performance, what steps does Johnson need to take the next day?

3. What, if anything, should be done about the attitudes of his two teachers, Mr. Brown and Ms. Silver?

4. If there continues to be divided opinions by staff members, what courses of action can be taken?

5. If the board does accept the year-round school proposal, what kinds of communication still need to be made to the community?

REFERENCES

1. Harold Hodgkinson, *A Demographic Look at Tomorrow.* (Washington, D.C.: Institute for Educational Leadership, 1992), p. 47.

2. James William Coleman and Donald R. Cressey, *Social Problems.* (New York: Harper & Row, 1987), p. 476.

3. Robert Bellah, *Habits of the Heart: Individualism and Commitment in American Life.* (Berkeley: University of California Press, 1985), p. 284.

4. Michael D'Antonio, "Tough Medicine for a Sick America," *Los Angeles Times Magazine* (22 March 1992):32.

5. Ibid., p. 33.

6. Marvin J. Cetron and Margaret Evans Gale, "Educational Renaissance: 43 Trends for U.S. Schools," *The Futurist* (September/October 1990), pp. 33–40.

7. Congressional Budget Office, Government Printing Office, Washington, D.C., 1990.

8. Harold Hodgkinson, *The Same Client: The Demographics of Education and Service Delivery Systems.* (Washington, D.C.: Institute for Educational Leadership, 1989).

9. National Education Association, *NEA Today* (September 1993), p. 31.

10. Sally Reed and R. Craig Sautter, "Children of Poverty," *Phi Delta Kappan,* June 1990, p. 130.

11. "Below the Line," *Time* (18 October 1993):20.

12. Ibid., p. 3.

13. Reed and Sautter, "Children of Poverty," p. 133.

14. House Select Committee on Children, Youth, and Families, *No Place to Call Home: Discarded Children in America,* 101st Cong., 1st sess., 1989, H. Rept.

15. E. D. Hirsch, Jr., *Cultural Literacy: What Every American Needs to Know* (Boston: Houghton Mifflin, 1987).

16. Joel Spring, *The American School 1642–1985* (White Plains, N.Y.: Longman, 1986), p. 331.

17. Jeffrey Kaiser, *The Principalship* (Mequm, Wis.: Kaiser and Associates, 1991), p. 97.

18. James S. Coleman, et al., *Equality of Educational Opportunity* (Washington, D.C.: Government Printing Office, 1966).

19. Hodgkinson, *The Same Client,* p. 3.

20. Coleman and Cressey, *Social Problems,* p. 479.

21. Ibid., p. 202.

22. Hodgkinson, *The Same Client,* p. 8.

23. Del Stover, "The New Racism," *American School Board Journal* (June 1990):14–18.

24. Hodgkinson, *The Same Client,* p. 5.

25. U.S. Bureau of the Census, *Statistical Abstract of the United States,* 1983–84 (Washington, D.C.: Government Printing Office, 1985), p. 64.

26. Reed and Sautter, "Children of Poverty," p. 135.

27. Hodgkinson, *The Same Client,* p. 16.

28. David Thigpen, "The Hidden Hurdle," *Time,* 16 March 1992, pp. 44–45.

29. Ibid., p. 45.

30. Trice Harrison and David Morand, "Cultural Diversity: Subcultures and Countercultures in Work Organizations," in *Studies in Organizational Sociology,* edited by Gale Miller (Greenwich, Conn.: JAI Press, 1991), p. 73.

31. San Bernardino Sheriff's Employees' Benefit Association, *Gangs, Groups, and Cults* (San Bernardino, Calif.: Stuart-Bradley Productions, 1990), p. 31.

32. Ibid., p. 37.

33. National Commission on Excellence in Education, *A Nation at Risk: The Imperative for Educational Reform* (Washington, D.C.: Government Printing Office, 1983), p. 136.

34. "Work in Progress: Ten Bellweather States," *Agenda* (Spring 1991):17.

35. Michael Rutter, *15,000 Hours, Secondary Schools, and Their Effects on Children* (Cambridge, Mass.: Harvard University Press, 1979).

INTERACTING TO CREATE A VISION

CHAPTER OBJECTIVES

In this chapter, you will learn

- How to develop a mission statement

- Some of the leadership responsibilities of the administrator

- How to manage time for long-range planning

- About two specific styles of leadership

- Some methods of accessing the ideas of others

- About different elements of school culture

- How the principal can implement his or her vision

CHAPTER OUTLINE

- The Principal as a Visionary

  Leadership Styles
  The Need for Visionary Leaders
  What Visionary Leadership Means

- Searching for Visionary Ideas

- The Principal's Role in School Culture

  Signs of School Culture
    Slogans
    Symbols
    Ceremonies
    School Heroes

  The Faculty Subculture

- Setting an Example

he past two decades have witnessed multiple appeals for more effective schools. An entire movement was created by the expressed concerns of parents and others about the adequacy of the public school system in America. These verbalizations were supported by research data and a number of commission reports. Despite massive efforts to revive public schools, many of the proposed changes have not secured the desired results.

Everyone wants effective schools. The quality of a school is important for students, faculty, and parents alike. All school-connected groups, including administrators, leaders, students, and parents, must be involved in the planning process if they wish to realize an effective school. All of these groups need to share a common educational vision for the institution. In attempting to develop the school's vision, a school group usually produces a **mission statement,** which guides program and curriculum planning, development, and ultimately, evaluation. A mission statement is a philosophical framework that defines an organization's main purpose, recognizes its special qualities, and establishes its overall direction. "The mission statement also serves as the basis for communicating within and outside the organization with those who are important to the school's effectiveness and success." [1]

All of these groups need to be continually involved in the process to maintain the sense of participatory decision making. Teamwork is an essential part of an effective organization, and one element of that concept is a common vision.

The Principal as a Visionary

t is logical that the one to assume the leadership role would be the school principal, since he is designated by position to be the school leader. Furthermore, research has indicated that the site-level administrator can make a difference in the effectiveness of a school. But there are many steps to achieving effectiveness. An effective school must have a sense of purpose and direction. If goals are well developed and clearly articulated, the sense of purpose will be clear to everyone involved. A principal can be successful in managing the goal-setting process. To achieve consensus and commitment from the staff, a principal will need a thorough understanding of the school and how the various parts interact. The principal must also have a clear vision of how the school will operate at some specific time in the future.

LEADERSHIP STYLES

Leadership, to be successful, must have a high quality of understanding between those who lead and those who follow. Leaders can be dictatorial, democratic, or laissez-faire; organizations survive if the followers understand and accept that particular leadership style. Two other styles defined in the literature by Burns are transactional and transformational.[2]

Transactional leadership is a status quo approach, a custodial form of operation. The leader deals with goals and values, but these are rarely new. The guiding philosophy might well be: *Don't fix it if it isn't broken.* The organization under transactional leadership is predictable and emphasizes problem solving.

The approach is that of a single-loop learning . . . in which efforts are expanded toward compliance with pre-existing norms.
    Single-loop learning follows these steps:

1. [Establish] a norm.

2. [Monitor] for compliance of that pre-established norm.

3. [Take] corrective action at bringing the organization back into compliance.[3]

In contrast, **transformational leadership** embraces creativity and looks upon existing practices or approaches as acceptable only if there are no better ways. The transformational leader uses personal influence to motivate the organization and its members to be risk takers. Members of the organization challenge the status quo through cooperative efforts. They create new answers to both old and new problems through a shared purpose. As Sergiovanni suggested, transformational leadership and fellowship operate from the heart as well as the mind and thereby exploit the highest level of moral response.[4]

THE NEED FOR VISIONARY LEADERS

Our educational programs, and our schools in particular, need visionary leaders. Change has always been inevitable, but the rate of change in our world is increasing; change happens on a daily basis. To adequately deal with change and, perhaps more importantly, to lead students to deal with future change requires school-site administrators who can facilitate change within the schools and districts.

Not all schools, of course, require a new sense of direction or purpose. However, as you may recall from Chapter 3, many schools are experiencing a sudden change in student population, a change in the community's involvement, and other trends. These changes may lead to the school's need to develop a new mission statement.

WHAT VISIONARY LEADERSHIP MEANS

To be an effective leader, one must be able to assess an organization's needs. One must also be able to project what the organization might become in the future. A leader who has these qualities is said to have vision. According to Sashkin,

> *Visionary leadership really means three things. It means that the leader is able to develop long-range visions of what his or her organization can and should become. . . . Visionary leadership also means that the leader understands the key elements of a vision, what must be included in a vision if it is to direct*

the organization into the future. Finally it means that the leader can communicate his or her visions in ways that are compelling, ways that make people want to buy in to the leader's vision and help make it happen.[5]

Traditionally, political and business leaders have brought about change by developing long-range views. In this century alone, we have witnessed the impact of a number of political leaders. Franklin D. Roosevelt, Winston Churchill, Mahatma Gandhi, and Martin Luther King, Jr. all created visions for their nations, developed committed followings, and then worked to solidify their ideas into a mission. The same qualities of leadership have been observed within some of our nation's businesses. Many times new executives have been hired to rescue floundering corporations and subsequently have developed new visions that have saved these companies. Lee Iacocca's commitment to Chrysler Corporation is a notable example. His vision, and the response of the company's employees to it, rescued the organization from potential bankruptcy.

Schools are neither nations nor profit-centered businesses, but they still require visionary leadership and often need to be overhauled, just like some businesses. Too often, schools, their faculties, and their administrators become stagnant, no longer seeking new ideas or attending to the changes in the makeup of the student population or the greater community.

Although it's the principal's responsibility to guide the development of the vision, others must share in both its creation and its implementation. Often, the school staff, the parents, and the students must modify their behavior so that the vision can become a reality through the daily operation of the school. Obviously, this is not a simple task, and there are no standard blueprints for accomplishing it. There is agreement, however, that the responsibility at the site-level is that of the principal. As Manasse states, "There is no individual with a better overall knowledge of the school, the staff, the students, the available resources, the needs, the expectations, and the intersections among all the above and the district and larger community."[6]

The visionary principal, therefore, not only must look at what the school is—both strengths and weaknesses—but also must have ideas about what it *can* be. For the creative principal, developing vision may be relatively easy, but it still may be challenging to develop vision among the school staff. For a vision to be realized, the work required to reach it must be one shared by the entire staff. It will require good planning as well as collaborative decision making throughout the entire process.

When we look at the long list of tasks required of a school principal, we can see that much of her time is spent on issues and situations that simply crop up. This leaves little time to reflect on goals or to engage in long-range planning. Most of the tasks that principals perform fall under the category of administration or management.[7]

Although management activities are necessary and cannot be ignored, a principal must find time for the "big picture." Perhaps the initial activity, other than dreaming of what a good school can be, is understanding the school and its culture. In order to take a good look at what exists, the visionary principal has to free herself from the countless meetings and interruptions that typically limit a principal's time for more creative tasks.

Appropriate use of time, therefore, is important. In his book *How to Get Control of Your Time and Your Life,* Lakein suggests many ways to save time and to avoid being trapped by other people's priorities.[8] For example, he suggests sorting tasks daily into three categories— *A*s, *B*s, and *C*s, with *A*s being the highest priority. Clarifying a vision would thus have a high *A* value. Therefore, it would warrant spending a major part of the day or week on this task. The others (the *B*s or *C*s of Lakein's system) would either be put aside or delegated for others to handle.

Lakein also suggests that every major goal be broken down into a list of tasks to accomplish to reach that goal. He also recommends that all leaders develop a daily "to do" list, to focus one's energies on the tasks that make up the goal. Developing a vision for the school will require a multitude of tasks. One of the first will be the gathering of ideas from other members of the faculty and staff.

Searching for Visionary Ideas

knowledge of any organization's history and culture is the foundation on which to build the future of the institution, but the politician, corporate head, or principal realizes that ideas for that vision will not be the sole inspiration. Although some inspiration may be born from insights and dreaming, most is generated by the ideas of others.

The leader is often able to formalize an idea and develop it more fully. For example, Winston Churchill, one of the century's greatest public speakers, attributed his approach to speaking to an American he met only once, in 1895, early in his career.[9] Churchill was able to take this person's six simple ideas, build on them, and develop his own oratory skills to the high level of mastery for which he was internationally recognized during his lengthy and successful political career.

School employees are a natural source for new ideas and concepts. Not only will the principal encounter fresh views about the school as he talks to his staff, but he also will gain insight into how others feel about the school. As a by-product, the principal also will gain knowledge about the relative strengths and concerns of those in each department or grade level. Later, after the principal has formulated the vision, he will be able to draw on his understanding of school staff to help realize the vision.

The principal should spend time talking to individual teachers and key groups that make up the organization of the school—the administrative team, the faculty advisory committee, departments, and grade levels—to develop collective ideas. This gives everyone an opportunity to share common concerns and discuss goals, but it also allows the principal to articulate his own philosophies about the school and its future. Members of these key groups must carry out the actions necessary to realize the vision. The principal especially needs the commitment of those who work on a daily basis with students; it is very important that these people embrace the vision. The principal should seek goals that faculty and others agree upon.

Eventually, as a result of these individual contacts and small group meetings, an administrator will formulate a mission statement. The statement provides an identity and unity for those who are part of a particular school or district. It provides a basis on which future decisions can be made.

The various groups and subcultures of the school (faculty, administration, parents, and others) may have a difficult time giving up old aspects of the culture and accepting new ideas. As Deal states, "In order to transform schools successfully, educators need to navigate the difficult space between letting go of old patterns and grabbing onto new ones."[10] A vision is influenced by a school's culture, which is a representation of what its members collectively believe themselves and the education program to be. If teachers have high expectations of students, and that is an accepted part of the school's culture, the students will achieve a high level of success. If teachers, parents, or students see the school as a "holding tank" for students (that is, without its own significant culture), then everyone will react accordingly. If the staff is cohesive, the culture will probably produce a shared focus; if it is dysfunctional, the focus will be scattered. But even with a cohesive and well-functioning staff, the goals may be outdated and the school may require new directions.

An effective principal will place a premium on communicating the agreed-upon mission statement or vision to all constituents. It is through effective communication that consensus, commitment, and programs for the future can best be realized. The methods for communicating a school vision are endless. They include school stationery, banners, buttons, book covers, logos, business cards, pamphlets, T-shirts, school pencils, and articles in local newspapers, to name but a few of the ideas for marketing the school's purpose and direction.

The Principal's Role in School Culture

s Deal states, "Powerful forces over the past decade have weakened the culture of schools, and changes in the educational environment have raised questions about whether existing cultural patterns are equal to new demands."[11] Although the principal of a school may not be able to combat community interests, public demands, or changes in demographics, she can build upon what exists as part of the school culture and refocus disparate views. Understanding the culture of a school is a prerequisite to making the school more effective. Vision can only be developed if the leader has a complete understanding of the organization itself. Specifically, the leader should,

1. Explore and document the school's history.

2. Begin praising the school's heroes and heroines.

3. Review the school's rituals.

4. Plan and carry out old and new ceremonies.

5. Call attention to the "folklore" of the school—from faculty and student alike.

A leader must search out the traditions at a school, maintain and build upon those that add to the desired vision, and help create and support activities that can be a part of the traditions of the future.

As Deal indicates, "Folklore and myth, tradition, taboo, magic rites, ceremonies of all sorts, collective representations, participation mystique, all abound in the front yard of every school, and occasionally they creep into the formal portions of life." [12]

If people want to make changes in a school to make it more effective, then they must understand the culture of the school. According to Deal, "Culture is an expression that tries to capture the informal, implicit—often unconscious—side of business or any human organization. It is often described as 'the way we do things around here.'" [13]

Although culture varies from one school to another, every school has one. It develops from both outside and inside the school. The local community may have held specific expectations for the school, particularly if it has remained stable. Parents, too, may have supported specific values for the school, which contributes to the school's culture. Within the school, the traditions and values of the faculty, administration, and students are all factors that make up the culture. As Manasse points out, "Excellent organizations have well defined basic purposes on which they focus their organizational energy and resources. Their leadership is strong and focused, directed toward creating commitment to purpose. Their leaders are aware of the value of symbolic actions and the influence of culture on productive organizational climates."[14]

Most organizations treasure their values, symbols, and beliefs. It gives purpose to the daily routine of the organization's existence. The U.S. service academies, for example, are rich in these signs of culture. Fraternities and sororities make much of the existence of symbols, and athletic teams have rallied around slogans for as many years as sports competition has been in existence. Likewise, most elementary and secondary schools have many traditions and customs that teachers, administrators, students, parents, and others support and pass on to the next generation.

SIGNS OF SCHOOL CULTURE

Educators have discovered that the "school spirit" of a school can be used to increase the enthusiasm of the students and sometimes the teaching staff. As the major universities and professional organizations have adopted mascots, slogans, and logos for their teams, so have schools at all levels.

■ SLOGANS

Businesses create lasting customers by their advertising mottos about services and products. Similarly, schools develop loyal followers among their current students, alumni, parents, and other community members with slogans, which can be based on overall history of achievement, a single event, a particular strength, or a perceived attitude. Often it is what the school stands for. Hardly anyone in America doubts that the name *Harvard University* stands for quality education because the school has had a lengthy history of success. If a school adopts a slogan based on its past achievements, such as, "A Dedication to High Academic Achievement," the students, faculty, and community expect these kinds of results and the expectation itself helps bring them about.[15]

A slogan can be based on a single achievement. For example, schools that have won state or national awards can turn these achievements into slogans that can last for years after the students responsible have graduated. Winning a state science award, for example, can lead to the slogan, "First in Science for the New Age." This slogan can apply as long as the school continues to emphasize science in its curricula.

Teachers who have a gift for motivating students and who have a reputation for high standards may also be the subject of a school slogan. School-site administrators may also help create a strong feeling for the school and student achievement. Many grade schools distribute bumper stickers such as the following to parents of achieving students:

We are proud parents of an honor student at _____ School.

My student goes to _____ School.

■ SYMBOLS

One of the most obvious symbols in any community is the school itself, particularly if it has been there for some time and alumni are members of the community. Schools of all levels often hold special places in the hearts of people who attended them.

At the school itself, the most prevalent symbol is often the school mascot. Some schools even develop other aspects of the school culture around its mascot. Elementary schools, for example, often choose animals as their symbol. For example, a school that uses a bear as its mascot may create "bear bucks" to award to high-achieving students who, in turn, use this paper money to purchase materials at the school site. Some teachers purchase rubber stamps that depict the school mascot and use the stamps to signify good grades on student papers or projects. In this way, the school mascot symbolizes strong academic performance.

At the middle and high school levels, mascots are the names of competing athletic teams. The teams have yells, cheers, and fight songs to urge the school to victory. In this case, the mascot symbolizes higher athletic achievement.

A mascot is only one example of a school symbol. Many other symbols abound at schools to motivate achievement. The students themselves must, of course, rally around the symbol as representing their school. Otherwise, it has no motivating force behind it.

■ CEREMONIES

Schools support ceremonies in a variety of formats. In the same way that football games begin with the traditional flipping of a coin, so do many schools start the day with a traditional ceremony. For example, many schools, particularly elementary schools, begin with a schoolwide meeting in which participants salute the flag and sing the school song. Other ceremonies include rallies, assemblies, student body officer retreats, and graduations. The presentation of awards (such as banners and trophies) to the school are ceremonies that encourage participation by onlookers as well as those directly responsible for the award.

Schools also have ceremonies for parents. There are open houses, back-to-school nights, PTA meetings, award or honors banquets, scholarship award meetings, parent conferences, and so on. Most ceremonies for faculty and staff recognize individual or group contributions to the school during the year or over a longer period of time. For example, some schools hold end-of-school-year awards breakfasts or luncheons to honor teachers for their work and dedication. Such ceremonies add to the school staff's morale and culture.

Schools also conduct ceremonies that single out leaders who are leaving the school for other sites or who are retiring. These ceremonies are also important to school culture. Former teachers who have already retired may be invited to share in the celebration. This helps build strong relationships between existing and former staffs.

■ SCHOOL HEROES

All schools have myths, legends, or stories about teachers or other employees whose contributions to the school have been woven into the culture of that school. Sometimes these are verbally passed on by teachers and students from one school generation to another. Teachers may become heroes by their very commitment to their profession. A teacher who turns down a larger salary in industry to remain in teaching, or a teacher whose students consistently win awards, becomes an important part of the school's history.

Students also may be subjects of school legends. Student leaders may be heroes based on a number of criteria, including their leadership qualities, scholastic achievement, or major accomplishment in athletics or other cocurricular activity. Student accomplishments often affect the tone of the school and, consequently, other students' behavior and performance. Some schools have helped support their heroes by creating graduate "Halls of Fame," with student pictures and data—year of graduation and accomplishment—prominently displayed. William McKinley High School in Honolulu, Hawaii, for example, maintains a number of pictures of famous graduates in its lobby. Oakland Technical High School in California displays a picture of former student and veteran movie actor and director Clint Eastwood inside the entrance to the school.

THE FACULTY SUBCULTURE

The school faculty also has its own subculture, with ceremonies, heroes, values, and beliefs. This subculture may center around personnel relationships, teaching assignments, or teaching strategies. The values and beliefs that teachers subscribe to are greatly influenced by their group affiliations. The many different faculty groups on campus may be defined by seniority, grade level assignment, department, age, gender, and so on. Groups may even be defined by where their members gather for lunch. As students are expected to adhere to the language, dress, and informal "rules" of their respective groups, so are teachers expected to behave like their colleagues.

Although most rules for faculty behavior are not significant, some attitudes and beliefs are, and the impact will often influence the total school program. For example, suppose the local union representative for teachers is highly respected and has stated strongly that to volunteer for any activity threatens the total profession. In this case, it will be difficult for an administrator to secure a volunteer from among the faculty.

When facing issues relating to faculty subculture, it's important for the principal to focus on common ground or on more flexible attitudes. Begin with problems that nearly all faculty see as important, such as pupil attendance, low achievement, discipline, or at-risk youth. This way, the faculty will begin moving toward the proposed vision. Strong schools generally have a balance between old and new values; it's beneficial to seek a similar balance between tradition and innovation.

Setting an Example

n order to further develop a vision for the school, the principal not only must voice her ideas but also must model the desired behavior. For example, if the proposed vision includes a mandate that something be done to "mainstream" at-risk students and the faculty commits itself to counseling these students at every opportunity, then the principal needs to lead the way. The principal must be on the grounds or in her office as needed. She must attend school events and take the opportunity to encourage, praise, and listen to the at-risk students.

Thus, the principal's involvement extends beyond the creation of a philosophical mode. He or she has to be involved in the implementation of the total vision. By doing so, teachers and others will be motivated to embrace the goal, and its parts, to help it become a reality.

Sometimes while developing a vision for the future, new ideas simply get out of hand. There may be too many creative ideas generated simultaneously, and the efforts to create a new, distinctive, productive school can appear to be chaotic and inappropriate. At such times, the principal can help articulate the vision in terms that are clear and widely understood. He may add, modify, or discard strategies, but the vision will remain the same. As long as staff sees the forward progress, any temporary roadblocks will be overcome.

Sometimes looking at the future in its totality is too demanding an undertaking and the principal needs to break the goal down into its various parts. This may take a series of planning sessions with different school groups, or with the entire staff, to help develop realistic steps. Change depends not only on wanting to reach an ideal but in knowing how to lead others there as well.

A school leader can identify and build on those aspects of the school's culture that support what he is attempting to accomplish. All schools are unique and need to be recognized as such, but there is also a commonality of purpose, which can be useful to the school vision. It is up to the site-level administrator to capitalize on both the uniqueness and the commonalities and to thereby articulate a direction for his school.

None of the activities discussed will bear fruit unless detailed action plans are a part of the process. As the mission statement or vision becomes a reality, plans need to be developed to capitalize on the strengths of the school. Opportunities for further progress will appear, as well as threats or limitations to progress made.

As strategic goals are agreed upon, the principal must develop action plans to carry out the objectives for reaching those goals. Professor Herman writes that "nothing significant and purposeful will take place unless detailed action plans are developed for each objective." Herman explains:

> *Each action plan should identify:*
>
> - *The specific tasks to be accomplished*
>
> - *The chronological order in which each task is to be accomplished*
>
> - *The person or persons responsible for accomplishing each task*
>
> - *The resources required to accomplish each task*
>
> - *The measurement to be used in determining whether or not the objective has been achieved at the qualitative level desired.*[17]

SUMMARY

1. In order for a school climate to be positive, there must be a vision for that school. A visionary principal can make a difference in a school's future.

2. In order to be a visionary leader, one must have a long-range view of what a school can and should become. The leader must also be able to communicate this vision to others.

3. The principal is responsible for developing a vision for a school. Implementing the plan requires the modification of others' behavior.

4. Visionary leadership requires time. A principal must be able to organize his or her day, week, and year so the majority of time is spent on high-priority tasks.

5. A school principal must actively seek ideas for the school vision. This will require meeting with individuals and the key groups that make up the school's internal structure.

6. Another aspect of the school that needs to be explored is the school's culture. The vision of the school of the future will require an understanding of that culture.

7. Old slogans, symbols, ceremonies, and heroes should be kept in the framework of the new vision. Newer signs of the school's changing culture should be developed in order to help support the new goals of the school.

8. Attitudes and beliefs among the faculty subculture may or may not be changed. The principal should focus on those that may and should be changed.

9. The principal's involvement in the vision extends beyond the creation of a philosophical mode. He or she must model the type of behavior desired in the new vision.

10. Creating a new school vision requires time for things to change. Realistic steps need to be taken rather than expecting to accomplish all of the necessary changes overnight.

DISCUSSION QUESTIONS

1. When do people at your school discuss values? How much time do you give to this task, and how deep do the discussions go? Have your discussions made an impact on your school for the future?

2. Has your principal sought ideas from other members of the school staff in relation to the school's future? How were these activities carried out? What were the faculty's reactions?

3. What faculty subculture groups exist at your school? List them, without revealing the membership. Do these groups help or hinder the progress of your school? Explain your answer.

4. How is education viewed from the district level in your district? What symbols are used at the district level to give support to strong education? Discuss these symbols with members of your class.

5. Do all teachers at your school support the same values and beliefs about what the school stands for? What positive and negative attitudes influence the school's progress? Which views have the greatest influence at your school?

ACTIVITIES

1. Interview your site administrator and/or other school leaders. Do they have the same idea of what the school vision is or ought to be? How do their ideas differ? Share and discuss the results of your interviews.

2. List the observed cultural aspects of your school according to the categories described in the chapter. How deeply embedded are these in terms of the school's functioning? Discuss with your class members those cultural aspects that you feel are the strengths of your school.

3. Ask your fellow students to list the major cultural aspects of their schools. Compare these lists for similarities and differences. Name and discuss the ones that seem to be the most unusual in terms of how they might help your school.

4. Break into small groups and develop a series of slogans or symbols that could be used by a mythical school. How would you use these in your vision for the school?

5. As a class, write a survey questionnaire to study cultural values for schools. Survey the faculty of each of your schools about the nature and strength of the school's culture. Use a scale of 1 to 5 for each item on the questionnaire. Share and discuss the results in class.

BULLDOZING A CAMPUS TRADITION

It did not seem as if it had been six months since Principal Bill Johnson had received his appointment to head Elm School. Frankly, being from out of the area, he had not felt that he had much of a chance at that time but had thrown his hat into the ring in order to gain the interview experience. Despite feeling that he had done well in front of the selection committee, he was still surprised when he had been offered the position.

The first half of the year had gone quite well. He had worked hard to communicate with both the students and faculty at Elm and felt that he was being accepted by both. Students and teachers had complimented him on some of the ideas he had brought to the school and a number of parents had either telephoned or stopped him at parent meetings to say that they also had liked some of his ideas. Some students —particularly some new students—had commented how much they appreciated his friendly but businesslike style with them.

There was one group, how-ever, with which Johnson felt he had not been successful. That was the senior class. He knew that it was difficult to follow the leadership of Pearl McLean, the previous principal, who had been the site admin-istrator at Elm for almost twenty years before her retirement. Johnson felt that he was follow-ing an institution rather than a human being when he first started in the fall, but he felt less and less threatened by her image as the year progressed. The senior class initially indi-cated concern about her retire-ment, but Johnson had not changed the school in any major way.

One of the senior class traditions bothered him, and he twice talked to the class officers about it. An area in the school's quad had been designated as "Senior Row" and a sign hung over the entrance to the area. The school's vocational depart-ment had planted trees and shrubs and had constructed benches for student seating.

Lately, there had been some problems with juniors trying to

"crash" the area during the lunch period, and a few fights had occurred. Although the individuals involved had been disciplined, the major problem was that the area was situated in the traffic lane between the four major classroom buildings that joined the quad. Unsuspecting nonseniors sometimes wandered into the area as they went from class to class and to lunch.

Last Wednesday, Johnson's concern about Senior Row became a major issue on his agenda. During lunch, some juniors had again entered the area, had argued with the seniors, and had arranged to meet at the area after school. A full-scale riot ensued, and it required all of the school's administrators, security personnel, and available teachers to quiet it. Even the local police had been called.

Several students suffered bruises, black eyes, and assorted cuts. Even two teachers had been roughly handled by accident; fortunately, though, no weapons had been used.

The faculty had been quite upset during the next day's faculty meeting, and the two teachers who had been injured were both absent from school. With all the extra precautions taken, no additional problems had occurred within the boundaries of Senior Row during the subsequent two days, but Johnson felt that something had to be done. So Friday afternoon he ordered the maintenance department to bring a bulldozer to the campus on Saturday and level Senior Row, except for any trees that had been there beforehand. The staff complied with his request.

Starting early Monday morning, there were numerous telephone calls from parents and former students of Elm School. The local newspaper sent a reporter to take pictures. Several parents threatened to go to the board of education, and members of the senior class threatened a strike if Senior Row was not reinstated. Even some teachers voiced their concerns.

The matter was to be a scheduled item on next Tuesday's board agenda. Johnson had an appointment today to discuss the matter with the superintendent.

DISCUSSION ISSUES

Past

1. What did Principal Johnson fail to do in assessing the school culture at Elm School? What steps should he have taken?

2. When the original problems surfaced between the juniors and seniors, what other steps should have been taken? Why?

3. Who else could Johnson have sought help from? Would these contacts have helped the overall situation?

4. Evaluate Johnson's action on Saturday. Was it the appropriate step to take? What other choices were available to him?

5. When the decision was made by Johnson to take the action he did, should he have involved others? If so, who?

Present

1. What can Principal Johnson do to mend the wounds between himself and the senior class? With the others in the community?

2. What are Johnson's options as far as Senior Row is concerned? What problems would occur if it were rebuilt?

3. Traditions are important in a school culture. Can they be tolerated, though, if they bring about problems? What steps could be taken to avoid such problems in the future?

4. Assuming that Senior Row remains as it is, what should be done with the area?

When should the suggested changes be made?

5. List some of the traditions of your own school culture. Do any of these have potential problems? Discuss them.

REFERENCES

1. P. J. Below, G. L. Morrisey, and B. L. Acomb, *The Effective Guide to Strategic Planning* (San Francisco: Jossey-Bass, 1987), p. 151.

2. James M. Burns, *Leadership* (New York: Harper & Row, 1979).

3. Larry W. Hughes, *The Principal as Leader* (New York: Macmillan, 1994), p. 66.

4. Thomas J. Sergiovanni, *Value-Added Leadership: How to Get Extraordinary Performance in Schools* (New York: Harcourt Brace Jovanovich, 1990).

5. Marshall Sashkin, "True Vision in Leadership," *Training and Development Journal* 40, no. 5 (May 1986):58.

6. A. Lorri Manasse, "Principals as Leaders of High-Performing Systems," *Educational Leadership* 47, no. 8 (May 1990).

7. Arthur Blomberg and William Greenfield, *The Effective Principal* (Boston: Allyn and Bacon, 1980).

8. Alan Lakein, *How to Get Control of Your Time and Your Life* (New York: Peter H. Wyder, 1972).

9. Thomas Montalbo, "Mr. Churchill's American Mentor," *The Toastmaster* (August 1993).

10. Terrance E. Deal, "Reforming Reform," *Educational Leadership* 47, no. 8 (May 1990):12.

11. Terrance E. Deal, "The Symbolism of Effective Schools," *Elementary School Journal* 85, no. 5 (May 1985):614.

12. Ibid., p. 606.

13. Ibid., p. 605.

14. Manasse.

15. Robert Rosenthal and Lenore Jacobson, *Pygmalion in Classroom* (New York: Holt, Rinehart and Winston, 1968).

16. Jerry J. Herman, "Action Plans to Make Your Vision a Reality," *NASSP Bulletin* 74, no. 523, p. 17.

EFFECTIVE COMMUNICATION AND CONFLICT MANAGEMENT SKILLS

CHAPTER OBJECTIVES

In this chapter, you will learn

- Why strong communication is important for gaining acceptance

- Why listening actively is the most important communication tool

- About four response tools that help people to listen actively

- Some ways to communicate with individuals and with groups

- Some methods and examples of conflict management

- How to avoid a negative school image through good communication

- How other school personnel can contribute to a positive communication program

CHAPTER OUTLINE

- Positive Communication Skills

- The Art of Listening Actively

  Response Tools
  Other Ways to Improve
  Communication

- Administrative Communication Tools

  Person-to-Person Communication
  Group Interaction

- Conflict Management

- Sharing Communication Responsibilities

  Avoiding a Negative School Image
  The Teacher's Role in Good
  Communication

Positive Communication Skills

he site-level administrator soon recognizes that the process of communication is what makes a school function well, both internally and externally. The skill of communication is both a verbal and a nonverbal process that brings people together so that they can mutually solve problems, share ideas, plan programs, and accomplish other things together.

Effective communication brings people together as they process information and, whenever possible, opens the channels for each participant to give feedback to the other. It is based on the relationships that are developed between those taking part in the process.

School leaders must sharpen their communication skills so that they can be successful in dealing with teachers, students, parents, and other members of the community. If the principal is not able to communicate well, the vision of the school will not be realized and the individual encounters and group meetings that are part of the principal's daily routine will not be productive.

As we communicate, we are trying to gain acceptance for what we say. It is therefore important to plan the message to communicate and the way in which it will be communicated. The best way to gain acceptance is to give reasons for the actions that have been or are about to be taken. Most people do not argue or disagree if valid reasons are presented. As a school administrator, it is important to provide time for faculty or parents to ask questions to verify that they clearly understand the implications of the issue under discussion.

Suppose, for example, that a principal is trying to improve her staff. She may believe that the strengths of a second-grade teacher would vastly improve the upper grades if she were assigned to an opening at the fifth-grade level. The principal needs to explain the rationale behind the change. The teacher should not simply discover the change on next year's printed schedule. Or consider this example at the secondary level. Suppose that a high school needs more beginning typing classes. This need causes a temporary shift from other business offerings, which changes a long-standing yearly schedule of one or more members of that department.

If the reasons are part of a complex, multifaceted problem, then it may take more than one session to explain, and the explanation may have to be presented in a variety of ways. Follow-up meetings, letters, school newsletters, and smaller group meetings are all vehicles for effective communication. When trying to persuade someone, the best form of communication is in person; a one-on-one situation is probably better than a group meeting. And it would be most difficult to imagine persuading someone to volunteer for a task or to give up something by requesting through an impersonal written memo or letter.

Effective communicators observe the reactions of those to whom they speak. Their body language and expressions are clues to their reaction to the speaker's message. Finally, administrators who are good communicators know how to use opinion leaders—staff members or community members who are in touch with public opinion—to spread information or ideas. The staff or community may use opinion leaders as sounding boards, an administrator may consult with the opinion leader to find out how others feel about a situation. If opinion leaders feel that others do not accept what has been communicated, the administrator can modify the approach.

The Art of Listening Actively

There is probably no single skill more useful for the site-level admin-istrator than the ability to listen. Administrative studies have consistently shown that about 75% of the contacts an administrator has in a school day are one-on-one meetings. Giving less than full attention during such an interaction can result in miscommunication and can damage morale.

It may be relatively simple to listen to an individual while seated in a quiet office with no interruptions. However, it is not quite as easy to listen with complete attention during the daily administration of a school with seemingly never-ending demands of students, teachers, auxiliary personnel, parents, and representatives of various community groups. Obviously, assorted people do not descend upon the principal all at the same time, but interruptions occur often. If the administrator's thoughts are focused on a meeting scheduled later in the day or week, or on one that has just ended, these thoughts can interfere with good listening posture. To successfully handle the daily demands of the school, a school-site administrator must be able to devote full attention to each issue at hand. Only then will the administrator be able to develop the tools necessary for effective communication.

Listening actually involves all parties. Guidance literature uses the term *active listening* to refer to the process. Dainow and Bailey explain, "Effective listening can only be assessed by the recipient: that is, if I as a listener have not managed to convey that I have done so, communica-tion has not taken place."[1] Therefore, the listener may use strategies to discipline his or her attending skills.

Before discussing some specific skills used by good listeners, it should be noted that observation is also part of the process. Siegman and Feldstein explain, "Face-to-face human communication involves more than the exchange of verbal messages. It includes patterns of visual interaction, facial expressions, gestures, body postures and movements, and tone of voice."[2] Eye contact, smiles, and nods all have meanings that are readily understood in the communication process, but others, such as hand movements, posture shifts, variations in posture, and body orientation of one person to another may not be as clearly interpreted.

With few exceptions, a person's movements cannot be precisely under-stood. However, body language often gives cues that help us develop inferences about the person's state of being. Although it pays to be watchful for possible body movement cues, it may be unwise to read too much into them.

RESPONSE TOOLS

Counseling literature discusses several listening responses, including requesting clarification, paraphrasing, reflecting, and summarizing.[3] These response tools not only help give direction to sessions but also communicate that one is paying attention.

■ REQUESTING CLARIFICATION

Typically, a listener might request clarification by asking the speaker a question about an ambiguous statement that he or she just made. The question should elicit further information about what the speaker said. Here are two examples of requesting clarification:

"Are you saying that one of the more difficult things for you to understand is when to discipline your child?"

"Are you saying that you feel the fifth-grade teaching assignment is not the correct one for you?"

Generally, the questions express the listener's feelings of confusion. The desired responses are usually rephrasing, summarizing, or illustrating the ambiguous remark. The purpose is to have vague statements brought into sharper focus.

Another situation in which the administrator might want to request clarification is when he or she has talked too much and wonders if the other person has understood. Here are some examples:

"I don't think I'm being very clear about this. What sense did it make to you?"

"Well, that's my view about the situation. What do you think of it all?"

■ PARAPHRASING

Paraphrasing is the rephrasing of the content part of the message. It avoids the use of an actual question but functions in the same way as requesting clarification. Paraphrasing allows the administrator to test what he thinks was said. This tool usually helps focus the speaker's thinking in a clearer manner. Although the main purpose is to test the administrator's understanding of what has been said, it is also a test of one's listening skills. When successful, the listener will have shaped the speaker's message into more precise wording and will have clarified mixed or obscure messages. Paraphrasing helps the speaker know when he or she is understood, and it encourages the speaker to continue. However, the paraphrasing must be accurate, of course. Here are some examples:

"Since your husband left, you have all the responsibilities and decisions about your children on your own shoulders."

"You aren't sure why you don't like to work with fifth-grade students."

■ REFLECTING

Reflection is an interpretive rephrasing of the speaker's affective expression. An administrator can respond to something expressed by reflecting what the person is saying or talking about. This kind of response, if used effectively, can also help someone feel understood. People often feel willing to communicate more freely with those who make efforts to understand them. This technique focuses on feelings rather than on content. It is difficult to master. Accurate reflection of the feelings and attitudes of another person requires empathy in addition to exceptional listening skills.

The listener must tune in to "feeling" words, watch for nonverbal behavior (body language and facial expression), and then verbalize these feelings using different words. Generally, reflection isn't necessary for expressions of strong emotions, which are obvious without words. Subtle emotions, though, are often expressed by words. In this case, the listener must tune in carefully to recognize feeling words. Then he or she must describe and observe the speaker's reaction to assess the effect and accuracy of the reflected statement. A listener can also reflect on a speaker's visual, auditory, or muscular expressions of emotion. Here are some examples:

"It looks like you're angry now." (visual)

"I hear you say that you're angry now." (auditory)

"You are feeling angry now." (muscular movement)

■ SUMMARIZING

Summarization builds on what the speaker has said and on the listener's responses. It can include two or more paraphrases or reflections or the entire message being presented. Summarizing can be used throughout a conversation to link several elements. Or it can be used at the end of the session to clarify all that has been said. Or, in some cases, it can be used over several conversations held at different times. Here are some examples:

"Now that you're assigned to teaching fifth grade, it's a lot easier to think about last year's assignment than to anticipate what's going to happen this year."

"You don't like taking physical education. You don't think it's important to learn, particularly if you're not an athlete."

Summaries of a long interview or a series of meetings could themselves become too long. It's important to select the highlights or general themes that accurately portray both content and feelings expressed. The main purpose of this technique is: (1) to show the speaker that progress has been made in exploring the issue, and (2) to open the discussion for a possible solution or at least a logical next step. Occasionally, a more explicit summarization may be appropriate to determine if the two of you have understood each other. Here are some examples:

"I just want to make sure I understand you correctly. You don't like the change to fifth grade, but you're willing to do it for the year as long as we consider you for a primary placement the following year."

"Even though you don't agree with the district policy of requiring athletes to take P.E. during the off-season, you will no longer refuse to dress for gym and will give it your best shot."

OTHER WAYS TO IMPROVE COMMUNICATION

If an administrator uses these four response tools well and accurately, the practice will lead to further exploration of the topic in question. They can be useful tools for obtaining additional comments from the speaker. Administrators must be careful not to overuse them, though.

Administrators often must communicate with students, faculty, and parents in the hallways, during passing periods, or at lunch. These are not the best surroundings for two people to communicate successfully, particularly if the problem requires complete understanding. There are, of course, ways to facilitate optimum opportunities for good communication to take place. Closing the door to one's office or classroom to ensure privacy and limit interruptions will improve the desired two-way communication. Planning before a possible confrontation will at least focus one's listening behavior. And simply listening and curtailing the urge to speak often lessens possible friction caused by charging into a discussion prematurely.

One of the most challenging school-site situations is dealing with irate parents. This interaction requires a great deal of tact and diplomacy. The parent may arrive unannounced, screaming about a school policy or a teacher who has upset his or her child. The verbal assault usually is critical, may be accompanied by a series of expletives, and may be uttered at a decibel level just short of a jet airliner. Without warning, it is impossible to plan for such an interaction. It would be easy at this moment to react in kind, but that would only expand the problem. Many educators have embraced an educational belief that has generally kept tempers at an appropriate, professional level at such times. The belief is, *At least this terribly upset, antagonistic parent is interested enough in his or her child to be there.* There are too many parents who are unwilling to take any interest in their child's schooling and are even unwilling to keep requested appointments to talk about their children's problems.

With a firm grasp of this point of view, a principal can then use some strategies to improve the situation.

1. Get the parent to sit down.

2. Lower your own voice to the level desired. The parent will generally approach the same volume.

3. Listen carefully and take notes.

4. Clarify misunderstandings by reflecting what is being said.

5. Always focus on the issue or child. Sometimes parents will talk about extraneous issues.

6. Promise to investigate if there are statements that seem out of line, and set a designated time to get back to the parent.

Most irate parents, treated in this way, will leave the principal's office with a much milder attitude. The basic skills required to implement these suggestions are simply the ability to listen. If the administrator listens well, the parents (or others) may even feel by the end of the conference that the problems are solved, even though the administrator let the parents do most of the talking. All the administrator may have to do is focus the discussion on the student's problem or the parent's disagreement, reflect what's being said, and ask questions that lead to a solution of the problem or disagreement.

Here are some additional suggestions to consider:

- Analyze past listening experiences: What made them successful? Why did they fail?

- Give the speaker undivided attention; be mentally and physically prepared to listen.

- Arrange favorable physical conditions for the meeting; consider lighting, temperature, furniture, and so on.

- Listen with sincerity to what the person is saying; be patient, because it sometimes takes time to share concerns.

- Avoid interrupting the speaker except to clarify.

- Listen for the main point of what is being said and also, at times, what is not being stated.

- Watch for gestures, facial expressions, and tone of voice that may reveal additional feelings.

- Develop emotional control; concentrate on what is being said and not on how it is being presented.

- Refrain from any sarcastic remarks, even to someone you know well.

- Focus on the problem in efforts to mutually find a solution.

Administrative Communication Tools

As mentioned previously, much of an administrator's time will be spent in one-to-one meetings, but there are times when this venue is impractical or inappropriate. Administrators can communicate in person or in writing. Either way, they can address one person at a time or many. Whenever possible, examine all venues and choose the most appropriate one.

PERSON-TO-PERSON COMMUNICATION

■ INFORMAL TALKS

Throughout the school year there will be hundreds of opportunities for what can be labeled as informal talks. These may include the casual unplanned meeting in the parking lot before or after school, during lunch, or as the administrator watches an after-school event in the company of a teacher, parent, or student. It may also be an unofficially planned meeting by either the administrator or one of the members of the staff.

The following situation is an example of an unofficially planned meeting. A young school principal at a middle school was asked by four female members of the staff to talk with one of the male teachers about his offensive body odor. This was not an issue that needed to be formalized by summoning him to the office. It certainly was not appropriate to address the issue in the form of a letter or memo. So the principal decided to try an informal talk.

A couple of days later, the principal "bumped into" the male teacher after school and shared the concern with him as a friend might have done. The teacher was most appreciative of the advice (at least verbally so) and thereafter took care of the problem. Nothing was mentioned of this issue again. The apparent chance meeting had been planned in advance, of course, in order to handle the situation. But the teacher didn't suspect this.

There are many insignificant issues (ones that may in time become major problems) that can be dealt with in this manner. For example, if a teacher has been negligent in some regard, the principal can drop by the teacher's classroom after school (or during a prep period) and share the concerns informally. Or he can attend extracurricular events at which there may be opportunities for dialogue.

The principal isn't the only one who can plan informal talks. This venue is a two-way road. Some teachers prefer to share concerns informally with the principal rather than call a formal meeting. Taking care of the problem in this way may be better for the administrator, too. The alternative might be having the issue raised at the regular faculty meeting. Even if the issue can't be resolved in the informal talk and has to be addressed later in a faculty meeting, at least the administrator will be better prepared.

This venue is also one of the best ways to communicate with students. Although principals have ample opportunities to meet with students regarding academic, disciplinary, social, or other kinds of problems, the vast majority of students are never referred to the office. According to Gray and Ward, students tend to equate the amount of time their principal devotes to them personally with the amount of care that he or she has for them.[4] Principals can increase the opportunities to talk with students by spending more time on the grounds during recess, passing periods, and lunch breaks. In fact, spending time talking with students at lunch time every day may be one of the best communication efforts the principal can make at his school.

■ PLANNED APPOINTMENTS

Most contacts between a principal and teachers, parents, and students are private, planned meetings. There are teacher evaluations, parent conferences to discuss student problems, meetings to address parent concerns, and so on. Throughout the school year, the school-site administrator has numerous meetings with individuals and small groups of people. The administrator may call the meeting or the other party may request it.

If the principal is scheduling the meeting, he or she should tell other attendees what the meeting is about beforehand. A memo placed in a teacher's in-box and stating, "See me in my office next Thursday at 3:00" may cause undue anxiety on the part of an employee. A note that reads, "See me in my office next Thursday at 3:00 to discuss next year's teaching schedule" would cause less tension.

The second habit that a helpful administrator should follow is preparing and planning for these appointments. For example, if a parent calls to complain about her child's teacher, it will pay to spend time discussing grades, discipline, and other matters with the teacher prior to the appointment. Another example is a meeting with parents who are concerned about the appropriate placement of their child at the school. A quick review of the child's cumulative record, a talk with a school counselor, or a telephone call to the district psychomotorist will be helpful and will facilitate the meeting.

Of course, if another person calls the meeting and neglects to announce the agenda, the principal cannot do much to prepare for the meeting. A well-coached secretary or assistant will ask the caller for the agenda. This will help the administrator plan for the appointment. The assistant can produce schedules, previous communications, or other documents for use during the meeting.

The principal may also need the expertise of other school personnel to discuss a child's problem or series of problems. The classroom teacher, the school nurse, the school counselor, a coach, and a district psychologist are additional resources to draw upon. It is the administrator's task to notify these other people about the nature of the meeting so they, too, can adequately prepare for it.

Teacher evaluations are a special type of meeting. Usually these are rather routine because most teachers do well and have nothing to be concerned about. However, there are times when a school-site administrator will not be able to offer a struggling teacher another contract. The timing of this kind of emotional conference is as important as the required planning. The ideal time for holding this kind of meeting is probably at the end of the school day, with no other scheduled appointments afterward.

■ WRITTEN COMMUNICATION

All messages intended to be preserved should be in writing. Oral messages are quicker and friendlier, but they can be forgotten or ignored. Most people consider written messages to be more formal or official. Such messages can be filed for later reference, if needed. School administrators are likely to write memos, letters, evaluations, thank-you notes, and other kinds of individualized written documents. See the appendix for examples of each kind.

Memos are considered to be less formal than letters and often do not require the filing of copies. Many administrators will even write memos by hand rather than have them typed to stress the informality. Memos often are used to remind people of meetings or to bring previously discussed items for a future meeting.

Letters are more formal than memos and are used for the operating business of the school. For example, a teacher would expect to receive a letter denoting a promotion, an official transfer, or a major accomplishment. Letters often are used to note a major breech of district policy or the negotiated contract. If parents cannot seem to remember previous agreed-upon strategies for helping their child, a letter can be both a reminder and part of the permanent file.

Evaluations must be written and usually are part of a district-adopted procedure. The teacher receives a copy of the document after discussing it in person with the site-administrator. Evaluations become part of a permanent file, which may be consulted if any legal difficulties arise.

Thank-you notes, like memos, are informal and often are handwritten. Teachers and others who do an exceptional job need to be promptly praised for their efforts. Sending a thank-you note is a simple, thoughtful gesture. Principals should send thank-you notes to faculty and staff more often. They might also consider sending thank-you notes to a few students and parents to show appreciation for their support in changing a student's attitude, behavior, or overall scholastic success.

A good time to send such notes would be after report cards come out or at the end of a school year.

GROUP INTERACTION

Both training and practice will generally improve a school administrator's abilities in appropriately handling the different kinds of group meetings that take place during the year. She must feel as comfortable when confronting a group of parents or addressing citizen's groups about the state of education in America as she does in a meeting of equals. Besides interacting with others through meetings and conferences, administrators also communicate with groups through the written word.

■ MEETINGS AND CONFERENCES

Staff meetings. These group meetings should be handled in a collegial manner so that important matters can be discussed and decided. Faculty members often think that staff meetings are used only for announcements, that they are more of a lecture by the principal than a sharing of ideas, and that they are held too frequently. The perceptive principal will, of course, be aware of teacher concerns about staff meetings and will take these steps to assure that positive practices such as agenda setting, timing, and faculty participation are followed.

In an article that originally appeared in *Psychology Today,* the National Association of Elementary School Principals offered these tips to make a staff meeting work:

1. *Determine if the meeting is required. Meeting when there's an issue at hand can be more effective than scheduling regular staff meetings.*

2. *Get the right people to attend.*

3. *Establish the meeting's purpose and time frame and stick to them.*

4. *Prepare and insist that others do so, too.*

5. *Review the results of the meeting before adjourning, and set specific guidelines for acting on them.*[5]

Staff meetings are the best way to deal with school issues. Sometimes, though, it is more appropriate to meet with smaller groups, such as the staff of one department or grade-level.

Planned conferences. These are generally more formal in nature and may have a set purpose. In-service programs and meetings to discuss gangs or drugs in the school are examples of planned conferences. The administrator may serve as keynote speaker. Or he may serve as facilitator, focusing the conference, outlining the format to be followed, and summarizing the results. With the trend toward more teacher empowerment, it would be better to have faculty members plan the topics and organize the meetings.

Mass meetings. All principals have numerous opportunities to address large groups of constituents, including PTA members, incoming parents and students from lower grades, graduating classes, and even an entire student body. This kind of mass meeting is not a forum for discussion. Rather, it is a presentation. The key, of course, is to anticipate what the audience will want to hear. A graduation speech might well be traditional, but a request from the parents or a representative of a feeder school may have a hidden agenda. Explore their needs and prepare for the presentation beforehand.

Use of the P.A. system. If there was ever any school instrument that has a history of being overused or misused it is the public address system. It is unsurpassed, of course, for the handling of emergencies. But it is inappropriate to interrupt the educational program of the entire school in order to contact two or three students. Many classrooms are equipped with individual phones. Administrators should use the P.A. system (and even classroom phones) sparingly. Teachers resent having their lessons interrupted, and rightly so.

■ WRITTEN GROUP COMMUNICATION

There is no way to predict how people will respond to a written group communication. There's no guarantee that everyone will even read the message. However, face-to-face individual meetings or staff meetings are neither practical nor desirable for all communication situations that arise. Several methods commonly used in schools can be adapted for the particular receiving group or to represent the personality of the sender.

A few representative examples are discussed here.

- *The daily or weekly staff bulletin.* This document usually is used for announcements and reminders; care should be taken that articles do not become too lengthy and that items are not repeated too often.

- *Newsletters.* This document goes out to parents or to special groups of parents who have students at the school. Newsletters usually report the school's or program's progress and may include student contributions. In some communities they are published in multiple languages.

- *Handbooks.* The most common of these are student, parent, and faculty. They need to be updated yearly and, in the case of both the faculty and student handbook, discussed at the beginning of the school year. (See the appendix for possible topics.)

- *The circulated clipboard.* This vehicle often is used in elementary schools to inform teachers of a last-minute change (such as a rainy day schedule). A student takes the notice to all teachers, who initial it to show that they have read it.

- *Monthly calendars.* These are used for students, teachers, and parents to remind them of the month's activities. Some schools attach this as a page of the regular newsletter.

- *Bulletin board notices.* All schools have strategic places to post information for both faculty and students. Care should be taken that all dated notices are removed on a regular basis so new information is noticeable and readable.

- *The school newspaper.* This student publication can be used to remind students of upcoming events. It also serves as a forum for student concerns.

- *T.V. shows.* Some schools have the facilities to produce their own school news show.

- *School marquee.* Most schools have a marquee on which a limited amount of material can be displayed. This is primarily for the people who drive by the school. The marquee can highlight special events, such as an open house or graduation.

Conflict Management

ome members of school faculties will inevitably have conflicts with one another. Substantial disagreements may occur over curricular objectives, policies, teaching practices, as well as emotional conflicts that often develop between people. "Major conflicts typically occur as the result of a minor incident that acts as a seed: a facial expression, remark, or word used in a memo is interpreted in a negative way. The need to be right sets the interpreter on an unconscious quest for data confirming the initial interpretation." [6]

The role of the school principal in such situations is to help those involved obtain resolution so the differences are lessened. The goal is to help analyze the conflict, determine both parties' needs, develop a resolution, and, if necessary, draft a contract for change. This is often difficult to do because of the emotional overtones that accompany these kinds of conflicts. However, administrative assistance increases the chance of success when independent attempts have failed to resolve the problem. Another strategy is to simply control the conflict so that the school is not adversely affected, even though the antagonism continues to exist between the individuals involved.

If an administrator wants to create the conditions for a constructive process of conflict resolution, she should use the attributes of the cooperative process, including: "good communication, the perception of similarity in beliefs and values, full acceptance of one another's legitimacy, problem-centered negotiations, mutual trust and confidence, [and] information-sharing." [7] As Walton suggests: "When facilitated by a third party, the conflict management process . . . can be educational or developmental for the participants, improving their skills for diagnosing conflict and resolving it through interpersonal dialogue." [8]

A principal must draw on many qualities to help resolve conflicts among staff members. He needs an understanding of human relations, an attitude of acceptance, and the ability and willingness to give emotional support to those involved in the conflict. One technique the principal can use is to hold discussions with each person separately to prepare them for future discussions with one another. Both disputing parties need to feel that they can be open about the situation and that support will be forthcoming from the principal to accomplish resolution.

The administrator can help each individual make his or her specific wants known. These can be specific (like a particular assignment, duty, or location) or subjective (like the manner in which the two parties interact). Differences should be negotiated to the satisfaction of everyone.

The administrator can then hold a conference between the two participants at a neutral spot. This may be the principal's office, another campus location other than the participant's classrooms, or even off campus. Timing is important; both parties should be available for as long as it takes to discuss the issue. The principal should arbitrate, keep the two parties focused on the point under discussion, and keep the discussion moving. Occasional observations about the discussion and about any agreements being developed are appropriate.

Although ideally a dispute should be settled in a single session, further discussions may be needed. If everything goes well, both parties will appreciate the principal's role and will want him to continue.

Above all else, the principal's role in such situations is one of being neutral. He should not use his or her position to resolve the conflict but should facilitate the process by allowing discussions to take place within an appropriate setting and time frame.

The principal has to be careful to concentrate on the issue at hand and allow the parties to express their feelings as well as actual events. According to Sandole and Sandole-Staroste,

> *The need to express one's sense of being restricted, put down, rejected, insulted, overlooked, unappreciated, slighted, confused, hurt, betrayed, bored, manipulated, or any other pinch brings us to the first of the conflict management skills: learning to describe behavior rather than to attribute and describe motives.*[9]

Burton and Dukes divide the mediation process into twelve stages. These are defined as follows:

1. *Initial contacts with the disputing parties.*

2. *Selecting a strategy to guide mediation.*

3. *Collecting and analyzing background information.*

4. *Designing a detailed plan for mediation.*

5. *Building trust and cooperation.*

6. *Beginning the mediation session.*

7. *Defining issues and setting an agenda.*

8. *Uncovering hidden interests of the disputing parties.*

9. *Generating options for settlement.*

10. *Assessing options for settlement.*

11. *Final bargaining.*

12. *Achieving formal settlement.*[10]

Mediating union contracts or labor–management conflicts may be somewhat different than solving conflicts between faculty members. But these twelve stages apply equally to both situations. The process is an art grounded in accepted practices like those listed. The school administrator must also keep in mind that conflicts are not ended until both parties have agreed that they have ended. And it must be fully understood that stability cannot last forever. Incidents will recur and both individuals are responsible for continuing a positive relationship. When incidents do arise, they will be able to take appropriate actions to deal with them.

Sharing Communication Responsibilities

ffective communicative skills are not limited to the school leader or other administrators. Members of the teaching and support staff have similar obligations because they, too, confront the public on a regular basis. All members of the school organization share responsibility for effective communication.

AVOIDING A NEGATIVE SCHOOL IMAGE

Whatever the contact between a community member and a member of the school staff (administrator, teacher, classroom aide, or bus driver), a message is conveyed about the school and the quality of its educational program. And the message may be longer lasting than the topic under discussion. All members of the school staff should use care in communicating with the public. They should try to represent the school in a positive manner. *Feelings are facts.* The way that students, parents, and others perceive a school will make a much stronger impression than any data.

For example, some teachers are masterful in the classroom as they work with students but, for whatever reason, appear defensive and antagonistic when confronting parents. Some administrators are also defensive. They may possess outstanding organizational skills or curricular knowledge but seem to adopt a confrontational mode when dealing with members of their own staff or community. No one expects a teacher or school administrator to be calm and understanding 100% of the time. But defensiveness does not help the communication process. All school personnel should be aware of the impressions they make and should work at honing their abilities to communicate effectively.

Even the routine daily contacts with the public can establish a negative image of a school. Handling incoming phone calls, school visitors, and new students are just a few examples of contacts that require care.

■ INCOMING TELEPHONE CALLS

There is probably no secretary or clerk who does not, at times, want to disconnect the telephone so it does not interfere with the many other tasks that need to be completed. However, many parents and others telephone the school for information or to share concerns about the school's programs. How these calls are handled may make the difference between a positive or negative feeling about the school itself. Support staff may be trained in appropriate phone skills, but handling hundreds of calls can take its toll. The principal should periodically monitor support staff to make sure that tone of voice or curt responses are not interfering with good school–community relations.

Explaining why someone is not immediately available, taking accurate messages, and assuring callers that someone will contact them later should all be part of the school's telephone courtesy. It is especially important to discuss phone courtesy with students who may be recruited to answer the school telephone. An irate parent may not realize a student is answering the call and may become angrier if an appropriate response is not forthcoming. The students should be given a list of appropriate responses, such as "He's not in. May I take a message?" or "Ms. _____ is off campus at this time. If you give me your name, I'll have her call you."

■ SCHOOL VISITORS

Some parents or others simply go directly to the school (without phoning first) to see a teacher or administrator. How they are directed and how quickly they get service also make an impression. All of us have felt positive about a business or institution when the receptionist immediately greeted us with the question, "May I help you?" These simple words do a lot to dispel concerns that may have brought us there in the first place.

Frequent checks on the attitudes that support staff convey toward visitors may improve skills, if necessary. Again, particular care must be taken if the regular staff is out to lunch and the office is being staffed by student or volunteer help.

■ NEW REGISTRATIONS

Sometimes parents show up at a new school with their children. Sometimes, students show up by themselves, particularly at the secondary level. Parents may bring documents about the child's previous education history, or they may not. If proof of immunizations is required, the clerk may need to explain this to the parent. Some parents need help obtaining immunizations or documentation for their children.

Some schools discourage students entering a classroom if the registration takes place considerably after the beginning of the school day. This policy should be carefully explained to the parents. However, if circumstances preclude the child returning home, then he or she should be welcomed into the classroom.

If the feedback from students, parents, or other groups is clearly negative about how they were treated by the administration, teachers, or support staff, then it's time to work on communication skills. A number of books, courses, and in-service programs are available to help in this regard. These can be used for the entire school staff, if the problem is universal. Or they can be tailored to selected school personnel if necessary.

The most important role of a school-site administrator is to observe potential problems and counsel those who seem to be unaware of the impressions they make. Several years ago, I visited a middle school and overheard a clerk assigned to handle student absences. The clerk was sarcastic and caustic to every student who came to the window to report. She certainly deserved an "A" for consistency, but her obvious disdain for students should have been corrected. Three months later, the same verbal abuse was still in evidence. A strong, alert administrator should have been monitoring that unacceptable behavior and should have worked with the offending individual to correct it.

THE TEACHER'S ROLE IN GOOD COMMUNICATION

A commonly voiced maxim is, *a strong school–community relations program starts in the classroom.* This principle is probably true. Many national educational polls report that parents obtain much of what they know or what they support about the classrooms and the schools from what their children report to them on a daily basis. It is therefore important for teachers to emphasize a strong academic program and to communicate the accompanying goals to the students. Communication means more than presenting a lesson. It also includes how the students are accepted and treated in the classrooms. The teacher who finds time to talk with his or her students individually in the classroom during the school week not only is doing a better job of teaching but also is helping establish a stronger community understanding of the school's purpose.

Good teachers have long understood and utilized this approach in their teaching, but even the best of them sometimes create communication difficulties with the very instructional approaches they use. The school-site administrator must be aware of the potential "hot spots" and must monitor them regularly and work closely with those teachers who regularly have problems. These hot spots include teaching methods, controversial issues raised in the classroom, homework assignments, assessment, retention and promotion, and discipline methods.

Schools should not expect or desire all teachers to think and perform in the same way, but the school administrator should understand that innovative teachers are sometimes misunderstood by students and parents. Some new teaching methods, in fact, may be unacceptable. The site-level administrator should visit classrooms often and take the opportunity to discuss experimental teaching approaches before they are used. The principal or teacher may decide to send an explanatory letter to the parents before the new program begins. In any case, the principal should be informed so she is prepared to address possible inquiries from parents.

The following example will give some perspective. Several years ago, a high school principal hired a beginning teacher to spearhead the development of a sophomore English honors program. In her eagerness to succeed, the teacher developed a 25-page syllabus for the students outlining the required readings and assignments for the entire semester. The students, being new to the high school level and being overly conscious of the need for high grades, balked at all of the required work. That afternoon, and all of the next day, the phone rang with calls from parents requesting to have their children removed from the program. In discussing the situation with the teacher, the principal found the teacher to be quite defensive but eventually receptive to the idea that she collect the syllabus from the students, symbolically tear one up, and tell the students that she would start over. She followed through with this plan, and the transfer requests slowed to a trickle. At the end of the semester, she reported that she had covered everything listed in the original syllabus, plus some additional work. The students hadn't complained about the work because by that time they had discovered the teacher's great strengths and were willing and able to complete the assignments on time.

Not all such situations have a happy ending, however. In the early 1950s, an elementary teacher was highly criticized by parents because he took the desks out of the classroom and replaced them with more comfortable furniture. He changed the lighting in the classroom so that there were centers with adjustable illumination for the project under way. He had the students working in groups rather than individually, gave assignments according to the students' interests and abilities, and emphasized a "class community." At another time or place, this teacher would have had droves of educators visiting his classroom. As it was, the principal bowed to community pressure and did not recommend a renewal of the teacher's contract.

In both instances, it would have been much better if the parents had been told about the exciting programs beforehand. Prior knowledge would have lessened parents' anxiety. And, in the second example, a good teacher may have been retained.

■ CONTROVERSIAL ISSUES

Schools must teach controversy if our students are to grow up with the ability to make judgments and grapple with the issues confronting them as adults. There are very few topics of educational merit that do not have opposing views.

If teachers want to include appropriate controversy for the age level or subject area, they should share their ideas and teaching materials with the principal beforehand. That way, the principal will be able to discuss the teacher's plans logically if concerned parents call.

Literary materials and textbooks are selected with careful consideration. If the site administrator reads (or even scans) the materials, he will be able to defend them. For example, it was easy for one high school administrator in the Midwest to defend a social science teacher's use of *The Daily Worker* in the classroom because he knew that representative publications of other "isms" in the continuum of economic and social beliefs were also included as part of the reading assignments for that course.

On the other hand, parents have the right to protect their children from materials that are against their religious beliefs. In the vast array of good literary publications, there must be others that teachers can use for any given purpose. However, no parent has the right to dictate what *other* students in the classroom can or cannot read. As one writer puts it, "Parents should be consulted [and] involved in the election process . . . as advisors and not as censors."[11]

■ HOMEWORK ASSIGNMENTS

Some schools and districts have mandated that homework be given in certain subjects on designated days. This is not a widespread practice, though, and it is generally not considered a good idea. However, most districts have adopted broad guidelines for the amount and kinds of homework that may be assigned at a particular grade level. Parents should understand that homework is a necessary and supportive aspect of the learning process.

Some teachers give too much homework and some give too little. This can cause difficulties when parents begin comparing teachers at the same grade level or for the same academic subject area. If problems occur, then teachers across a grade level or within a department may need to set appropriate standards.

Most concerns about homework seem to surface when students do not understand the purpose of the assignment or if the homework is used to discipline the student. Teachers should be encouraged to discuss the purpose of homework with their students at the beginning of each school year. They should also be encouraged to seek other approaches for classroom discipline. Teachers may wish to provide parents with guidelines about their homework policies, the purpose of an assignment, and the responsibilities of the parents in support of these activities.

■ GRADES AND THE PUPIL PROGRESS REPORTING SYSTEM

There is probably no area that creates more negative reaction from parents than grades. Some parents believe that when teachers grade students they are, in effect, grading the parents as well. Many parents react defensively about the marks their children receive. Although no plan of action will completely curtail problems at the grading periods, teachers can reduce the problems. There are some suggestions that have proved to be helpful in the communication process. Pass along these suggestions to teachers.

■ Remind parents about district policies on grading, and follow the policy. For example, a district might endorse a policy of no "F" grades without a previously mailed progress report.

- Keep a well-documented grade book. A parent will react less negatively to "Your son missed 19 of 25 assignments" than "He missed a lot of his assignments this semester."

- Sit with each student independently and communicate academic progress. Review the grade prior to the issuance of the report card. This strategy will greatly limit the number of complaints. Students have a much more difficult time telling their parents, "I don't understand why I received such a low grade," when the teacher has carefully gone over the facts with the students.

- Involve guidance counselors, as appropriate. At the high school level, grades and credits affect graduation and college admissions. Counselors should report to parents about their youngster's academic standing, especially during the senior year. The number of earned credits may determine whether a student will take part in the graduation ceremony. In many states, grades have a major bearing on a student's eligibility for extracurricular activities.

■ RETENTION AND PROMOTION

Despite many studies regarding student retention, there still seems to be no consensus regarding its effectiveness. Research indicates that students suffer trauma from being held back and that students who are retained actually perform worse than those who are not retained. Teachers encounter pressure from their colleagues to retain students who do not perform at grade level.

In the 1980s and early 1990s, there was a movement to get tough with academic standards. Several states adopted proficiency tests at designated grades; to move on to the next grade level, a student would have to pass the test. Despite these efforts, the problems of poor performance still exist. A 1986 study in New York City indicated that 40 percent of the city's children who were retained dropped out before the end of high school as compared with 25 percent of students who had not been retained.[12]

Although many schools have adopted discipline policies, these are sometimes interpreted differently by the teachers. Some schools leave classroom discipline completely up to the teachers. Classroom misbehavior and misbehavior outside the classroom both must be monitored closely. Whereas most teachers have the skill to handle routine classroom disturbances, some do not. Most teachers set reasonable classroom standards, monitor their students appropriately, and rarely call for assistance from the administrative staff. Others, however, refer students to the office for the slightest infraction (not having a pencil, for example).

Not all teachers who overuse the office staff for disciplining students are poor teachers. But they do need in-service training on discipline. They need to learn which problems to handle themselves and which ones require outside help. Appropriate behavior models and special in-service programs available to teachers can improve this situation.

In a study by Vredevoe, students report several factors as important in a school discipline program. In order of importance, these factors are:

1. Interpreting the reasons and purposes of the rules

2. Fairness in enforcement

3. Treatment that recognizes the maturity of the student

4. Consistency in enforcement

5. Enforcement without embarrassment, whenever possible

6. Observance of rules by teachers

7. Opportunity to participate in making rules in areas where students are capable.[13]

Adhering to these criteria does not in itself create a strong discipline program. However, they are worth the attention of any school staff. If parents or students voice concerns about the discipline program, it may be appropriate to examine this list of criteria with faculty, an advisory committee, or an ad hoc committee of parents.

SUMMARY

1. Positive communication skills are a must if a site-level administrator is to be effective in dealing with the many people that he or she will encounter. People often obtain their impressions of a school by the quality of the communication efforts.

2. The most important skill of the site-level administrator to develop is the art of listening. The ability to be a good listener improves communication and helps avoid misunderstandings.

3. For working with staff, students, and others within the school, the willingness to follow an open-door policy will improve communications between the administrator and those groups. Although the administrator cannot always be available, the appearance of accessibility can improve relationship with staff, parents, and students.

4. Dealing with irate parents is never pleasant but can end with better results if the administrator adopts some techniques. Listening can be an important stance to take. Keep in mind that at least the parent is interested enough in their child to approach the school.

5. The principal can use many communication tools, both verbal and written, including one-on-one talks (informal and formal), memos, letters, and group meetings.

6. Gaining acceptance of what is being communicated is more difficult than simply expressing an idea. This usually requires additional planning. Probably the best technique to use is to give reasons for decisions made.

7. One of the roles of the school principal is to monitor conflicts between staff members.

8. The routine daily contacts of outsiders with the school are often lasting and form the basis for one's image of that institution. These include interactions with administrators, teachers, classroom aides, or bus drivers.

9. A strong school–community relations program starts in the classroom with the teaching approaches and personal attitudes of the teachers. Parents often get their impressions of a school from what their children tell them.

10. For various reasons, some teachers are not as strong as they ought to be in communicating with other adults. A strong school administrator will watch for the common classroom communication problems and will help teachers avoid or overcome them.

1. Why are teachers, administrators, and others sometimes negative when communicating with parents and others? What can you, as the school administrator, do to improve the situation?

2. What options does a school administrator have in dealing with a member of the clerical staff who continues to respond negatively to school visitors?

3. What steps would you, as the school administrator, take if an irate parent went directly to a classroom and verbally attacked the teacher at that location?

4. When are thank-you notes appropriate? Some teachers have more opportunities to show their skills (for example, coaches and music teachers); how can an administrator balance this form of praise?

5. Suppose you were a site-level administrator and your opinion leaders indicated a lack of understanding of an issue by parents. You had already sent home a newsletter about the issue. What methods would you now use to increase or gain understanding and acceptance?

1. Observe the office at the beginning and close of the school day. Analyze how office staff interact with students, parents, and others. Share with your fellow students your recommendations, if any, for improvement.

2. Observe listening skills in others at your school. Are there differences among faculty members? Does the site-level administrator always

listen? Is there a need to improve this skill on the parts of staff members? Report your findings to the class.

3. Analyze your staff meetings in terms of strengths and weaknesses. What have been the strongest and weakest aspects of these meetings? After looking at the weaker aspects, state how you as the school administrator would have improved these meetings.

4. Bring to class your student, parent, and faculty handbooks. In small groups, discuss the strengths of the handbooks. Compile a list of items that you think would be of importance, but that are not included in your school or district handbooks.

5. Discuss the six types of classroom "hot spots" discussed in this chapter. Describe a realistic scenario for each one. In small groups, discuss how you would go about resolving the problem. Share your agreed-upon process with the rest of the class.

GRADS' NIGHT OUT

For the past three years the seniors at Elm School tried a number of grad-night pranks that were upsetting to both the school's administrative and teaching staff. Three years ago they hung posters throughout the school campus; these were innocent enough. Last year, they filled all of the classroom door locks with glue, and it took a locksmith to make the locks workable again. It did not seem appropriate to do anything about the matter, so no investigation was made or penalties assessed.

This year, the rumors about a variety of senior shenanigans circulated around the campus. Some of the more sensible students brought them to the attention of Bill Johnson, the school principal. Johnson knew that he should head the matter off, and he tried talking to the officers of the senior class. Although all of them concurred with Johnson that the activities were getting out of hand and did little for the good name of the class, they felt that they had little power over the more rowdy seniors.

The rumors persisted and Johnson met with the student body council, which included a number of influential seniors. They, too, agreed that the acts were inappropriate. But they also reiterated that, although their efforts might stop a few from participating, they could not influence all members of the graduating class.

With only five weeks to go before graduation, Johnson was continuing to receive comments from both students and faculty expressing concern. There were now rumors that some of the students were going to disrupt the graduation ceremony itself. Something had to be done, and quickly.

Johnson met with his faculty advisory council, which decided that Johnson, as school principal, should address the entire twelfth-grade class. A week later, the assembly was held in the school auditorium. Principal Johnson was popular with the students at Elm School. He spent almost every lunch period on the school grounds, attended all of the sports events, and supported the student council and other school organizations

in their special projects. When he strode to the microphone, the seniors gave him a standing ovation.

His heart sank a bit at the recognition, but he knew he had to deliver an ultimatum to the students. He had worked hard on his talk and started by reminding the students of all they had accomplished during their four-year stay at Elm— the high scholastic records they had set, the number of scholarships awarded to the students, the high number of Merit Scholars, the athletic championships, the music and art awards. The students cheered at every accomplishment; the audience was riveted to his every word.

Then he got down to the reason for the assembly: the appropriate behavior expected from a class that had accomplished so much. He talked about how faculty, students, and parents were concerned about the actions of the past classes and the rumors that had been circulating around the school. Then he touched on the graduation ceremony itself and the rumors that something

would occur at that occasion. Finally, he said that misbehavior would not be tolerated at a graduation because it lessened the program for everyone— students, parents, and faculty. There was a subdued silence after he finished. Then a sustained round of applause followed. Johnson walked off the stage with the feeling that he had fulfilled the desires of his administrative council and that his words had perhaps saved the day.

During the next three weeks, rumors all but disappeared, although a few students reported plans for disrupting the event and a few parents called to express concerns. But Johnson knew he had made the point in his speech, and he was certain the students knew he meant business.

This particular year was the largest graduating class in Elm School's history, so the school did not have room at its own campus for the ceremony. The staff had arranged to hold the ceremony at the football stadium of the neighboring university. In view of the size of the class, both the superintendent and the board president were on stage for the program.

The graduates marched in and took their seats facing the stage. The flag salute was led by the senior class president. Then the first of the student speakers rose to give her talk. At that moment, several things seemed to occur simultaneously. Two smoke bombs went off on opposite sides of the assembled group of seniors; a string of firecrackers began popping in the midst of the group, causing a number of robed students to leave their seats, knocking over others seated in front of them; and a barrage of water balloons were hurled at the platform guests.

Principal Johnson looked to both his right and left and observed the superintendent and the board president looking at him with anticipation. He was expected to act, and his action would have to be appropriate to stop what could be the greatest disaster in Elm's history.

DISCUSSION ISSUES

Past

1. When the pranks took place in the previous years, how should everyone's concerns have been communicated to those responsible? What communications were sent to the students?

2. When the rumors started this year, Johnson met with two leadership groups. Comment on and evaluate these communication strategies. What else might have taken place?

3. What are the students' attitudes toward Johnson? What is Johnson's attitude toward the student body?

4. Was the senior speech a defensible communication technique? How could it have had greater impact?

5. A few rumors still survived the senior talk. Could these bits of communication have been used to forestall what would occur? What communication techniques could Johnson have used?

Present

1. What should Johnson do at this moment? What kinds of messages is he giving to the parents, the community, the board, the faculty, and the students, whatever he decides to do?

2. Assuming that nothing is done and the program proceeds as scheduled, what can Johnson anticipate for next year's graduation?

3. Assuming that there are other outbreaks during the ceremony but that the program continues despite the interruptions, what can Johnson anticipate for next year's graduation?

4. Regardless of the decision made by Johnson at that moment, how should he handle the negative media coverage that will be generated?

5. How should a principal deal with the parent of a student who causes the disruption, if the parent responds, "Boys will be boys, you know"?

REFERENCES

1. Sheila Dainow and Caroline Bailey, *Developing Skills with People* (New York: Wiley, 1988), p. 53.

2. Aron W. Siegman and Stanley Feldstein, eds., *Nonverbal Behavior and Communication* (Hillsdale, N.J.: Lawrence Erlman Associates, 1986), p. 5.

3. William H. Cormier and L. Sherilyn Cormier, *Interviewing Strategies for Helpers: A Guide to Assessment, Treatment, and Evaluation* (Monterey, Calif.: Brooks/Cole, 1979), pp. 62–72.

4. John W. Gray and Allan L. Ward, "Improving Communications Between Student and Principal," *NASSP Bulletin* 58, no. 384 (October 1974):3–12.

5. *NAESP Communicator,* National Association of Elementary School Principals (November 1989) p. 2.

6. Richard J. Mayer, *Conflict Management: The Courage to Confront* (Columbus, Ohio: Battelle Press, 1990), pp. 28–29.

7. Richard E. Walton, *Managing Conflict: Interpersonal Dialogue and Third Party Roles* (Reading, Mass.: Addison-Wesley, 1987), p. 49.

8. Ibid., p. 6.

9. Dennis J. D. Sandole and Ingrid Sandole-Staroste, eds., *Conflict Management and Problem Solving: Interpersonal to International Applications* (New York: New York University Press, 1987), p. 48.

10. John Burton and Frank Dukes, *Conflict: Practices in Management, Settlement and Resolution* (New York: St. Martin's Press, 1990), p. 31.

11. Franklin Parker, *The Battle of the Books: Kanawha County,* Phi Delta Kappa Educational Foundation Fastback 63, 1975.

12. *Teacher* (August 1990), pp. 10–11.

13. Lawrence E. Vredevoe, *Discipline* (Dubuque, Iowa: Kendall/Hunt, 1971), p. 24.

INTERACTING WITH SCHOOL-BASED GROUPS

Determining the Needs of Groups

hen considering school–community relations, one often thinks of groups or agencies that are outside the school organization, the multiple communities discussed previously. Although there are various groups and subgroups on any campus or in any district, four major groups within the school need attention and an opportunity to voice and receive communication: students, teachers, classified personnel, and the administrative team.

Site-level administrators have daily contact with many of these groups and assume one of two things:

1. Daily contact is sufficient for communication purposes.

2. Seeking out opinions and concerns is not needed if students or staff have not raised any issues.

Neither assumption is accurate; by embracing these feelings, principals can become complacent and, because of the press of other duties, overlook or ignore potential problems. As indicated in Chapter 3, the demographics of school change, as do students, teachers, classified personnel, and others. The demands, the concerns, and the problems also change because of these shifts. To offer the leadership necessary to manage the accompanying challenges, school administrators must recognize early on these remodeled structures.

Within-school groups have the same needs as those outside the school. For each group, site administrators need to answer the following questions:

- What are the expectations concerning the educational program?

- What elements of the school operation are seen as strengths?

- What elements of the school operation should be changed?

- What kind of information is needed, and how is it being presented now?

Major Internal Groups

By discussing each group separately, we can focus on some methods of communication targeted for that group. We will start with the largest group on any school campus—the students.

STUDENTS

The education of students is the reason for the existence of schools and all adults who are employed there. But beyond the teaching of facts, concepts, and ideas, adults have the opportunity to communicate with young people as they are growing and maturing. The best classroom teachers understand this and try at every opportunity to talk with students in classes, in small groups, or on a one-to-one basis. They often become the heroes of the school's culture.

When graduated students return to their old schools and discuss the teachers they remember, they generally do not mention the subject matter as much as they focus on the teachers' willingness to interact with them as individuals. As one reviewer said of Samuel Freeman's remarkable book *Small Victories:*

> *Siegel suggests a model accessible to all those prepared to use their intelligence, their wit, their education and their decency on behalf of their students. Her particular heroism is not beyond the reach of many, many teachers, and one*

has the sense that there are in fact many like her, working without praise or recognition.[1]

Unfortunately, not all teachers appreciate this approach or are willing to give that much of themselves. For those who do, the results have double value: Students feel more positive about school and themselves; because they have made extended efforts to know their students, teachers are more understanding of them.

Some years ago, when I was a high school principal, one of the continued powerhouses of basketball in the league was nearby Ramona High School of Riverside. When Coach Tommy Williams was asked about his ability to produce league-leading teams each year, he commented: "I don't do anything special, except possibly my sending all but one of my players to the showers each day and working with the remaining one for a half-hour to forty-five minutes by himself!" What student would not react positively to that kind of approach? Coach Williams was not only an outstanding basketball mentor but also understood the value of communicating with students as a teacher should. Therefore, one task of site-level administrators is to encourage teachers to take this kind of approach inside or outside their classrooms.

Few teachers can send all but one student elsewhere while working with the remaining one, but opportunities for one-to-one encounters arise daily. Some examples are the following:

- Teachers often have students work quietly and independently at their seats. This is the time to talk with an individual student at the back of the classroom.

- Ask a student to remain after class for a short discussion about an issue or a problem.

- Opportunities present themselves at various school activities. Attending an event and commenting on the student's success afterward show a teacher's interest in a student and his or her commitments outside the classroom.

Anxiety is another common problem among students, particularly in relationship to grades. Pressures from home, peers, and their own long-term goals cause many students to be concerned about their report cards. Despite receiving low marks on tests and papers, some students maintain unrealistic views about how well they are doing in school. Whether it is misunderstanding or self-delusion, they often seem "shocked" upon receiving a failing or near-failing grade on the school report sent home to their parents. Most teachers remind students briefly and casually throughout the quarter or semester if they are not doing well. School counselors may also do so. But these efforts seem not to alter the final evaluation.

One middle school physical education teacher met with selected students for an individualized conference, with grade book in hand, to discuss the grades the day before they were sent home to parents. The teacher displayed interim grades and explained the grading process. Not only was there better understanding about the grades, but also students usually vowed to the teacher that improved effort and attitude would ensue in the following quarter.

School personnel other than teachers should also place such communication efforts high on their agendas. For example, school counselors and deans are generally allocated time to deal with students on an individual basis. The site-level administrator should ensure that not too many auxiliary tasks (for example, scheduling, disciplining, and duties) which interfere with the primary role of counseling are assigned to these professionals.

Administrators, too, must seek opportunities to hold two-way communication with students. Students expect certain things from their administrators, and much of one's time can be spent fulfilling these desires. The research in this area of education is somewhat limited, but one study indicates that successful principals

- Create and maintain a safe and orderly environment.

- Enhance a student's self-esteem, sense of responsibility, and ability to get along with others.

- Help students grow academically.[2]

Some students will be referred to the principal's office for a variety of reasons, often negative; these contacts acquaint the administrator with those so chosen, but the majority of students are not referred to the office. Efforts to communicate with them about these major expectations, as well as other interests, need to be taken.

Principals should communicate with individuals and groups of students. Even though coaches and activity sponsors deal directly with the teams and support groups, the principal needs to show interest in these same groups, without "looking over the staff's shoulders." Many other groups, which may not have official school sanction but do meet, may appreciate a principal's expressed interest. These groups may have common interests or simply may gather during lunch.

Other communication methods are the following:

- Talk to students at assemblies. Usually one-way communication does little toward the gathering of information.

- Visit each class on a regular basis. Students will have more opportunities to share concerns. At the secondary level, the homerooms can be used for this approach.

- Visit with the student council. If the elected members are responsive to those who chose them, they can relay the expressed concerns of their constituents.

- Eat lunch where groups of students meet. Meaningful discussion sessions with students can arise.

- Invite groups of students to have lunch. Do not limit this only to recognized school leaders because they may present a distorted view of students' feelings about school problems.

- Seek out the at-risk students for a series of personal contacts, which might make a difference in their lives.

TEACHERS

Communicating with the teaching staff is an essential aspect of the principal's job. This task actually begins prior to the beginning teacher arriving at the school. Some administrators will have the opportunity to interview prospective teachers. In some districts, teacher candidates are interviewed by the district's personnel department. Regardless of the procedure for selection of new teachers, the site-level administrator should contact the person prior to the opening of school.

Principals also must maintain open communication with experienced teachers and teachers who are not full-time staff members. In the next pages, we discuss various communication methods to use with teachers at all levels of experience and employment.

■ WELCOME LETTERS

A number of items can be covered in a welcome letter (see sample in the appendix), but beginning teachers are particularly concerned about (1) their assignments (grade level or subject), (2) how they can secure teaching materials and textbooks before beginning the school year, (3) when and how they can get keys to their rooms, and (4) starting dates and times.

Sending such communication a month before school starts can establish a positive feeling between the teacher and the principal, as well as providing the administrator an opportunity to give the neophyte needed information. If other teachers are willing to do so, they can be tapped as "buddy" teachers for those newly recruited teachers, and their names (and phone numbers) can be included in the letter as potential contact people.

If candidates are within driving distance, they may wish to visit the school before it opens. If this is the case, dates and times the principal is on campus should be included in the letter. Teachers who have been hired from other states may also find principal availability to be a time when they can ask questions about the school, the curricula, and the district's philosophy.

■ ORIENTATION MEETINGS

Districts usually have two or three days of orientation for teachers before the arrival of students. The district will schedule some of this time for its meetings, but the site administrator will have time to work directly with new teachers on the staff. The number of new personnel will undoubtedly determine the kinds of meetings scheduled. If only one teacher is being added to the faculty, a one-to-one meeting in the principal's office or the teacher's room can be arranged; if several teachers are involved, a more formalized group meeting may be required.

Some items to consider discussing are the following:

- The first day of school

- Attendance/lunch count procedures

- The actual school schedule (for example, recesses)

- Referral procedures

- Supplies and equipment

- Disaster-preparedness procedures

- Special program schedules (for example, art, music, rainy day, GATE)

- Procedures for using the daily/weekly bulletin

Some elementary and secondary schools have developed teacher handbooks, which contain such items as maps, duty schedules, teacher assignments, school policies, a calendar of the year's events, and sample school forms. This document can be used with new staff, not to go over it page-by-page but to highlight specific topics. This also allows the new teacher to ask questions about procedures and the principal to stress the most important ones.

New teachers will want to talk to others, and it is the principal's responsibility to introduce them to other members of the faculty (or department), particularly the "buddy" if they have not already contacted one another. Finally, because all teachers need time in their classrooms before the opening day of school, avoid overscheduling meetings during this traditional orientation period so that valuable staff time is not wasted.

■ CLASSROOM VISITS

Every school district has a planned series of classroom visits and follow-up conferences, certainly a way to communicate with new teachers and other teachers who are part of this process.

Some schools and districts require teachers and administrators to meet at the beginning of the year to develop goals and specific objectives for the school year. The local teachers' union sometimes controls how many meetings can occur, so the principal must ensure that the contract is not violated. Limits also exist on times when meetings can be held. For example, the district may require that a principal develop goals and objectives by a certain date. Thus, not only must she be aware of and follow union mandates, she also must be familiar with district policies and mandates.

Both techniques are clearly established, successful methods of teachers and administrators working together to improve schools. But why not go beyond these formal get-togethers? Why not casually drop by a new teacher's room a few weeks into the fall semester and ask, "How are things going? Is there anything I can do to help?"

Both formal and informal techniques can do much to bolster morale and establish rapport, as well as air possible problems that may be easily resolved. This relationship to staff can also be used with veteran teachers. All you must do is have time to listen and follow through with any situation that requires your help.

Another effective method involves the administrator doing numerous walk-throughs, especially at the beginning of the school year, to allow teachers to become at ease with his presence in the classroom for the more formal evaluations.

The principal needs to schedule these walk-throughs so that every teacher, new and veteran, is visited in this way. At the elementary level, some principals can visit every classroom several times a week. At the secondary levels, faculties are often larger in number, and this could be an impossible task. However, walk-throughs could be planned department-by-department, and the assistant principal(s) also could have a participatory role. If time is scarce, however, the important faculty to include in these walk-throughs are the new teachers.

After each visit, the administrator should leave a positive note about something she saw going on in the classroom. Teachers often report this communication means much to them because they are reassured by the positive comments.

■ FACULTY MEETINGS

One major vehicle that schools use for interactive communication is the faculty meeting. Teachers are too often heard complaining, however, about these meetings having nothing to do with their grade level or subject area. Administrators need to understand these concerns and take a look at the proposed agenda to ascertain if entire faculty attendance is required to accomplish what is proposed. If not, they need to consider other group-meeting options, which include the following:

- Hold faculty meetings for selected grade levels or departments.

- Schedule certain items pertaining to all faculty at the beginning of the meeting and dismiss early the faculty that need not be present for subsequent items.

- Hold meetings for designated staff (beginning teachers, for example) to discuss an annual event that other faculty members are familiar with and whose attendance is optional.

Accommodating the faculty in this manner, however, can cause miscommunication. Faculty who do not attend scheduled meetings sometimes feel that they do not know what took place. It's wise, then, to avoid discussing any items that are not part of the agenda. Issuing accurate minutes so *all* teachers will understand what has taken place at these meetings is another method to alleviate this potential problem.

All faculty should get together periodically, so the preceding is *not* meant to imply that staff meetings are to be avoided. The analysis of the agenda and the frequency of staff meetings is probably the best method to use to measure the need for different types of staff meetings. If the items are only announcements, the items seem to be geared to one grade level or one department, or the meetings seem to have no legitimate purpose, then some of them can and should be eliminated.

Sometimes districts mandate a specific number of staff meetings. The number may have been negotiated with the teachers' union, so avoiding them would clearly be in violation of contract. This is where teacher empowerment, however, can be used: Have teachers develop, or at least help plan, the agendas for the scheduled meetings. If they are to be called *staff* or *faculty meetings*, then those members ought to be at least involved in some of the planning.

Besides faculty, grade-level, and department meetings, faculty also attend committee meetings. These committees meet for such purposes as dealing with specific aspects of the curricula, the handling of designated funds, or the planning of social events. Some schools also operate with faculty advisory committees, which meet on a regular basis to discuss school issues and develop recommendations for the entire faculty. These groups can also serve as a conduit for voiced concerns that might not be expressed in meetings of the total teaching force.

■ INTERACTING WITH PART-TIME FACULTY

When thinking about your communication with faculty, don't overlook those educators who are not on your full-time staff. Many schools function with teaching personnel who serve several schools; these individuals are often specialists in areas like music or speech therapy and work with students one or more days a week. Include these individuals when faculty meetings or special activities are held. They may not choose to attend (or may not be able to), but that you have included them as part of your staff is important. Occasionally, take time to talk with them on the days they are scheduled at your site. They, too, may face problems that you can help solve.

Substitute teachers, other members of your part-time teaching staff, are often ignored. Large school districts may have a cadre of full-time substitute teachers, but most districts use appropriately credentialed individuals from the community. Regardless of how they are employed, this group of teachers need to be met when they come to serve your school. Greeting them as they arrive, introducing them to your regular staff the first time they enter your school, dropping into the classroom during the day, or asking them "How did things go?" as they leave at the end of the school day are all ways to establish rapport with those who may well have the toughest job in education.

As indicated earlier, the principal may not always be available to personally perform these professional contacts. Many times, when substitute teachers arrive on campus, the principal will be occupied elsewhere. If the school has an assistant principal, delegate this task to that individual. If there is no other administrator on the campus or if the one designated is also busy, the office secretary can act as the principal's liaison.

What is important here is that some plan be in place so that these individuals are helped to get started, particularly the first time they are assigned to your campus. A copy of the lesson plans (if there are any), a bell schedule, a map of the school, and a copy of the district substitute handbook are all items that should be given to the substitute teacher as he or she arrives. Don't forget any special events scheduled for that day.

Knowledge about a planned fire drill, an assembly, or a shortened day will help the teacher when working with the students in the classroom.

■ SCHEDULING APPOINTMENTS

Whether approaching a young, beginning principal or a seasoned veteran of administrative challenges, teachers will bring their professional or personal problems to the person who holds that position. This does not mean that they wish the principal to always solve their dilemmas, but they do desire a sympathetic ear. Simply being available is one key to this aspect of the job. Ingari argues that by increasing the opportunities for informal contact between principal and faculty, the level of mutual trust and understanding between them can be greatly increased.[3] That does not mean that a site administrator can *always* be available. He must follow a schedule to complete some of his own goals, and his hours on the job coincide with those of the teaching staff. It does mean that it is best *not* to schedule appointments at certain times. Alerting the secretary to these reserved times will lessen interference from the outside.

These key times seem to be the half-hours before and after school and sometimes the lunch breaks. An administrator cannot organize the day so that she can be available during all recesses (elementary school) or all preparation periods (secondary school); there would not be time to do anything else. Teachers soon adjust to the principal's operating procedure as far as accessibility is concerned and eventually comply with these times. A principal can also attend extracurricular events (athletics, drama productions, musical events, and so on) to increase the opportunities to talk with coaches or other faculty members.

The method used by Dr. Kenneth P. Bailey, former principal of Pacific High School in San Bernardino, California, is perhaps one of the best examples of availability for teacher concerns and requests. Dr. Bailey, who took great pride about his rapport with his teachers, would regularly seat himself and his secretary in the teacher's lounge before the beginning of the school day. Teachers would bring their requests or stated needs to him for discussion; as decisions were made, the secretary would take appropriate notes, and the approved requests would be expedited immediately. This organizational approach or a similar one would not be appropriate for personal problems, but it could hasten decisions on routine requests and establish the feeling that the principal honestly cares about teacher needs.

CLASSIFIED PERSONNEL

All school administrative staff should appreciate the contributions to the daily operation of the school made by classified personnel. They include clerical staff, custodial and maintenance staff, cafeteria workers, instructional aides, and bus drivers. These people answer phones, attend to minor student emergencies, handle supplies and moneys, serve the food at lunch time, keep the rooms and grounds clean, and do hundreds of other tasks. We are aware of their contributions, but how many times do we share our appreciation for their efforts? How often do we take time to find out their concerns or ideas for the improvement of the school's operation?

Because classified personnel contribute to the functioning of a school, the site administrator should provide opportunities to communicate with them. This communication should be two-way. The administrator can make sure that all of these personnel receive copies of the daily or weekly bulletin, copies of newsletters, and other written materials. But there should also be a way for them to voice their ideas and concerns.

■ CLERICAL PERSONNEL

The number of clerical personnel assigned to a school will vary depending on the level of school and its enrollment. Small elementary schools may have only one secretary—the principal's—whereas a large high school may employ several secretaries (or administrative assistants) throughout the school site. The secretary makes appointments; transmits information about school courses, activities, and programs; arranges group meetings and the use of school facilities by student body groups, faculty, and others; takes and transmits messages; handles requisitions for school supplies; and is responsible for registering and enrolling students. The secretary also may deal with budget items. Other clerical personnel prepare and assemble materials for members of the staff, keep records, handle phone calls, and so on.

Because clerical staff are the most familiar with the operation of the office, administrators should solicit their ideas and concerns about how the office runs. One-on-one talks can be held, or periodic group meetings might be scheduled for these purposes. Ask staff members to help develop an agenda. Listen to their contributions.

■ CUSTODIAL PERSONNEL

Each school has at least one daytime custodian available, whereas some may have several throughout the school plant as well as groundskeepers. The head custodian inspects heating, electrical, air-conditioning, and water equipment and makes minor repairs and adjustments; supervises other custodial personnel; and coordinates the daily operation of the school plant.

Those who work under the supervision of the head custodian sweep, mop, and vacuum floors and floor coverings; clean bathrooms; wash classroom walls and windows; and so on. In general, they take care of the housekeeping at school. During school breaks, they clean the building more thoroughly and restore it.

Night crews may be assigned to school classrooms daily or on alternating days. They may have more than one school to clean and may work under the direction of a district department rather than the school-site administrator. Nevertheless, the administrator should try to meet with all of these individuals at a time convenient to both the day and night people. Such meetings will generate closer working relationships and will enable custodial workers to voice their ideas and concerns.

Custodial staff should be notified of special events such as an open house or a music performance. They may need to prepare for the event beforehand. They also may have suggestions for smoothing out potential problems concerned with the event.

■ INSTRUCTIONAL AIDES

Most schools today use noncertified (that is, nonfaculty) personnel in the classrooms. These people are often assigned on a part-time basis and often work directly in the classrooms under the supervision of teachers. They work with small groups, tutor individual students, prepare and grade student assignments, and generally help the teacher execute lessons.

Primarily, instructional aides need to communicate with the teachers they work with. They also need to communicate with each other and with the site administrators. Participants should schedule meetings during the school year to facilitate planning, scheduling, and other related concerns.

■ CAFETERIA PERSONNEL

The people who work in the kitchens do not have a broad view of the operation of a school, but they obviously perform an invaluable service to the school. Breakfast and lunch programs are especially important services at elementary schools. The cafeteria manager (usually found in secondary schools) orders and stocks foods, inventories supplies, and keeps records. This person assists in planning menus, supervises all preparation and serving of food items, and maintains sanitation and safety standards for food service, as required by the county or state health departments.

Other cafeteria staff work under the supervision of the cafeteria manager and help prepare and serve food to the students and faculty. They are often responsible for the collection of moneys and lunch tickets on a daily basis. Cafeteria personnel can make suggestions about the organization of meal times and can share problems they encounter. Instead of scheduling formal meetings, the administrator might drop in to the kitchen facilities infrequently; cafeteria staff generally are not on the school site the entire day.

■ MAINTENANCE PERSONNEL

The staff in the maintenance department provide routine scheduled tasks (for example, painting) at a school site, and they take care of emergency maintenance requests. A variety of skills are supported by the maintenance department, including carpentry, electrical work, and plumbing. These workers are assigned jobs and are supervised by district personnel. It is important to be aware of what they contribute to the school.

One high school principal I know routinely talks with maintenance personnel *each time* they work on his site and sends a thank-you note to the supervisor *each time* about what was accomplished. One day this principal arrived early to school and found graffiti on ten concrete columns along a walk surrounding the central courtyard of his school. He immediately called the maintenance crew and, by the time the majority of students arrived at school, each column had been cleaned and repainted. The workers were more than happy to respond to the emergency call for a principal who appreciated their efforts.

■ BUS DRIVERS

Some schools operate without student buses and others transport students via public transportation or contracts with private companies. Many school districts, however, own their own vehicles and hire their own drivers, who become part of the total staff.

Drivers transport students to and from school along designated routes and transport students on field trips. Bus drivers bear the responsibility of student safety and adherence to state laws and regulations. Bus drivers routinely turn their backs on thirty or more students at a time, twice a day. Some drivers are assigned to buses equipped to handle students with special needs.

An annual meeting with the bus drivers to discuss student behavior may reap major benefits. If necessary, administrators can ride the bus if drivers report troubles. Problems do occur on buses, and drivers need whatever help the site-level administrator can provide to appropriately deal with them. Drivers need the opportunity to communicate these problems to administrators and be heard.

THE ADMINISTRATIVE TEAM

Another important group to communicate with on a regular basis is the administrative team at the school. The size and make-up of this group will depend on the level and enrollment of the school. Frequently at small elementary schools there is really no team structure to speak of. To paraphrase the *Pogo* comic strip, "I have met the team and it is me."

Many site-level administrators are in charge of a school entirely by themselves. However, middle and high schools often have assistant principals, deans, counselors, department chairs, and security personnel, who meet regularly to discuss school issues. The principal decides which team members should attend. The purpose of the meetings is to improve education, so the team must operate as a unit. Team members should feel free to contribute ideas and to question or challenge those of others. By so doing, some school problems will be avoided, and team members will be able to work together to solve common problems that do arise.

Meeting times and frequency will depend on several factors, including the responsibilities of team members. A newly appointed principal may wish to hold meetings more often at first to establish rapport with other members of the team, to develop an understanding of each of their responsibilities and roles, to ascertain what is occurring in all aspects of the school program, and to develop relationships that will ensure a consistent philosophy for the school's operation. As time passes and these goals are mutually attained, the meetings may be held less frequently.

Consulting with Opinion Leaders

Among the entire school staff, a few individuals will come to the forefront as extremely well informed about the feelings of their particular constituency. Sometimes these opinion leaders are the appointed heads of their groups (department chairs, head custodian, and so on), but sometimes they are just individuals whom others confide in.

Regardless of their title or position in the group, they can be of immense help to the administrator. Opinion leaders have their fingers on the pulse of their constituent group. They are amazingly well-informed about many aspects of the school. And they can be tapped to measure the feelings of those they represent or know. Their insight, knowledge, and contacts among faculty and staff can be of value to the site-level administrator. The site-level administrator should listen to opinion leaders and accept the information without evaluating it and without divulging the sources to others. Otherwise, the administrator will lose the opinion leader's trust.

If the principal is new to a school, other members of the administrative team may help identify opinion leaders; otherwise, they will probably seek out the principal in some informal manner. The value of the information can be appraised in terms of its accuracy and the person's willingness to share data without malice toward others. If the information is inaccurate or the person seems vindictive, the principal will learn to disregard the information in the future.

Group Conflict Management

hether the principal is effective when meeting one-on-one does not necessarily mean that she will be as effective when working with a small group or when addressing a large meeting. Effective spoken communication with groups of employees requires special skills. For example, a conflict of interest may arise between two different types of employees at a meeting. The situation will require the principal's tact. If only one group worked at a school site, the challenge of communicating would be minimized. But most schools have many internal groups. Sometimes the groups have a difference of opinion about issues such as hours of work, changes of schedules, peak demand periods, new district policies, and teacher empowerment.

The site-level administrator's role in conflict resolution (usually, as mediator) can become a major one. Union representatives, members of the district administrative staff, and board members may also be involved. As mediator, the administrator should follow these steps:

1. Attempt to secure all facts in the situation.

2. Attempt to reveal each disputing party's perceptions of the other and of the conflict issues.

3. Try to secure compromise.

Conflicts that are out in the open and understood are less of a concern as those that "are unspoken and misunderstood."[4] This underscores the need to meet with internal groups of a school site to learn about potential problems brewing.

School-site administrators are often unaware of the conflicts between individuals or groups of employees, mainly because those involved are reluctant to voice their concerns either privately or in a public forum. When the conflicts surface, the wise administrator should be willing to help mediate them if possible. However, the principal is not always the best person to do this. Teachers may not trust the objectivity of administrative personnel, the problems may be too sensitive to share with others, or the principal may be part of the conflict itself. These are important issues, though, and the administrator should try to help when appropriate. He can also contact district personnel and outside agencies to help mediate and to resolve conflict.

A Value for Communication

The goal of these communication efforts is to identify the people within the school community and then reach out to them. Each group has its special interests and needs, but they are all part of the total school structure. Each group should be given the opportunity to voice its concerns and offer its suggestions for the improvement of the school.

Most teachers and classified personnel consider communication to be one of the major concerns about the operation of the school. Better communication skills lead to improved relationships. By obtaining feedback from each of the enumerated constituencies, the perceptive administrator may avoid symptoms of dissatisfaction and low morale. The site-level administrator cannot do much about salaries, teacher burnout, or personal problems, but he can encourage all school groups to voice their needs and *attempt* to do something about them.

Consider the results of a Western Electric Company experiment conducted in the 1920s concerning working conditions for the company's employees. Some work groups were given better lighting, some were given poorer lighting, and others received no change in lighting. What happened? Productivity improved for all groups. The results indicated that when programs of change are implemented, subjects expect the program to be effective. The effect of *any* change introduced can be greater than predicted, based on knowledge of the change itself.[5]

The following example should clarify the point. A few years ago, a California high school district was facing the possibility of cutting one hundred of its teachers in addition to as many members of support groups due to state funding cuts. As the financial negotiations with the state progressed, the superintendent of the district visited each of the school sites monthly to share the progress made. The teachers and other groups knew that they were being apprised of all up-to-date information, and the superintendent's efforts avoided a major morale problem even though the results of the actual negotiations were not known for some time.

Satisfaction by all school groups is important for the successful operation of the school. Obtaining systematic feedback from individuals and groups about the problems and issues that affect them helps keep morale at a high level.

Above all, remember that it does little good to schedule meetings and listen to everyone's concerns unless you follow through on suggestions.

Many different ingredients contribute to good human relations. Gorton and Schneider outline six essential ingredients. These qualities, which follow, reflect the values that we all strive for:

1. *Be sensitive to the needs of others*

2. *Attempt to explain the reasons for your actions*

3. *Try to involve others in decisions about the school*

4. *Be open to criticism; try not to be defensive*

5. *Be willing to admit mistakes and to make changes*

6. *Be honest and fair in your interactions with others.*[6]

SUMMARY

1. The site-level administrator needs to communicate with internal groups as well as those outside the school. All schools have numerous groups, with students being common to all levels.

2. All groups should be included in the usual communication vehicles, but efforts should be made to create a two-way system of communication to seek out and solve school-site problems.

3. The school principal must be sensitive to the needs of students and should set an example for his or her staff in reaching out to the students, as appropriate.

4. In addition to the usual methods of working closely with student groups, the principal needs to spend time each week talking with students, carefully listening to their school and personal concerns.

5. New teachers need to feel a part of a staff even before they come to the school. Three methods for the principal to help establish this relationship are the welcome letter, the assigning of "buddy" teachers, and orientation activities.

6. The faculty meeting is the main vehicle for communicating with teachers. Teachers do not always view faculty meetings positively, so the principal needs to analyze both their purpose and the organization of such meetings.

7. Classified personnel include clerical workers, custodial staff, maintenance staff, cafeteria workers, instructional aides, and bus drivers. Administrators should find opportunities to meet with all of these groups on campus, either individually or in planned group meetings.

8. If the size of the school warrants, efforts need to be taken to establish and carry out a smooth administrative team concept. Planning together will help develop teamwork and a common operating philosophy for the well-being of the school program and for those who are members of faculty and staff.

9. The site-level administrator has a major role in resolving conflict among members of faculty and staff.

10. Most teachers and other school staff consider communication to be the most important factor in the efficient and effective operation of the school. Good communication improves morale and overall satisfaction.

1. Why is it important to include all internal groups in a principal's communication efforts?

2. What kinds of concerns might you expect to hear from each of the internal groups listed in the chapter? Why do you feel these would be forthcoming?

3. With the advent of unions and the trend toward teacher empowerment, what resistance would you expect to encounter if you were to begin a systematic program of meeting with each internal group at your school?

4. What efforts are made by your current principal to communicate with your internal groups? Do you feel they are successful? Why or why not?

5. What kinds of things does a beginning teacher need to know? Who do you think would be the best source of supplying each of these things?

PRINCIPAL FAILS TO KEEP APPOINTMENT WITH UNION PRESIDENT

For the past several years, contract negotiations with the teachers' union were getting more difficult. A few districts had called strikes, although most of them had been short-lived. Anytown's teachers' union had increased its demands for salaries, fringe benefits, and a voice in decision making over the past few years but there remained an amiable working relationship between the union and the school district.

Principal Bill Johnson wasn't thinking of this as he prepared for his meeting with Eric Sanders, the union president. Sanders was also on the faculty at Elm School, and the two had been professional colleagues ever since Johnson had assumed the principalship. Johnson just finished gathering information on beginning- and end-of-school-year class sizes over the past five years at Elm. Sanders had asked for the data during last month's meeting, but Johnson was not able to provide it; he promised to supply it today.

1. Use your lunch period at your present school to observe the students. Report to the class the various kinds of student groupings that you observe.

2. With your principal's permission, develop a survey questionnaire and give it to selected school groups. Share the results with members of your administrative class.

3. What written materials does your school use to communicate with internal groups? Bring these to class to share with your fellow students.

4. Without divulging names or positions, list the opinion leaders on your campus using descriptions of their responsibilities. Share the reasons that you selected the ones you did.

5. Bring in the agendas of several of your past faculty meetings. Analyze them together in terms of items for selected faculty or total faculty.

Suddenly, the door to his office came open with a bang. Startled, he looked up to see Olive Silver standing in the doorway with two students with her. Silver was almost livid and started to explain the problem.

"Let's close the door first, Ms. Silver," Johnson suggested. He got up from the desk and shut his office door. A few minutes later, Sanders arrived at the secretary's desk for his scheduled appointment. The secretary, upon request, rang Johnson's inner office.

"Mr. Sanders is here for his 2:30 appointment," she related.

"I'm in the middle of a serious discipline situation," Johnson replied. "Tell Mr. Sanders that I can't see him right now," and he hung up.

The secretary turned to Sanders and said, "He can't see you." The union president left hurriedly with no reply to the secretary.

The problem with the two students and Olive Silver took longer than it should have. The students were admittedly wrong in what had taken place, but the teacher was not immediately satisfied with the students' apology or the scheduling of a parent conference the following day. She wanted more, and it took much of Principal Johnson's patience and skills to put the situation in perspective. It was after 4:00 when the door was finally opened and the students and teacher left.

Johnson asked his secretary if Sanders had left any word. On hearing the reply, he made himself a mental note to talk with Sanders the next day. He then busied himself with the other messages on his desk.

The next morning when Johnson got to school, he found a letter on his desk from the union headquarters. It read:

Superintendent Williams:

A month ago I asked Principal Johnson to give me the information about class size over the past five years. He did not have the information at that time, so a meeting was scheduled for 2:30 today.

When I arrived for the meeting his door was closed, and when his secretary rang his office he refused to see me.

What's going on here? Why isn't the principal willing to share the information with our union? We negotiated class size more than five years ago. Are these agreed-upon policies being ignored? Why the secrecy?

I also believe that the behavior of one of the district administrators to a representative of our teachers' union and a member of his own teaching staff was outrageous.

I would like to put this matter on the agenda for the next board meeting. I feel this whole situation is a breakdown of the positive relations we have held with the board and the district ever since our organization was selected by the teachers to represent them.

Eric Sanders, President
Anytown Teacher Association

cc: Bill Johnson, Principal
Elm School

Johnson was stunned by the letter and began to read it for a second time. He was almost halfway through when the intercom rang and his secretary said, "Superintendent Williams is on the line and says it is imperative that he speak to you right now."

DISCUSSION ISSUES

Past

1. How do you think Johnson should explain the situation to the superintendent? What recommendations do you think the superintendent should make to Johnson?

2. How did Johnson view the relationship between Sanders and himself? How did Sanders view the relationship between Johnson and himself? How did these views affect this particular situation?

3. What is the relationship between Johnson and Olive Silver? What impact did that relationship have on this situation?
4. What techniques of communication could Johnson and his secretary have used to avoid this situation?
5. Read Sanders' letter carefully. What are the union president's attitudes about the district and administration? Why do you think these have developed?

Present

1. What communication techniques should Johnson and Williams use to reestablish the positive relationships that existed before between the district and the union?
2. Assuming that Johnson and Williams contact Sanders about his letter, how do you think Sanders will react?

3. What changes need to be made by both Johnson and his secretary to see that this kind of situation does not occur again?
4. Situations of a serious nature (in this case, discipline) do happen when other plans have been made. How can these conflicts best be handled so that no one is offended?
5. Sanders may have talked to other union members before writing the letter. What impact will this have on the district? At Elm School?

REFERENCES

1. Samuel G. Freeman, *Small Victories* (New York: Harper & Row, 1990), book jacket.

2. Carrie Kojimoto, "The Kids-Eye View of Effective Principals," *Educational Leadership* 45, no. 1 (September 1987):69–74.

3. Sandro Ingari, "A Case Study in Human Relations," *NASSP Bulletin* 60, no. 401 (September 1976):104.

4. James Lipham, Robb E. Ramkin, and James A. Hoeh, Jr., *The Principalship, Competencies and Case Studies* (New York: Longman, 1985), pp. 218–219.

5. Robert Rosenthal and Lenore Jacobson, *Pygmalion in the Classroom* (New York: Holt, Rinehart and Winston, 1968), pp. 164–166.

6. Richard A. Gorton and Gail Thierback Schneider, *School-Based Leadership, Challenges and Opportunities* (Dubuque, Iowa: Wm. C. Brown, 1991), p. 263.

INTERACTING WITH PARENTS

CHAPTER OUTLINE

- The Rationale for Parent Involvement

- Parent Conferences

  Parent Concerns
  Conference Strategies
     Guidelines
     Step-by-Step Conferencing

- Parents of Special-Need Students

- Parents as School Volunteers

  Recruiting Volunteers
  Training for Volunteer Programs
  Why Plan a Volunteer Program?

- Special Events for Parents

  Planning Special Events
  The Administrator's Role

- Parent Classes

- Advisory Committees and Site Councils

- Home Meetings with Parents

  Setting Up Home Meetings
  Orientation for Parents of
     Kindergartners

- Parent Newsletters

The Rationale for Parent Involvement

Parent involvement in schools has long been supported by educators throughout our nation as not only being a positive school–community relations tool but a necessity for student success. In 1990, California went a step further by passing Assembly Bill 322, which required all school district governing boards to adopt a policy on parent involvement.

As Solomon explains in an article on this state's policy: "In California the policy on parent involvement was inspired and informed by an earlier initiative on curriculum reform. Thus the parent involvement policy supports the state's major goal of improving student learning."[1] Although the assembly bill requires districts to adopt policies, it gives both the districts and the schools a great deal of leeway to adapt parent involvement to the needs of their students, families, and communities.

Not all states have mandated such participation, but the legislation seems to make sense. As Henderson points out, the National Committee for Citizens in Education (NCCE) published two studies, *The Evidence Grows* and *The Evidence Continues to Grow: Parent Involvement Improves Student Achievement,* which "strongly [suggest] that involving parents can make a critical difference in school improvement efforts to raise student achievement at all socioeconomic levels."[2] How much difference it makes seems to be tied to the planning, the comprehensiveness, and the length of the parent involvement.

These two NCCE studies described about 50 educational studies, which identified some major benefits of parent involvement in schools. A subsequent NCCE study, *Taking Stock,* validated the earlier ones. When parents are involved, students—particularly those labeled as at-risk—do better in school. Their success shows in the form of higher grades and test scores, long-term improvements in academic achievement, and improved attitudes and behavior; also, more school programs are successful, and the schools are more effective in general.[3] With these positive results, it's no wonder that California and other states passed legislation to require active participation.

If such partnerships are to be developed between the schools and the students' families, then the school system must make sure it develops worthwhile relationships. Therefore, the traditional parent involvement approaches (participating in PTA, attending open houses, reading newsletters, and so on), which are still important, are not sufficient. Schools need more active parent participation. This can be challenging. The demographics of school communities have changed and continue to change. Education backgrounds vary, language skills vary, ethnic and cultural backgrounds are different, and family situations are different. Meaningful parent involvement, therefore, must also be different and varied.

The site-level administrator is responsible for developing a plan for parental involvement at his or her school. The plan should be comprehensive and should include various ways in which parents can be informed about school and can actively participate in the learning program. Any program of involvement should be based on the demographics of the school site. There are increasingly more single parents and working parents who are not able to meet with school personnel during the day. Even if they were able to meet briefly, the contact would not be enough to build long-term involvement.

Parents also need to make an effort. In one study, 89% of the parents surveyed indicated that the major method of learning about the school was from what their child told them.[4] Parents have many other alternative ways of learning about their children's school.

Remember the three basic principles to follow when purchasing property: "Location, location, location"? Let me paraphrase that axiom: When inviting parents to school events, the three principles are planning, planning, planning. This holds true for the monthly PTA meeting, the quarterly parent conference, the annual open house, and back-to-school night. Those schools that follow this advice seem to realize the most success in these endeavors. They are even more successful when all staff members are involved in the planning.

Parent Conferences

here are many kinds of parent conferences, including those called by parents concerned about their child's schooling, those called by the teacher or the administration for some disciplinary problem, or routine conferences to discuss student progress. Without exception, planning should precede the conference. In planning, teachers might consider some topics that are likely to concern parents, including academic performance, social development, emotional development, and classroom behavior.

PARENT CONCERNS

Parents are particularly concerned about basic skills at the elementary level. If a student is having any problems academically, the teacher needs to discuss these problems in detail and describe specifically what is being done about them. Parents of secondary students often have more concern over grades. An up-to-date grade book is the teacher's strongest evidence to share with the parents about a particular mark.

If a student performs far beyond what is expected or performs far below the norm, the teacher should tell the parents. Although comparisons with an average can be of value, the teacher should resist comparisons with other students by names or siblings.

Most parents are concerned about how their youngsters relate to others. At the elementary level, information about working and playing with schoolmates may be of importance. At the secondary level, parents may be interested in how their child works on group projects or how willingly the child participates in class discussions.

A child's emotional development may seem different at school compared with home. How a child handles stress, unfamiliar tasks, success, and failure are all worth reporting to parents if they seem to be factors in the student's learning process.

Emotional development may be reflected in the student's classroom behavior, which itself may be a subject of concern. In fact, some parents are more concerned about their children's behavior than their academic achievement. The teacher's comments and evaluation of the behavior as it relates to other youngsters will be of interest. The teacher should note particular problems as well as strengths.

If the teacher has offered the student special help in a subject area, he or she should inform the parents. The teacher should also report the student's reaction to the offer. The report might indicate gains made or the student's unwillingness to accept the help, for example.

CONFERENCE STRATEGIES

Teachers should try to establish rapport with the parents when they arrive. Then they can deal with specific issues supported by specific observable examples. To close the meeting, the teacher then summarizes the issues. Parents need to know how their child is performing and what is being done to improve performance in both academic and related areas.

Other strategies, in addition to the ones for opening and closing a meeting, can help teachers conduct successful parent-teacher conferences. Teachers—especially first-year teachers, who may not have much experience with parent-teacher conferences—may need some training. The school could sponsor in-service sessions, with optional attendance for veteran teachers.

■ GUIDELINES

One school district in California developed a handout for teachers to use in preparing for conferences.[5] These materials include a one-page form that helps parent and teacher focus on the child. The form is reproduced here as Figure 1.

STUDENT	
Strengths	**Needs**
Plans for School	**Plans for Home**

Also included are preconference activities for students (for example, writing an invitation to their parents), a form for the parents to complete (as "homework") and bring to the meeting, a discussion of how to handle "special parents" (the abusive parent, the timid parent, and so on), as well as a summary of good communication skills for teachers. The handout outlines four alternatives for handling angry, abusive parents. These are:

- *Listen without saying anything.* Sometimes this causes the parents to collect themselves, stop their outburst, and move on to the purpose of the conference.

- *Acknowledge the parent's anger.* A calm statement such as "I hear that you're angry" will sometimes halt the outburst.

- *Tell the parent how you feel without becoming emotional.* An example would be, "I feel uncomfortable when you raise your voice like that."

- *Stop the conference.* "I don't think it will be helpful if we continue. Let's plan to get together at another time."[6]

Any school or school district may prepare its own conference preparation materials tailored to its own needs. The guidelines should take into account the character of the school and the community it serves.

■ STEP-BY-STEP CONFERENCING

To be successful, all conferences require good conferencing skills. Following a step-by-step sequence in planning and delivery helps. The following sequence of steps prepared by Lawrence and Hunter are appropriate for all types of conferences.[7]

1. *Establish reasonable expectations.* The major obstacle to parent-teacher or parent-administrator conferences is the time frame. Sometimes both parties are unrealistic in what can be accomplished. Greeting one another and establishing rapport, dealing with the parent's attitude (defensive, argumentative, challenging), and just trying to understand one another better all consume time. Therefore, both parties need to be realistic and focus on the major issues regarding the student.

2. *Establish the conference objective.* If the parents have asked for the conference, then they will be apt to bring objectives to the meeting. Likewise, if the teacher has initiated the conference, he or she will take the leadership in conveying the purpose. However, all conferences should focus on mutually agreed-upon objectives for productive communication to take place.

3. *Prepare for the conference.* All types of conferences require preparation, which includes reading records, consulting with others as needed, and organizing any additional data. Sample student work, an up-to-date grade book, anecdotal records, and other relevant items may be needed. Formulating questions or practicing how things might best be stated can also be of help.

4. *Make an opening statement.* The idea is to allow parents to relax and feel comfortable no matter what the reason for the conference. For a teacher-initiated conference, the teacher might say, "I'm pleased you were able to come today. I wanted to discuss . . ." For a parent-initiated conference, the teacher might say, "I'm glad to see you. How may I help you?"

5. *Formulate the message.* The teacher or administrator should state the message in language that the parents can understand, avoiding jargon. All statements should avoid emotional overtures (for example, words like *lazy* or *immature*). All communication should be aided by **enabling statements,** which allow for hope in the future or support the parents in what they are doing.

6. *Check back.* This is a common counseling technique that conveys, "Let me be sure I understand what you said." This technique (checking back) increases understanding. It helps determine if what one person said and the other person heard are the same.

7. *Close the conference.* Reviewing what has been said, particularly if there have been verbal commitments, is an important closing step. In some challenging situations, the teacher might send a written summary to the parent following the conference; however, this summary should also be verbally agreed upon at the conference. The teacher should express appreciation to the parent for attending the conference.

8. *Judge the success of the conference.* Initially, the parent may seem satisfied with the conference; long-term success should be judged by observable changes in student behavior at school following the conference. If either person thinks that things did not go well, then they should plan subsequent meetings.

Parents of Special-Needs Students

ducators have tried to achieve universal and effective education for children with physical, behavioral, or cognitive disabilities. Designing an effective educational intervention and developing meaningful individualized education programs (IEPs) are essential to the goal. The IEP team includes the individual, family members or advocates, and program staff. The program staff often includes regular teachers, a psychologist, and a special-education teacher. According to Wang, Reynolds, and Walberg:

> *All levels of treatment decision making originate with [the IEP] team. The members are responsible for determining the acceptability of a proposed treatment for the individual. This committee also decides if the proposed treatment meets the criteria for further review and monitoring by a higher level committee.*[8]

In an earlier publication, Wang, Reynolds, and Walberg describe the purpose of the IEP:

> *Public Law 94-142, particularly the mandate for IEPs, has provided a structure for decisions regarding curricular conduct for handicapped students. With a means of prioritizing goals and matching them to individual students' needs, the IEP has rationally focused on balancing academic, social, and vocational emphases in providing a total curriculum package.*[9]

The parents of special-needs students are an essential ingredient of the learning process and must be involved in their children's education. Parents can intensify the learning at home and can reinforce what has been taught at school. However, the quality of the relationships between school personnel and parents must be kept at a high level. Both parties must be willing to communicate and cooperate in the planning and implementation of the instructional program. Meetings can consume a great deal of time, especially during the planning process.

An IEP is based on the student's past performance, his or her strengths and weaknesses, attitudes toward school, leader's observations, analysis of the test data by the school psychologist, and the parents' knowledge of their child. The program sets goals and strategies, suggests curriculum materials, and defines assessment strategies.

Most parents are cooperative when they are involved in an IEP meeting. Some, however, are defensive about their child's disability or about other school programs. Parents may respond strongly to labeling the child by his or her disability; indeed, some children are labeled incorrectly. For example, there is ample evidence that minorities and those of lower economic status have been identified incorrectly because of factors other than those that should be considered.[10] A site administrator's skills in conflict resolution may be tested in this type of situation.

School administrators should seek and offer support services to the teachers who work with disabled children. This support may include coordinating with parents and specialists as appropriate; procuring educational supplies, materials, and equipment; and providing in-service training. If this type of support system is in place, parents will be more inclined to champion the program. However, if parents still want a detailed explanation of the program, the administrator should provide it.

Parents as School Volunteers

Another important method of communicating with parents about a school's programs is to have them contribute to the operation of the school. Only a small number of parents devote time to the school on a daily basis, but there are many ways to schedule parents as their availabilities permit—one day a month or even a year, in the evenings or on weekends, or during breaks. The enterprising principal will look for opportunities to pair availability and tasks to be undertaken. For example, the athletic department at one high school requested that the principal get some equipment painted at the school site. Rather than asking parents in general to volunteer to do the painting, the principal called some parents who worked as professional painters. Five fathers volunteered to help, and none of them had ever participated at the school before. On one Saturday morning, with all of their mechanized equipment and expertise, they were able to paint the equipment in a few hours.

In what other ways can parents help a school function? There are thousands of ways. Here is a list of ten common methods of involving parents in volunteer situations.

- *Tutors.* Many students need additional help and a one-on-one relationship with an adult. Tutors usually work with students according to their availability but on a regularly scheduled basis.

- *Story readers.* Reading to children is not as time-consuming as tutoring but is a valuable way to help students directly. It gives students an opportunity to hear stories read aloud by others or to read stories to someone who listens.

- *Guest speakers.* Parents can speak to the class about careers, hobbies, travel experiences, and many other topics that fit into the curricula.

- *Fund-raisers.* Volunteers can call or personally contact businesses for fund-raising efforts, such as donations for prizes and awards.

- *Publicity helpers.* Parents can help make phone calls or create publicity releases to mail to parents or release to the media.

- *Library volunteers.* School libraries can use volunteers to reshelve books, mend books, help students locate resources, and so on.

- *Field trip chaperons.* Volunteers can help keep track of students on school outings.

- *Bake sale volunteers.* Parents can furnish and help sell food at fund-raising events.

- *Sports coaches.* Many schools do not have adequate faculty to head all of the sports teams or to serve as assistants. Parent volunteers can help with coaching responsibilities.

- *Clerical assistants.* Parents can help teachers in the classroom with such clerical tasks as preparing student awards, scoring tests, typing letters, setting up materials, and so on. They can also help prepare the school newsletters.

It is easier to think of ways that parents and other members of the community can aid the schools than it is to get their commitment to help. Every school community has a cadre of families that are stable, long-term members of the community. This group of permanent residents can be a foundation upon which to build a strong parent volunteer program. By contrast, many families enter and leave the community within the same year or at least within a couple of years. These community members are less likely to commit time as volunteers.

RECRUITING VOLUNTEERS

How much time can a school administrator realistically expect of volunteers? This question is difficult to answer because communities differ in many ways. Single-parent families may not think they have the time to spend at the school. Some parents with limited education feel intimidated by teachers and are reluctant to work alongside them. Others may travel a great distance to and from work each day and would not be available to work on-site. Everyone *can* contribute. The administrator should not assume that volunteers are completely unavailable. For example, the principal at one elementary school in Fontana, California, developed a program that attracted parent volunteers like moths to a flame. The school logs as many as 7000 hours of volunteer time in a single year and averages almost 6000 hours a year.

The program started as part of the requirements of the school's Chapter One program but grew to an all-school program after the initial federal program push. It is based on three key elements: (1) initial contacts, (2) matching volunteer with task, and (3) a reward system. When parents enroll their youngsters, they are introduced to the principal, who conducts them on a personal tour of the campus. He gives them a strong sales pitch about why they should be a part of the volunteer program. Of course, not all parents are willing to commit themselves initially, but other school personnel make follow-up contacts to secure a commitment. Because these efforts are time-consuming, the administration and the staff must believe that such a concentrated campaign will benefit the school as well as ensure that the parents understand what is taking place within the walls of that school.

The second requirement is matching the parent with the tasks to be completed. There is a major attempt to tie the school activities with particular interests and talents listed by the parents on a questionnaire. The school has thirteen task centers with such options as counseling, listening, crafts, art, creative expression, applied mathematics, reading, cooking for the primary grades, and construction. Parents also can assist in many of the school's special programs. They work with individual or small groups of students to help support their educational progress in some manner.

Some parents are not willing to work directly with children but are still interested in becoming a part of the parental support effort at the school. These parents develop materials for teachers, make educational games, or complete other tasks at the school. The key is to ensure that those parents who volunteer have something to do. It also means developing a sophisticated system of pairing the parent with the task that he or she is capable of doing and willing to do.

What is the payoff for the volunteers themselves? There is, of course, the positive feeling that everyone gets when they contribute to a worthy cause. But the school also has built a reward system into the program. The first time a parent comes to school to participate, a staff member takes the parent's picture. All pictures are prominently displayed in the front office, where other parents and interested students can see them.

At the end of the school year, the school holds an awards ceremony and invites the superintendent of schools and the board members. At this gathering, each volunteer for that year is honored with a certificate of appreciation, designed to convey the school's concept of school–community solidarity.[11]

A second successful example of recruiting volunteers can be found at La Mirada High School in Los Angeles County. This school's group of parent volunteers was born out of budget cuts. When the board of education cut nurses from the school, parents reacted by forming the "MOD (Mothers on Duty) Squad." Although their initial task was to staff the nurse's office, they soon expanded their services to the attendance office, the library, and the career center. The key ingredients for La Mirada's volunteer program are worthwhile tasks and recognition. "MOD Squad" participants are honored at the Senior Awards Assembly each year.

Once parents are recruited as volunteers, they will need to learn how to participate effectively. At an orientation session, they can learn about the school's philosophy and any pertinent policies. This meeting is particularly important for the parents who will be working in the classroom. They need to know what are the teachers' roles and what teachers will expect from them. In subsequent training sessions, volunteers can learn how to work with individual students or groups of students. Volunteers should learn effective ways of reacting to students (and some behaviors to avoid). Training sessions should also cover teamwork.

Teachers need training too, especially if they have not had aides or other volunteers in their classrooms before. Teachers need to know what they can expect from a volunteer. They also must learn how to plan for volunteers; they should have a meaningful task to do each day. Teachers also should learn what to do if a personality clash exists between themselves and the volunteers.

WHY PLAN A VOLUNTEER PROGRAM?

Although involving parents and other members of the community is an important task, the site-level administrator must understand that the accumulation of logged hours of participation is not an end in itself. All of the efforts made to organize, develop, and sustain such a program should lead to improved education at the school site.

Through the volunteers' experience and expertise, the school should benefit in many ways. The human resources alone will allow the school staff to tackle aspects of education that simply cannot be explored otherwise. Additional benefits will be the volunteers' expanded awareness about the school and its educational programs. This should lead to improved skills in working with their own children at home which, in turn, may be reflected back into the classroom. Developing meaningful parental involvement will take time away from other administrative tasks. Research indicates, however, that the results will more than pay for the effort.

Special Events for Parents

Many opportunities for communicating with parents have become rather traditional in schools. These are the annual open house or the back-to-school night. "Open house" generally is held in the spring and focuses on academic progress made during the school year. The main purpose of back-to-school night, which is held at the beginning of the school year, is to acquaint the parents with their children's teachers. Special academic events that are open to all parents may, in fact, appeal only to the parents of the participants. Music recitals, science fairs, scholarship awards ceremonies, athletic banquets, and school plays are examples of programs that attract limited parent attendance.

PLANNING SPECIAL EVENTS

All of these events are important public relations vehicles, no matter what the attendance. Again, planning is the key to their success. Schools that spend the time focusing on the program well in advance of its actual date report the greatest participation. Planning sessions must involve the teachers from the beginning. Teachers should work together to select a theme for the event ("Writing Through the Grades," for example). Teachers should also have the opportunity to help each other prepare for special events such as open houses. Veteran teachers may help newer, less experienced teachers compile portfolios or folders of representative student work. Teachers usually place these on the students' desks so their parents can thumb through the work and see how their child has progressed.

Some teachers are masters at creating bulletin boards and displaying student work. Others may need help. If the teachers have an opportunity to meet and visit each others' classrooms, then they may all be able to create classroom environments to impress the parents. What can the principal do to facilitate? She may be able to secure release time for teachers, schedule meetings for them to share expertise, or cover a teacher's class for a brief time while he visits another classroom.

The site administrator has a number of specific tasks to do to attract parents to these events. After all, if the teachers are going to prepare for the event, they deserve an audience. The administrator can:

- *Send out invitations.* Use a variety of approaches, including flyers, announcements in the school newsletter, press releases, local radio station community spot announcements, a telephone tree, and personal letters from the students to their parents.

- *Share the sponsorship.* If any parent groups (such as PTA, booster clubs, or foreign exchange programs) are operating as part of the school community, ask them to cosponsor the event. Set up tables where they can recruit for their own organizations.

- *Clear the calendar.* Make sure that any groups that use the school plant regularly, such as adult education or community groups, have been notified well in advance.

- *Set up directions.* Make sure that parking areas and entrances are clearly marked. A night custodial crew might be assigned to help. Student guides and directional signs may help direct parents to the appropriate location. If traffic around the school is a problem, notify the local police about starting and ending times.

- *Help teachers avoid parent conferences.* During an open house or back-to-school night, teachers do not have time to hold individual parent conferences. Announce this in your letter or bulletin sent home to the parents. Announce it again during a general meeting prior to visiting the classrooms. Provide a sign-up sheet in every classroom for follow-up parent-teacher conferences.

- *Encourage teachers to enlist students' help.* Display student work (such as art work or writing) in classrooms and other permanent display areas in the school. Students may conduct science experiments in the classrooms; perform skits, songs, or dances for parents; serve as guides; or act as hosts in each room. Their participation increases the chances that their parents will attend the event.

After the event, the administrator should meet with the school staff to find out what went well during the event and what could be improved. If the administrator keeps a notebook or file on each type of event held, he will be able to consult his notes when the event is held the following year.

If possible, the principal should write a follow-up note to all parents who attend the event. This gives the principal an opportunity to thank parents for their continued school support. One principal I know of even wrote a note to each family that didn't attend the event, indicating that he had missed them that evening. Not surprisingly, attendance the following year for that event increased.

Parent Classes

Not all parents have adequate preparation for parenting, so it can be worthwhile to offer classes or seminars on topics of interest to those parents. Education is not the sole responsibility of teachers; parents are teachers, too, and in most cases are the longest lasting and most important mentors. Here is a list of topics that might appeal to parents:

- Respecting learning and achievement

- Talking with children about school and their personal concerns

- Reading to children or reading together

- Limiting the use of television

- Providing additional learning experiences from family outings

- Showing concern for children's interests and talents

- Providing a balanced diet

- Supervising homework—setting a time and place to work

- Showing consistent love and affection

- Setting appropriate behavior standards at home and school

In Omaha, Nebraska, the district and other citizen leaders of the community have developed the Familyness Project. Professionals from the community attend parent meetings and address issues such as coping with anger, encouraging your child, building self-esteem, satanism, drugs, gangs, and understanding adolescents.[12]

Not all parents are able or willing to attend classes, but they still may be open to learning about issues that affect their children. Instead of setting up classes, the school district can prepare materials to send home to parents as part of a parent handbook or simply as a separate publication. In fact, print materials also may supplement parent classes. The outline below is taken from a one-page handout developed by the Fountain Valley School District in California.

Ways Parents Can Help Students at Home

1. Develop a study plan.
   a. Confer as a family and agree on effective times for study. The time should be the same each night.
   b. Help students budget their home study time.
   c. Gradually guide the student toward an independent and effective use of study time.
   d. Help the student develop a plan that provides an appropriate amount of time for recreation, family activities, and rest as well as study.

2. Provide a good environment for study.
   a. Set a definite place for study, with needed equipment and adequate light.
   b. Make sure the location is quiet.

3. Show interest and provide guidance.
   a. The parents' role should be one of offering encouragement; parents should not take the role of the instructor.
   b. Take time to display interest in homework and be available for questions or discussions. Avoid undue pressure.
   c. Encourage a study atmosphere in the home by reading during the student's study time.
   d. Encourage students to broaden their knowledge by making use of various community resources.

e. Help the student see the significance and value of the homework assignments.

f. Use family trips to stimulate and increase knowledge.

g. Stimulate and praise your son's or daughter's progress.

4. Give students practical arithmetic problems at home—adding, subtracting, multiplying, and so on.

5. Encourage students to read for pleasure. If the students are not able readers, read to them to develop interest.

6. Make newspapers and magazines available to students and discuss with them things that happen in the news.

7. Take students to the library for resource materials or for practice in using the library.

8. Take an interest in schoolwork and encourage students to discuss what they have learned.

9. Give students practice spelling tests.

10. Encourage students to watch educational television programs.

11. Look over children's work papers and folders and give them praise and encouragement as appropriate.[13]

Advisory Committees and Site Councils

f the schools really want parent involvement in the public schools, then parent participation in the decision-making process should be supported. In a Harris poll taken in the early 1990s, 90% of respondents favored "involving parents much more in making decisions about their children's schools."[14] The move toward parent empowerment suggests that parent advisory committees are both desirable and necessary. In fact, several states have mandated the formation of such groups; others are following suit. However, advisory committees are not without their problems. Typical problems include the following:

- The committee must develop procedures for selecting members, particularly if the group represents all geographic, ethnic, and economic groups.

- If the committee does not establish a sense of direction, it may search for problems to justify its existence.

- Some committee members may have their own agendas.

- Committee members may lack the background to address school problems and may need in-service training.

- Committee members may lack the experience to make group decisions and may need in-service training.

- Some faculty members and other parents may react negatively to an advisory committee.

- The school administration must devote time to the development, nurturing, and encouragement of the advisory committee.

Unless mandated by state law or a board of education edict, the administrator should not establish an advisory committee if he or she does not think that parents can contribute substantially to the educational process. The administrator should carefully select the committee members so the group represents the cross-section of students enrolled at the school. Then the administrator must clearly define the objectives, function, limits, and authority of the committee.

Most people who serve on advisory committees prove to be dedicated, sincere, and supportive. Their comments and recommendations usually are helpful to the administration in preparing annual school reports, establishing spending priorities, addressing comprehensive school plans, planning curriculum modifications, and so on. To maximize a committee's efforts, a site-level administrator must spend time with the group. He should offer training for new members and whenever special situations arise that warrant training. He should keep all members informed about both the strengths and the weaknesses of the school operation. He should use the strengths of the committee members to help solve existing problems and reward the committee members for their willingness to serve the school.

Forming an advisory committee can be a stimulus to developing and maintaining a school that is responsive to community problems and concerns. Such a committee can go a long way toward establishing community spirit. Committee meetings allow parents to talk with each other about specific needs of the school. The group can become a nucleus of support as well as a conduit of positive information to other parents. Sometimes committee members can share their knowledge about other schools in the community that internal school personnel may not share. They also may have contacts that can help solve problems beyond the scope of the district or school board.

Home Meetings with Parents

espite all of the methods of involving parents, there are still those who are not used to attending school events or are unwilling to do so. The obvious alternative is to go to them. One way to accomplish this objective is to schedule a series of small, intimate meetings with parents and the site-level administrator in their homes. Many schools throughout the United States have organized such meetings and have reported a strong turnout and ongoing interest.

SETTING UP HOME MEETINGS

How might an administrator set up such parent gatherings? One middle school principal called the feeder elementary schools and asked their principals to name four or five reliable parent leaders whose children would be attending his school the following year. Since each of the feeder elementary schools represented a different geographic area of the community, he then called these parents and asked them to call other families in the area to host meetings. The school district supplied each of these area coordinators with a list of all parents in that geographic area. The principal also furnished each coordinator a set of dates when he was available to attend these meetings. Most meetings were scheduled for the fall, when parent interest seemed to be at its highest. Most meetings were in the evening, but some were during the day. The number of people invited to each home varied from 10 to 25, depending on the size of the host's meeting space.

The meetings themselves usually cover a "state of the school" message by the principal, followed by questions from the parents. Usually, the newest parents to the school have the most questions. Most parents reflect the concerns that their children bring home. Often, these "concerns" are simply rumors, so the parent meeting provides a great opportunity to squelch such rumors. The meetings also provide an opportunity to listen carefully to parents' sincere and reasonable concerns. An administrator should approach the meeting without defensiveness. There is much to be learned from interested parents.

Meetings need not be restricted to the school year. The administration at Mt. Carmel High School in the Poway Unified School District in California, for example, found that many parents preferred meeting in the summer. The National Association of Secondary Principals recommends that teachers or specialists accompany the principal to parent meetings and that all school officials prepare to share the successes of the school as well as listen to the concerns of the parents.

ORIENTATION FOR PARENTS OF KINDERGARTNERS

Many schools provide a kindergarten fact sheet along with the registration packet, which gives a brief overview of class times, the date and time of an orientation meeting, and a description of the curriculum covered in the first two weeks of school. When parents return the registration forms, they may receive an information sheet or booklet that discusses skills that parents can practice with their child prior to entering school (tying shoes, distinguishing their first and last names, using the restroom properly, keeping track of personal property, and so on). The information sheet also may suggest that parents visit the school building with their child before the first day of school; talk about school in a friendly way; and try to respond to the child's fears and doubts in a positive, reassuring manner.

Each year when a new class of kindergarten students begins its school experience, the administrator should take extra time to make the students (and their parents) feel welcome. After all, those children will probably attend the elementary school for seven years. Even before school begins, the administrator might send a welcoming letter to all parents of incoming kindergartners, which might explain what kindergarten is all about and what is expected of a kindergartner. For many parents, their children's school may be a new experience. It is helpful to know ahead of time that kindergarten learning includes working and playing together, respecting the rights of others, being a good listener, following directions, completing assigned tasks, keeping the work area clean, working as part of a group, and increasing one's attention span, among other things.

The kindergarten teacher and administrator should plan the parent orientation meeting as a team. It is extremely important during this orientation to make parents feel comfortable about entrusting their children to the school. The orientation should be held before the first day of school and should include kindergarten teachers, the principal, instructional aides, the nurse or health clerk, a school secretary, a custodian, the librarian, the PTA president, and any other support personnel who may come to know the kindergartners. The principal may talk about attendance, tardiness, enrollment (especially if class size is large), the safety of students, the school information packet, and other important topics. She should introduce support personnel, who should speak briefly on specific topics that they deal with. For example, the secretary might explain how to check a child out of school early, and the health clerk might talk about the need to verify absences. The PTA president may wish to address issues such as volunteer survey forms, PTA meeting times and place, and some special events planned for the year.

Finally, the teachers should summarize the kindergarten program and tell parents what they can expect during the school year. Teachers should not try to give too much detailed information; they will have an opportunity to give more in-depth information at back-to-school night, which usually is scheduled within the first or second month of school.

Some of the issues regarding orientation for kindergarten apply to transfer students. If a school receives several transfer students in a two- or three-week period, the principal may wish to hold an informal orientation meeting for the parents of these transfer students. (This applies to students of all grade levels, not just kindergartners.) The meeting will help parents become acquainted with the operation of the school. It also will let them reflect their children's concerns about their new school.

Parent Newsletters

Despite all efforts to involve parents in a volunteer program, parent classes, or as participants at school events, there will be some parents who will not participate in any of these activities. The school can still communicate with these parents through the school newsletter. (Parents can be encouraged to respond to the newsletter to foster two-way communication.) The newsletter can be published on a monthly basis or less frequently, if the budget is limited. Parents still will learn more about the school than they would from the local media.

Remember that the newsletter may well be the only link with some parents, who may judge the school by the quality of its publication. Careful writing and editing will help develop a favorable impression. So will an attractive design.

Because the newsletter represents the school, it needs to look professional in every respect. If necessary, the principal should seek help from staff members to plan the masthead and logo, type style and size, and general layout. As needed, a skilled staff member should check the articles for accuracy, style, grammar, and spelling before the newsletter is printed and distributed. Articles should be specific and factual and should appeal to parents or other adults. They should be written in standard English (and possibly other languages) and should not use jargon.

The kinds of items that are appropriate for school newsletters are editorials about the goals of the school, parent contributions to the learning process, information about past and future school programs and events, the school curriculum, test scores, pending educational legislation, and services provided by the school. Some schools occasionally feature student contributions—class stories, poetry, and so on. (Generally, though, the PTA newsletter is a better vehicle for student work.) A monthly newsletter might include a calendar of upcoming events that can be clipped and posted at home. Most importantly, though, the newsletter should be serious. If the school takes it seriously, then the parents will, too.

Two words of caution here about publishing the school newsletter in other languages: (1) The translator should understand English and the second language well and should be able to translate into the appropriate dialect; and (2) the school should find out which families prefer the non-English newsletter, because some people are offended when others assume they cannot read English.

SUMMARY

1. According to some research studies, parent involvement makes a critical difference in school improvement. The degree of improvement seems to be tied to planning, comprehensiveness, and length of involvement.

2. Although traditional activities for parents (going to PTA meetings, reading the school newsletters, participating in school events) are still important, parents should be more involved. The principal should help develop a plan for parental participation.

3. There are many kinds of parent conferences and a variety of issues to discuss; teachers and administrators can sharpen their skills for conducting them appropriately. Schools may prepare conference guidelines and conduct in-service sessions on conference skills for teachers.

4. The parents of special-needs students are essential to the learning process. They can intensify learning at home and reinforce what the child learns at school.

5. Parent contributions to the operation of a school can enhance programs in a variety of ways. An enterprising principal needs to look for tasks, as well as times, to match the skills of the parents with the jobs to be done.

6. Many traditional school events, such as open house, back-to-school night, recitals, and banquets, are important public relations events that benefit from long-term planning.

7. Some parents need help understanding their roles in the learning process. Parent classes as well as materials that can be sent home can help with parenting skills.

8. Some states mandate school-site parent advisory committees. This movement suggests that such committees are desirable and necessary.

9. If parents do not attend special events at school, the administrator can attempt to hold such events in parents' homes or locations more convenient to their homes. Depending on the community, these meetings can be held in the afternoons, evenings, Saturdays, or during school breaks.

10. Newsletters can inform parents about school-site events in the past and future. All articles should be specific, factual, and interesting, and should avoid the use of professional jargon.

DISCUSSION QUESTIONS

1. Does your school show any signs that the parents are becoming more or less involved? If so, why do you think these changes are taking place?

2. In general, do you think that traditional school events for parents are successful? Why or why not?

3. Do you think that a series of parent classes would help the cooperative relationship between schools and parents? In what topic areas do you see the greatest needs for such classes?

4. What do you see as the strengths and weaknesses of parent advisory committees? Does your school have one? If so, what contributions has it made to the functioning of the school?

5. Of all the parent groups associated with your school or district, which are the most active? In what ways do these groups help your school?

1. Check with your site-level administrator and list all of the ways that parents are involved at your school. Share these with other members of the class to compare both the numbers of participants and the kinds of tasks undertaken.

2. Without using real names, summarize the most difficult parent conference in which you were involved. Be specific. Ask your fellow students to describe techniques that might have made that conference more successful.

PARENT EMPOWERMENT TAKES TOO BIG A STEP

It had been a good summer. Principal Bill Johnson had gotten a good rest and completed twelve more units toward his doctorate. He had many new ideas he wanted to try at Elm School. The courses he had taken had been stimulating and challenging and had been taught by those who were currently working in the field. When he returned to campus before the beginning of the school year, the newly elected PTA president called to make an appointment with him. The discussion led to the subject of parent empowerment; Johnson was pleased that he learned something about the issue from his classes that summer.

The PTA president talked about the idea of greater freedom for her organization—freedom to set the agenda, hold committee meetings, and produce the PTA newsletter without having to clear these routine tasks through the principal's office. Johnson thought that these requests were in line with his own professional desire to be more open-minded, and he eagerly agreed with each suggestion. He even thought that not having to sanction every little request would free him up to begin some of his new ideas. The meeting with the PTA president ended with both parties seemingly pleased with the new way things were

3. Gather copies of invitations that your school has sent to parents for school-sponsored events over the past year or so. With other students, evaluate the strengths and weaknesses of these invitations.

4. If your school has a parent advisory committee, ask the principal if you can attend one of its meetings as an observer. Share with your class the agenda items covered and the principal's role at that meeting.

5. Bring a copy of your school newsletter to class. Compare it with those of other schools. List at least five ideas you can use in the future.

---

going to be conducted. Later, a couple of other officers stopped to congratulate him on his openness to suggestions and his trust in their organization.

The first two PTA meetings of the year had gone smoothly, and Johnson was pleased at how confidently the president conducted them and how little he had to do beyond organizing the facility. At the next board meeting, he was taken by surprise. One of the PTA committees had evidently proposed (and the board had adopted, without his knowledge) a program for a series of parent skill classes to be taught in the evenings by teachers of the Elm School staff.

The union contract was very specific about teacher hours at the school site. Because things had been running so well under the guidance of the new PTA president, and because other members were supportive of the new organizational approach, Johnson was reluctant to say anything. He decided that it was simply an oversight; perhaps the program had been presented at the board meeting when he was out of town at an administrative conference. He didn't remember reading about it in the minutes, though, and he usually read the minutes thoroughly.

The program called for each of four teachers to conduct a two-evening program, so he decided he could "twist some arms" to obtain the necessary volunteers. Two of his teachers were always eager to display their talents in front of a group, and another owed him a favor and was quite willing to be one of the four staff members. The fourth teacher was a little harder to convince, but finally she agreed.

Actually, the classes had gone well. Attendance was better than expected. The PTA officers were all pleased with the effort and some positive comments were voiced by both the participants and the teachers conducting the sessions.

When Johnson walked into

REFERENCES

1. Zelma P. Solomon, "California's Policy on Parent Involvement," *Phi Delta Kappan* 72, no. 5 (January 1991):360.

2. Anne Henderson, "Parents Are a School's Best Friends," *Phi Delta Kappan* 70, no. 2 (October 1988):149.

3. National Committee for Citizens in Education, *Taking Stock* (Washington, D.C., 1993).

his office this Thursday morning, he was not surprised to find a letter from the PTA president, who often left him notes about things for him to do or materials the committees needed. He opened the note and read it.

Mr. Johnson:

The PTA committee on teaching has decided to begin two new activities starting this spring:

(1) Each year the Elm School PTA will select among its members a committee to evaluate the classroom teaching of every teacher at Elm. For those who have not earned tenure, recommendations will be made as to whether they should be retained on staff. For those who have tenure, the committee may wish to recommend improvements in their teaching to the standards we think should be appropriate for the students at Elm.

(2) Starting next year, Elm School PTA will select among its members a committee to interview and recommend to the board of education the employment of new teachers at Elm School. We realize, of course, input from the school principal will be needed to determine the appropriate grade-level positions.

Mrs. Charles Smith
PTA President

Johnson was in a state of shock and disbelief. His summer classes now seemed too theoretical. Those discussion groups on parent empowerment had not prepared him for this turn of events. What should he do?

DISCUSSION ISSUES

Past

1. In what ways did Johnson fail to communicate with the PTA president at their initial meeting? What can we deduce that Johnson probably failed to get out of his summer classes?

2. What other opportunities did Johnson have to communicate with the PTA during the school year

4. Juleen Cattermole and Norman Robinson, "Effective Home/School Communication—From the Parent's Perspective," *Phi Delta Kappan* 67, no. 1 (September 1985):49.

5. Upland Unified School District, "Parent–Teacher Conferencing" (Upland, Calif., 1987).

6. Ibid.

7. Gerda Lawrence and Madeline Hunter, *Parent-Teacher Conferencing* (Beverly Hills, Calif.: TIP Publications, 1978).

prior to receiving the letter? What stances should he have taken?

3. Many of the items suggested by the PTA president seem innocent enough. Where did Johnson go wrong in his agreement?

4. What role does a principal have in working with parent advisory committees? How can one balance a democratic approach with being "on top of things"?

5. What does the letter tell you about the attitude of the PTA committee members? Why do you think these attitudes exist?

Present

1. What communication approach should Johnson take immediately, now that he has received this letter?

2. Some school districts have implemented parent empowerment in both ways suggested in the PTA president's letter. What are the strengths and weaknesses of this level of parent empowerment?

3. If a copy of this letter got into the hands of the faculty, what reaction do you think would be forthcoming? How do you think Johnson should anticipate this potential event?

4. If a copy of this letter got into the hands of the union representative, what reaction do you think would be forthcoming? How do you think Johnson should anticipate this potential event?

5. If a school or district desires to implement parent empowerment, what communication strategies need to be followed? And with whom?

8. Margaret C. Wang, Maynard C. Reynolds, and Herbert J. Walberg, eds., *Handbook of Special Education, Research and Practice,* vol. 4, *Emerging Programs* (Oxford, England: Pergamon Press, 1991), p. 138.

9. Margaret C. Wang, Maynard C. Reynolds, and Herbert J. Walberg, eds., *Special Education: Research and Practice* (Oxford: England: Pergamon Press, 1990), p. 39.

10. Ibid., p. 104.

11. G. Keith Dolan, "What Volunteers? Can They Be Found?" *The Networker* 2, no. 1 (Spring 1979), pp. 38–39.

12. Nancy Bednar, "Building Better Families: School-Community Cooperation," *NASSP Bulletin* 76 (December 1992), pp. 93–94.

13. Fountain Valley School District, "Ways Parents Can Help Students at Home," Fountain Valley, Calif., 1987.

14. Louis Harris, "The Public Takes Reform to Heart," *Agenda* (Winter 1992), p. 18.

INTERACTING WITH THE COMMUNITY

CHAPTER OBJECTIVES

In this chapter, you will learn

- How to form alliances with community groups interested in supporting education

- How to secure leadership for the PTA or other parent-sponsored school group

- How to work as a team member with the district office

- How to appeal to the board of education without overstepping bounds

- Why it is valuable to work with local service clubs

- Several ways that local institutions of higher learning can serve the school

- How to draw on resources, such as community leaders and public institutions

- What contributions the business community can make to education

- How to set up a school–business partnership

any groups and individuals in the surrounding community support the schools. Others might if they knew how to help the school's educational efforts. One of the first tasks for a new site-level administrator is to identify the major groups that make up the community. The late Dr. William S. Brisco, Professor of Education at the University of California, Los Angeles, and a former superintendent of Santa Monica Unified School District, often told his students that when he initially assumed the superintendency at that location he literally walked the city's streets to become better acquainted with both the people and the organizations of the area. This method may not be practical for all new school leaders, but it shows that any administrator should make an effort to become knowledgeable about the geography and citizens within the boundaries of the school district.

There are, of course, less strenuous avenues for obtaining the information desired. Inroads can be made by:

- Talking with the former principal at the school

- Talking with other members of the administrative team or the superintendent

- Talking with one's contemporaries at the same administrative level

- Talking with community leaders

- Reading back issues of the local newspaper to find out about groups and individuals who may want to support the school

- Attending meetings of the local chamber of commerce

These suggestions serve as starting points in locating potentially useful and interested community groups.

The Education Community

Many community organizations are already involved directly in education. The principal of any school will know about these groups but may not think of them as useful community resources. These include local parent organizations, the district office, the board of education, service clubs, and local universities and colleges.

PARENT–TEACHER GROUPS

For the first and foremost organization, one does not have to leave the confines of the school itself. Every school is supported in its endeavors by organized parent groups. Probably the most widely recognized is the PTA (Parent Teacher Association), a local organization with state and national affiliations. Some schools choose to develop their own independent groups, which are often called PTOs (parent teacher organizations).

The PTA or PTO can be one of the school's strongest partners. Most members are dedicated to the proposition that schools can be improved and are willing to work to that end. From its national origins in 1897, the PTA has worked toward bettering schools at the local, state, and national levels, so its avowed purpose has been well established.

The key to success for a PTA or PTO at a specific school site is the leadership of interested parents. Some schools have a tradition of electing quality leaders; in these schools, a new principal can lead simply by supporting the activities of the PTA or PTO.

If, however, the PTA leadership is not apparent among its members, or seems to be waning, then the site-level administrator needs to do something to improve the situation. One place to start is to seek out parents with potential leadership qualities. To discover these individuals, a principal can:

- Closely observe parents at meetings and note those with enthusiasm and a high degree of interest in the functioning of the school

- Ask your teaching staff to give you the names of those who have exhibited high interest in the school

- Call the principals of feeder schools and ask them to recommend incoming parents who have shown a spark of leadership in the past

- Review your list of family names for those who are recognized as ones who regularly contribute to the functioning of the community as a whole

The principal can then contact select parents and enlist their support in improving how the PTA functions. If possible, the principal should make these efforts along with the existing PTA board or its nominating committee; she should not appear to usurp the organization. However, a school leader certainly has the right and responsibility to obtain the strongest leadership for the PTA.

What if the school doesn't have a parent teacher organization? The principal can initiate one. He should gather a slate of officers to represent all ethnic groups, economic levels, and geographic areas within the school boundary. The initial slate of officers also should represent several grade levels so that they do not all leave the school at the same time. Obtaining parents who are willing to serve as officers of the PTA at the high school level is particularly challenging. Although the student body is generally larger than at the feeder schools, fewer parents are active in the PTA once their children leave elementary school. Some parents simply burn out; some parents devote their time to other support groups (booster clubs, band parents, and so on). Most students no longer actively solicit their parents' membership as they get older.

Once the group has been established or rejuvenated, it needs to develop realistic, meaningful objectives for the year. Goals should be widely discussed and agreed upon. Otherwise, planning meetings can evolve into gripe sessions or arguments about what is best for the school.

A principal can help the group plan meetings that will be meaningful to other parents. For example, if drugs are a concern in the community, the PTA can plan a series of meetings that focus on this problem. If gang activity is increasing in the community, the group can plan meetings on this topic. Strategies for student success at school is another topic. A survey of the parents, either at the first meeting or by a newsletter poll, might help determine issues of concern to parents.

Meetings should be advertised through a variety of methods—the PTA newsletter, the school newsletter, invitations, and the telephone tree. Although leadership may come from dedicated parents, the site-level administrator's support is a necessary ingredient. To be successful, the organization will require time from teachers, administrators, and clerical staff.

Most of all, a principal can support parent groups by communicating openly with the members. He must be committed to all parent groups associated with the school. This can be especially difficult at the high school level, where more parent groups exist; each group adds something different to the functioning of the school. At some schools, an administrative delegate attends PTA board meetings on behalf of the principal. Still, the principal should attend whenever time permits or when a major issue surfaces.

Typically, PTA board meetings and schoolwide programs are held either in the afternoon or in the evening. Both time periods create problems, particularly for working parents and for teachers who want to participate. No time will satisfy everyone, but it is probably best to retain the meeting times already established. If attendance begins to slacken or word comes through the grapevine that there is a concern about the designated time, then poll the parents and schedule a different day or time.

THE DISTRICT OFFICE

This group certainly is a vital part of the internal educational program's operation. Often, though, it is distant from the school site. Like all organizations, school districts are a bureaucracy. Large districts have layers upon layers of administrators who can help—or sometimes impede—the programs of the local school. Smaller districts have fewer employees, but their organizations still constitute bureaucracies, which tend to move slowly. One of the major problems is obtaining approval for any exception to a policy. District rules and regulations are obviously necessary; however, as any competent administrator understands, the purpose of an administrator is to make exceptions to rules and regulations! A principal must therefore discover ways around the unintentional roadblocks of the bureaucracy.

One of the best ways is to develop a reputation for being a team player. When the district office asks the principal to complete a task, such as complete a questionnaire or submit a detailed budget, she should just do the job (and quickly) rather than gripe about it. She will earn the reputation of being a team player, which will cause less anxiety. Her reputation will spread quickly among the staff at the district office.

To expedite requests or obtain needed support, the principal needs to cultivate friendships with those who run the departments for business, personnel, curriculum, maintenance, and so on. She needs to learn where the power lies: A secretary, for example, can be very important in obtaining an appointment or expediting a work order. This does not mean ignoring the chain of command, but seeking out those who can get things done without unnecessary delay is a useful strategy. For major projects (a curricular change, for example), a principal may need the approval of the head of that department. Discussing the issue with that individual *before* submitting the proposal may help establish a positive inclination about approving it. Seeking advice from district personnel will further develop the principal's reputation as a team member.

Although secretaries and administrative assistants can sometimes help avoid bureaucratic snags, they also can be part of the problem. Sometimes it is a challenge to get past the assistant when trying to talk with his or her boss. When I was a principal, I couldn't seem to bypass the secretary to talk to the associate superintendent of personnel until I discovered that the secretary left for home at 4:30. After that, the associate superintendent himself answered the calls. Finally, I established a regular line of communication without having to make an issue about the roadblock. To find out who the expediters are, one can either ask colleagues or simply discover for oneself. These expediters should be thanked both privately and publicly for their help. By so doing, the administrator is apt to receive the same kind of help in the future.

THE BOARD OF EDUCATION

If the administrator had to single out one outside group with whom to develop positive community–school relations it would be the board of education. The site administrator wants board members to think positively about the school and to be aware of faculty accomplishments. Unfortunately, it's the superintendent's job to work directly with the board of education. The principal should not interfere.

Most people elected or appointed to local boards are motivated and dedicated to improving the schools in their communities. However, a few may have some personal charge against the district or schools. How the public views the makeup of the board may be changing. Danzberger et al. comment: "A finding that is related to the increased representativeness of the local boards is the perception that the number of board members who represent special interests on very specific ideological positions is also growing."[1] Although the principal most likely will have an opinion about such vested interests, it is much better to avoid identifying with board politics. Individual agendas of board members will affect the superintendent. But such issues should not involve site-level administrators or teachers.

As an employee of the board, a principal needs to communicate with its members in a positive, friendly, and professional manner. The principal may know some members of the board as neighbors, friends, or colleagues. But it is better to avoid seeking such relationships with board members. Using a personal relationship to obtain some item or decision regarding the school is unjustifiable.

The site-level administrator may have direct contact with board members whose children attend his school. On occasion, board members visit the school site to observe some aspect of the curriculum. The principal will also have direct contact if he is called upon to explain a facet of the school program at one of the scheduled board meetings.

Because principals do not meet with board members unless the superintendent invites them to, the opportunities for school–community relations with the board are limited. It's a good idea to send invitations to all school-related events to board members. They should also receive copies of the school newsletter and other publications. If the board room has space, the principal can offer to display examples of student work in that location. These are all appropriate ways to communicate with board members.

SERVICE CLUBS

One way to become known by members of the community is to join a local service club. Kiwanis, Rotary, Lions, Optimists, and Exchange are the most widely recognized groups. These clubs meet weekly for breakfast, lunch, or dinner; arrange for guest speakers on subjects of interest to the group; and discuss community projects.

Service clubs are more popular with high school principals than elementary school principals, probably because the geographical area served by the high school more closely matches that represented by the club's membership. Secondary administrators have assistant principals, whereas elementary principals often work without appointed help. This type of organization may allow secondary principals the time to attend the meetings. Belonging to a service club is not mandatory, but it gives the administrator an opportunity to meet people who represent various businesses and professional groups. The membership may include opinion leaders who can share insights with the site administrator.

Obtaining membership is not difficult, and most service clubs constantly seek new members.

A new administrator may wish to visit several service clubs as a guest. That way, the administrator can select a group with the most appropriate membership. Whether the principal decides to join a club, any of these organizations can still be a part of the school–community program. Many service clubs even seek worthwhile community projects to support. They often are willing to support student programs that are unique and have a measurable benefit to the students. Some service clubs have well-established national projects that could help some students directly. One national project, for example, furnishes eyeglasses to needy students.

Service clubs have limited budgets and should not be viewed as "money machines." Club members often are willing to support activities in ways other than financial. They may help run one of the school's athletic programs, for example, or participate in a school event that cannot be organized by the faculty alone. If a club turns down a school's request for help with a program because the club doesn't have the funds or is involved in other projects, the staff should not give up on that group. A year or two later, the same organization may be looking for a worthwhile community activity and may reconsider the proposal.

Most service clubs meet weekly and often need guest speakers. Schools can foster worthwhile communication by sending students and faculty members as scheduled speakers or performers. The club may welcome the school band or choir, foreign exchange students, the debate teams, and others. Some clubs are even willing to include a five-minute "state of the school" message by a student at their meetings on a regular basis. This keeps the members of the club apprised of events occurring at the school and offers the student an opportunity to speak regularly to an adult group.

UNIVERSITIES AND COLLEGES

A school that is located near a college or university may find opportunities to work with higher education faculty. Many college instructors are willing to serve as educational consultants. Their expertise can help bolster a curriculum need, or they may give in-service help to staff members. These services often involve fees. Universities and colleges can be part of the school–community relations program in other ways, too:

- *Field trips.* Students can visit the university or college on a field trip, and they will benefit from seeing the campus and finding out what college is like. Some departments (science, drama, and art, for example) will arrange demonstrations to entertain and challenge visiting students.

- *Guest speakers.* Most schools of higher learning have a speakers' bureau that includes those professors who are willing to go to school sites to speak. These talks usually are free. Speakers often address topics unrelated to their teaching specialty but of interest to them.

- *Tutors.* If the local college or university has a teacher preparation program, college students may be required to tutor for a specified number of hours. Tutoring is an important fieldwork task. Students and classroom teachers will benefit from their contributions.

- *Student teachers.* Schools of education need to place student teachers at a variety of grade levels and subject areas. Being a resident training teacher is useful professional experience for regular teachers, and it gives them an opportunity to work with students in smaller groups. In addition, such a program can be an excellent source of new teachers in the future.

- *Recruitment representatives.* Recruiters from major colleges and universities often visit high schools to inform students of the requirements and programs of their institutions. All students will benefit from the information provided by the recruiters. However, those students seeking college admission will especially benefit. What they learn may broaden their views but also narrow their choices.

- *Researchers.* Some schools of education seek students to participate in research studies or special programs in reading, mathematics, or other subject areas. Participation in these programs requires parental permission. Students usually benefit academically from participating; they learn firsthand about research, they enjoy the special attention, and they gain from helping others.

The Public Community

ll towns and cities are rich with resources that schools may draw from: community leaders, including ordinary people, who have something to offer; professionals; government workers and other officials; and institutions such as museums and libraries. Schools should seek opportunities to combine these community assets with appropriate school programs. The Philadelphia Parkway School Project, for example, brought most of its high school classes to various facilities within that historical city. Such a dramatic step toward community involvement isn't necessary. Every school can take advantage of the public community around it in less major ways. The site administrator should work closely with his teaching staff to ascertain program needs and then be aggressive in seeking alliances with the desired resources.

COMMUNITY LEADERS

All citizens are potential contributors to the education of youth. Nearly everyone serves in that capacity to some extent anyway, as a parent, volunteer, professional, or worker. Consider, though, how people might serve as community leaders, too, working directly with students at the school site.

- *Seniors.* Many schools hold grandparents' day and invite students' grandparents or other older citizens to come to class. Some schools enlist the help of seniors on a regular basis (one hour a month, for example) to read to children, listen to the children read, talk with the class, and so on. How about enlisting support from a local senior center? Adopting a senior to share some time with a class regularly may benefit both parties.

- *High-interest presenters.* Develop a resource file of individuals who are willing to share life experiences, travel, occupations, or hobbies with young people. The school district may already have a file that you can add to. Screen the presentations to make sure they are grade-level appropriate.

- *Foreigners.* Many foreign visitors or people who have just moved here from another country are willing to share their lifestyles and customs with others. High school foreign-exchange students are an excellent resource; they often can relate well to students and know what cultural differences will be of interest.

- *Alumni.* All schools—not just high schools and colleges—have alumni. Programs can be developed whereby students from an elementary school who are now at the middle school or high school can return regularly as tutors, as coaches, to help run school events, or as judges for competitions. Likewise, alumni of middle schools and high schools may also volunteer. Develop a clipping service, and send letters of congratulations to those who achieve awards, scholarships, elections, and so on. They are the future adults of the school community.

- *Police officers.* Some schools and districts sponsor courses at the middle school and high school levels in which police officers teach about law enforcement and youth rights. Some have even developed "ride around" programs, in which students have accompanied officers in their patrol cars. Many elementary schools have become involved in D.A.R.E., a drug abuse prevention program.[2] The D.A.R.E. curriculum was designed by professional educators to be taught by police officers knowledgeable about drug culture.

    A school principal should establish a smooth working relationship with the local police so they can handle common problems together. The police may need to help with crowd control, student conflicts, and extra patroling of the school area on weekends if problems occur.

- *Firefighters.* Young children look up to firefighters and enjoy visiting with them. Most local fire stations have regular programs whereby they visit the school with one of their trucks or encourage a class to visit the local station. Students may learn about school and home safety and other useful information.

- *Elected city officials.* Representatives of all levels of political office are more than pleased to visit schools or send someone to represent them at school functions. Their offices are also available to students studying city, county, or state government. It's surprising how seldom city officials are asked to help. One teacher in San Diego, California, requested that a representative from the city manager's office visit his political science class to explain how the city runs. The city manager himself came—and returned every year. He stated it was the only speaking request he had ever received.

INSTITUTIONS

- *Museums and art galleries.* Many towns and cities may not have these kinds of institutions. Those that do should use them. Field trips are the obvious approach for student participation. Some museums and galleries will send staff or volunteers, who bring exhibits and printed materials to the school. With some planning and organizing, they may even be willing to host a private showing and tour for students, a worthwhile community endeavor.

- *Libraries.* Most schools maintain their own libraries but do not have the budgets of county and city libraries. Encourage students to visit the local branches to broaden their access to research materials. In rural communities, mobile book libraries may augment the school reading program. Elementary teachers should encourage their students to participate in the summer reading programs sponsored by public libraries.

- *Parks, national monuments, and special structures.* Most regions have something special to offer—historic landmarks, monuments, architectural treasures, areas of natural beauty, and so on. Like museums, they are appropriate field trip destinations. Students learn to appreciate their community in the context of a history, science, or art lesson.

- *Military installations.* Most military facilities have designated days when the public may visit. All have program speakers. They may also have special programs for schools. One unique approach was used at McGaugh Elementary School in the Seal Beach School District in California. The principal invited sailors stationed in the community to come to his school to read to the students. Fourteen volunteered the first time; now, more than 50 arrive each time the program is held. There is even a waiting list of sailors wanting to participate.[3]

The Business Community

working relationship with the business community is not a new strategy for schools, but it is an ever-expanding one. As Turnbull states,

> *With financial resources dwindling across the country, the school district has found the business community to be a valuable educational resource. Local companies offer a reservoir of knowledgeable professionals who contribute time and expertise to enhance the efforts of the community schools.*[4]

Thomas W. Evans, chairman of the Education Committee of the Presidential Board of Advisors on Private Sector Initiations, has estimated that 60,000 business-sponsored projects are currently underway in U.S. schools.[5]

Not long ago, the contributions of businesses to schools were limited to materials, tours, and scholarships. Many businesses recently have gone far beyond those efforts and are now working directly at the schools with the teachers, administrators, and, perhaps most importantly, the students. These efforts are not limited to *local* business establishments. As a spokesperson for a major automobile company states, "American companies spend $2.4 billion on education, apart from paying about one third of the state and local taxes in this country that support schools. . . . At Chrysler we've got a dozen separate education programs going on. We think all of them are working."[6]

STATEWIDE EFFORTS TO MANDATE PARTNERSHIPS

Many people consider the leadership of business to be crucial to improved public education if the present system remains intact. In the summer of 1991, members of the California Business Round Table, the California Chamber of Commerce, and the Industry Education Council for California for the Year 2000 met to discuss issues regarding business–school partnerships. The California group proposed seven strategic imperatives:

1. Develop performance-based assessment models.

2. Develop and support school autonomy.

3. Link schools and students with business and community.

4. Strengthen the teaching profession.

5. Develop student-focused instruction.

6. Move the education system into the information age.

7. Assure the provision of adequate facilities.[7]

Other states are developing similar mandates. For example, West Virginia has restructured its school system in a major way. Spring comments on this state's efforts:

Training became a key part of [the] strategy to improve its schools. Today, the involvement of companies such as GM, C&P Telephone [a Bell Atlantic Company], Ashland Oil and IBM has created in West Virginia what some observers regard as the best example of corporate investment in retraining teachers and administrators.[8]

In Ossing, New York, the General Electric Management Development Institute has adopted Anne M. Domer Middle School and has contributed programs for both students and faculty. They have provided judges for the school's science fair, furnished speakers at school career breakfasts, and supplied videotapes about countries covered in the school's social studies program. For the teachers, the institute has held personal computer workshops; provided minicourses on science, technology, and economics; and presented awards to teachers for unique contributions to the school.[9]

Hartsville High School in Hartsville, South Carolina, developed a similar arrangement with a program built around career goals and teacher recognition. Students shadowed community businesspeople at their jobs and received job counseling. The businesspeople honored teachers by department each month and substituted in the classrooms while the teachers attended the awards luncheon.[10] A final example demonstrates the strength of the business community's influence. A community alliance in Grandview, Missouri was formed among the school district, city hall, the chamber of commerce, and the local water district. Together, the alliance succeeded in passing a bond issue that boosted public confidence in both the schools and other economic development programs.[11]

THE KEY TO SUCCESS: LONG-TERM COMMITMENT

National programs run the gamut. Some furnish classroom materials to specific schools or purchase materials for specific curriculum needs. Some programs employ local youth during the school year. All of these programs are worthwhile. But the best ones establish a long-term commitment of business people working with schools to improve the entire educational program.

This commitment goes even deeper than the adopt-a-school programs, which offer resources and personnel to schools. Some new efforts, for example, focus on a particular school problem identified by both school personnel and business representatives. These coordinated efforts have become contracts of sorts. Spring writes:

> In some communities, a formal relationship was established between business and the schools. In the early 1980s, business leaders and the Boston schools signed a formal compact stating that the schools would improve the quality of graduates to meet employer needs, and, in exchange, local businesses would give preference to graduates of Boston schools. A similar alliance was established in Atlanta.[12]

Small cities and towns face problems with obtaining business support. This is mainly because the businesses themselves are small and have limited resources. Neither personnel nor sizable financial contributions are likely from a single business concern in a community that has no major companies. Therefore, partnerships may not be appropriate for small school districts.

The focus for many of the major school–business partnerships has changed. The goal is to have an impact on both the students and the schools. According to the U.S. Department of Commerce, "The reality is that the future of business depends on the schools preparing students with skills and work attitudes that will enable employers to compete in an uncertain and highly competitive market place."[13]

Partnerships vary across the United States, but schools typically ask businesses to share people, equipment, facilities, and technology. Schools benefit from access to talented, highly trained people who are willing to share their business experiences and the educational materials funded by a particular company.

Potential partnerships should consider what will benefit students most. They should plan for a long-term relationship. Partnership programs should be evaluated regularly, and the results should be shared with the public. (See Chapter 11.) These business partners, like other groups, need to be recognized for their contributions to the development of our youth. One article in an educational journal summarizes the advantages of these partnerships as follows:

Benefits to Business

1. Better understanding by young people of how the economy works and an appreciation for private enterprise.

2. A better educated workforce.

3. More stability in neighborhoods where corporations produce and sell.

4. Better informed consumers and voters.

5. Training in vocational education that more nearly matches what employers need.

6. Employee satisfaction from working for a company that does good things for the community.

7. Bottom line results in productivity and product quality resulting from education and training improvements.

Benefits to Schools

1. A broadened base of support for the educational system.

2. Greater recognition of schools and what they contribute to business and the economy.

3. Business people to come into the schools and help educate students about careers and job opportunities.

4. Use of partner's facilities and personnel for instruction.

5. Follow-through on school's and partner's commitment to the importance of experience in learning.

6. Financial resources, which are usually in short supply.

7. Access to state-of-the-art equipment.

8. Support for appropriate education legislation.

9. Help on management problems.

10. Access to job placements for graduates.

11. Graduates who have a better understanding of how the economy works.[14]

Several business- and community-related programs have been developed for at-risk students and dropouts, including adopt-a-student programs, work programs, peer counseling, adult tutoring, and summer enrichment programs. In addition, some programs provide incentives for students to stay in school. All of these programs are long-term.

DEVELOPING NEW PROGRAMS

In California, as in some other states, grant funds are available to start up proposed partnerships. The California Educational Initiative Fund (CEIF) is a group of 11 large corporations that has dispensed money to California schools for more than ten years. These grants are competitive and the number of applicants has been increasing yearly.

Grant funds are not the only approach to developing partnerships. Site-level administrators must be aggressive in seeking help from businesses. Getting started is generally the most difficult step. School staff and business representatives should mutually want to establish a partnership. As they consider the partnership, they should determine specific objectives and the steps needed to turn the goals into reality. This may require a committee of educators and businesspeople working together to develop the details of the proposal.

After the necessary negotiations have been completed and the commitment has been made to share in the education of our youth, both groups still must heed some cautions. Consider the example of distributive education, a work-study program whereby students attended school for part of the day and worked a limited number of hours at a local business establishment. By working with one or more students, the business owner gained an impression about young people and their educational attainments. An eager, dedicated student brought forth positive comments; a student who did not handle directions well or who lacked the needed academic skills led to negative reactions and complaints. As a result, some businesspeople generalized their experience and formed negative impressions about all students and all schools. Open and honest communication is necessary to the partnership's success. Some students will view the program as an opportunity to goof off. Some will not measure up in spite of their efforts. School staff should heed the voiced criticisms. They may need to develop criteria for student participation as well as a placement service, which will demand constant supervision and follow-through. School personnel should be involved in these programs in order to smooth out any problems.

COMMUNITY SERVICE PROGRAMS

Students need to learn at an early age how they can serve their communities. Some businesses and community groups provide opportunities for students (especially high school students) to work directly with them to serve the community. These opportunities improve school–community relations and give students the chance to commit themselves to worthwhile projects. The late John F. Kennedy said during his inaugural address on January 20, 1961: "And so, my fellow Americans, ask not what your country can do for you; ask what you can do for your country."[15] Although Kennedy's plea for community service is ingrained in many Americans who grew up during the 1950s and 1960s, subsequent generations may need opportunities to cultivate the values.

Former President George Bush signed into law (November 1990) the National and Community Service Act, which provides funds for community service in schools and colleges. Conrad and Hedin qualify the impact of the act: "Actually the idea of service being a part of the school experience has reappeared in cycles throughout this century and has been a consistent, if less than dominant, feature of educational reports and reform proposals for the last 15 or 20 years."[16] At the secondary level, students may receive credits for their service. Regardless, most students who take part in service programs are highly supportive of them. According to Conrad and Hedin,

> A consistent finding of research into service and other kinds of experimental programs is the high degree to which participants report that they have learned a great deal from their experiences. In a nationwide survey we conducted of nearly 4000 students involved in service and other experimental programs, about 75% reported learning "more" or "much more" in their participation program than in regular classes.[17]

At Thomas Jefferson High School in Los Angeles, approximately 500 students (18% of the student body) have taken part in the Humanitas program during its first seven years. The students have raised money for individuals in need, worked in a seniors home, helped residents with personal problems, and tutored younger students. Reports indicate, "Overall attendance at Jefferson is about 76 percent. For three-year Humanitas students, [attendance is] 96 percent. Participants also have a lower dropout rate—only 3 percent—and an amazing 98 percent of Humanitas graduates go on to college." [18]

The Grant Foundation reported that all young people need more positive contacts with adults and opportunities to participate in community activities such as local crime prevention and neighborhood cleanups. Older youth singled out Vista, Peace Corps, and Youth Conservation Corps opportunities. Similar opportunities for community involvement need to begin earlier. Today, there are more than 3000 school-based service programs, which point at a growing awareness of the value of service. [19] Student councils are ideally suited to carry out proposals for service programs. Council members often are dedicated to their school and its image in the community. Other student groups also may be willing to commit time and resources to community work.

BUILDING GOOD RELATIONS WITH NEARBY BUSINESSES

Students of all grade levels have daily contact with small businesses adjacent to an urban school site. The students often eat there, shop there, or simply hang out there. Their actions are judged by the owners of these establishments as being typical of a school's population. Adults often generalize about particular age groups, especially teenagers. Businesspeople may even try to limit student patrons with signs that read: "No more than three students allowed in the store at one time."

If businesses are in close proximity to the school, the site administrator may want to speak with the owners at least once a year to find out if any students are causing problems. A positive effort to "mend broken fences" can be a powerful tool toward offsetting a negative predisposition toward students. Student leaders and organized student groups also can create goodwill with the business community.

A final word about working with the business community: Keep businesspeople informed of what schools are doing. When schools are being criticized, local groups need more than ever to communicate with schools. Including external groups in the educational process can be a win-win situation for everyone.

SUMMARY

1. Many groups and individuals in the community are supportive of the schools. One of the first tasks of a school principal is to identify those groups and individuals who are interested in helping the school's educational efforts.

2. Almost all schools have either a PTA or PTO, which has proved to be a strong school partner. Strong leadership in these groups is a necessity and the principal can play a role in securing parents with leadership quality.

3. The school principal needs to actively support all of the PTA's programs despite supporting other school-related groups. This attitude will require administrative, teacher, and clerical time.

4. School districts, like all organizations, are bureaucracies and can move slowly as well as appear to impede progress. An administrator must learn to avoid the unintentional roadblocks but must also be a team player.

5. A successful school administrator will know where the expediters at the district are and will cultivate their help. When help is provided, some form of thank you is always appropriate.

6. The principal is an employee of the board of education and needs to communicate with its members in a positive, friendly, and professional manner. Generally, it is better to avoid using or seeking friendships with board members to the school's advantage.

7. Service club affiliations are not required of a principal, but tapping the resources of such groups can be beneficial to the school. These groups may be willing to lend a hand for a worthwhile educational project.

8. Universities and colleges have a great deal to offer students at all levels. Students can take field trips to the institutions, professors may visit as guest speakers, and college students may tutor or serve as student teachers.

9. All communities have people and places with something to offer students. Schools may draw upon such resources as seniors, professionals, public officials, museums, libraries, and parks. Teachers should carefully weave their resources into the curriculum.

10. Businesses are expanding their efforts to work directly with schools. Knowledgeable professionals are contributing time and expertise to school programs as well as funds to support specific educational goals.

DISCUSSION QUESTIONS

1. Is the PTA or PTO an integral part of your school? What are its major strengths and weaknesses, according to you and your fellow faculty?

2. Do you think your district office has a bureaucratic image? Why or why not?

3. Is your local board of education representative of the district, considering its makeup? Why or why not? If not, what problems, if any, have been caused by this lack of representation?

4. Does your school principal belong to a service club? If so, does the club benefit the school?

5. In what ways do colleges and universities take part in the operation of your school? Could they be more helpful? If so, how?

1. List the external groups discussed in this chapter. Talk with your administrator to see how many are currently involved at your school and share the results with your fellow students.

2. Think about the following statement: *The purpose for an administrator is to make exceptions to rules and regulations.* List two situations in which you think this is true and two in which it is not. Discuss with the class.

BUSINESS TRENDS

Principal Bill Johnson was a dedicated reader of professional journals. He was convinced that for a busy site-level administrator it was one of the few ways you could keep up with the trends and changes reshaping the American education scene. Recently he came across some articles that championed the involvement of the business community with the public schools. *Phi Delta Kappan, Thrust for Educational Leadership,* and the *NASSP Bulletin* all featured articles on the subject. So did *Business Week, Time,* and other news magazines.

Elm School District worked with a number of local businesses in the past, but most of the relationships were based on the need for funds. Although Elm School received contributions for scholarships, teaching materials, and grant money, Johnson thought there was a major need to develop an honest collaborative approach between his school and the business community.

Working closely with the district's superintendent, Johnson formed a joint committee of teachers, administrators, and businesspeople to develop some long-range programs for the school. Businesspeople were released to work directly with students on the school site, students were invited to use some of the equipment located at the business sites, business workers volunteered to tutor and

3. Attend a board meeting. Observe how various members of the district office communicate with board members. What generalizations are you able to share in class?

4. Poll the teachers at your school to find out how they incorporate community resources into their curriculum. Also find out how they *would like* to use community resources. Discuss the differences, if any, in terms of how a school site administrator could bring the two lists closer together.

counsel students who asked for help, and plans were set for some companies to hire students during the summer.

The joint committee wanted the greater community to know what they were doing, so they planned the first annual Business–School Community Forum and invited parents, teachers, and interested community members. The local newspaper and chamber of commerce supported the event. Interest was so strong that the forum had to be scheduled in the community auditorium.

On the evening of the event, the auditorium was nearly packed. Johnson introduced the committee chairperson who, in turn, introduced the keynote speaker, an up-and-coming business leader who owned a new business in town. Johnson had never met or heard him speak but had been told that he was a gifted orator and possibly a candidate for political office in the future.

Johnson was enthralled with his speech, and so was the audience. The speaker all but mesmerized the group as he recounted his first year as part of the community and his background before he came to Anytown. Then the speaker shifted the topic to education. Johnson could not believe his ears. The speaker seemed to be denigrating education in America, the state, and the local community. Among his statements were:

"Our schools are failing American industry!"

"Teachers do not care about kids but are only interested in tenure and their salaries."

"At our colleges, academics have taken a back seat to Mickey-Mouse, spoonfed education courses."

Johnson sat bewildered as the speaker continued. Committee members on the stage shifted in their seats. The audience grew restless. He could see groups beginning to talk, and some people, including a few teachers, began to leave. There was nothing he could do at the moment, but what would this do to the business relationships he had worked so hard to establish?

5. Take a drive around the business sections within your own attendance area. List community agencies that could be useful to your school and discuss that potential with your fellow students.

DISCUSSION ISSUES

Past

1. What communication mistakes were made in the planning of the program? Could the situation have been avoided? How?
2. Most of the activities created and supported by the joint committee seemed worthwhile. How did this community forum go wrong? What should have been undertaken instead of the forum?
3. Were the teachers and others correct in their decisions to walk out of the meeting? What messages do these decisions convey to other members of the audience?

4. What communication techniques did the speaker use? Could these have been predicted?
5. Is Johnson correct in thinking there is nothing he could do at the meeting? What alternatives are open to him?

Present

1. Johnson will inevitably be asked questions immediately after the program is over. How should he reply to these questions? Is there anything else that he should do that evening?
2. Johnson should meet with individuals or groups starting the next day. Who should be included and why?

3. What steps need to be made to keep the joint business–school committee on an even keel? How can this group still serve the school?
4. After the forum, how should Johnson deal with the teachers? The union representatives? Members of the board of education?
5. What will happen to the committee if its members agree with the keynote speaker? How can their views benefit education in Anytown?

REFERENCES

1. Jacqueline P. Danzberger et al., "School Bonds: The Forgotten Players on the Education Team," *Phi Delta Kappan* 69, no. 1 (September 1987):57.

2. "Teaching Kids to Never Take Drugs," D.A.R.E. America, Los Angeles, 1991.

3. Principal John M. Blaydes, a talk given at Sycamore Elementary School (Upland Unified School District, Calif., January 19, 1992).

4. Sharon Turnbull, "Tapping Community Resources," *Thrust for Educational Leadership* 21, no. 5 (February/March 1991):41–44.

5. Robert Rothman, "New Emphasis for Partnerships Urged," *Business Week* (12 November 1986), p. 5.

6. Lee Iacocca, "Changing Needs and Responsibilities," *Agenda* 2 (Winter 1992):59–60.

7. Operation Education, "A Brighter California: What We Want from Our Schools by the Year 2000," California Chamber of Commerce (1992), pp. 3–18.

8. Joel Spring, *The American School 1642–1985* (White Plains, N.Y.: Longman, 1986), p. 335.

9. John Humphrey, Richard Maurer, and Bellamy Schmidt, "How to Develop a School–Business Partnership," *NASSP Journal* 72, no. 507 (April 1988):105–107.

10. H. Kenneth Dinkins, "A Plan for Community Involvement: Adopting a School," *NASSP Journal* 76, no. 2 (October 1992):106–107.

11. Tony Stansbury and David Westbrook, "Allies in Excellence," *The American School Board Journal* 178 (September 1991):32–33.

12. Spring.

13. U.S. Department of Commerce, "Counties—Employees, Payroll and Establishments," *County Business Patterns* (Washington, D.C.: Bureau of the Census, June 1983).

14. Jack Oaks and Diane Thomas, "A Second Investment," *Thrust for Educational Leadership* 20, no. 5 (February/March 1991):12–18.

15. John F. Kennedy, "Inaugural Address," in *A Question of Character: A Life of John F. Kennedy,* by Thomas C. Reeves (New York: The Free Press, 1991), p. 234.

16. Dan Conrad and Diane Hedin, "School-Based Community Service: What We Know from Research and Theory," *Phi Delta Kappan* (June 1991), p. 774.

17. Ibid., p. 748.

18. Diane Dismuke, "Helping Community, Helping Themselves," *NEA Today* (September 1993), p. 15.

19. William T. Grant Foundation Commission on Work, Family and Citizenship, "The Forgotten Half: Pathways to Success for American Youth and Young Families," *Phi Delta Kappan* 70, no. 4 (December 1988):280–289.

INTERACTING WITH THE DISTRICT ADMINISTRATION

CHAPTER OBJECTIVES

In this chapter, you will learn

- Why administrators must func-tion as part of the school's bureaucracy

- About some roles of a district superintendent

- About the role of a district communications specialist

- How a superintendent can keep the board of education well informed

- Why board meetings should be organized and businesslike

- About board policies that reflect concern for school–community relations

- Why the board of education may select advisory groups to study issues

- How a district can rally support for bond issues

- About some kinds of district publications for internal and external groups

chools operate within, and are part of, a bureaucracy. Schools are organized, to a great extent, like businesses and are managed accordingly. It is imperative, therefore, that a site-level administrator, as a middle manager, learn how to function as part of that bureaucratic organization.

Through astute observations and discussions with colleagues, site-level administrators will soon become aware of the strengths and weaknesses of the various departments at the district level. This will allow them to work effectively and productively with many different offices and people. Although principals usually work through the district superintendent, they do work directly with other district-level administrators, such as assistant superintendents, program directors, business managers, and maintenance supervisors. This is particularly true in large districts.

As part of the district administrative team, a principal must use his or her best communication skills to work effectively with the district's divisions and the personnel who lead them. District office administrators rely on the support of site-level staff to help them carry out their programs and policies. Principals are designated to communicate and interpret the philosophy and policies of the district to others.

The Superintendent's Role in School–Community Relations

o understand the school–community relations of a district, a principal must understand a little about the superintendent's role. Knowing what communication problems a superintendent faces, for example, may help a principal avoid the tendency to be critical of the decisions made at the district level. School superintendents and other district-level administrators must maintain effective relations with the community and their colleagues who operate at the site level. They must be acquainted with key personnel and must understand the power structure both inside and outside the school district. The tactics of how to relate with the representatives of various groups are not unlike those discussed in previous chapters. But the constituency of these groups is broader and the interests manifested are more diverse.

By the nature of his or her position, the superintendent must interpret the schools to the public and must shoulder the criticism for whatever goes wrong—or whatever is thought to have gone wrong—in the operation of the district. For example, if some difficulty occurs on the school bus, at a school site, or in the adoption of a new reading series, it's the superintendent who must face the irate parent or the demanding pressure group if the problem has not been resolved at the school-site level. Therefore, the responsibility for the district communication system lies with the superintendent.

The Blumbergs report the results of interviews held with 25 superintendents of school districts. They write that "dealing with situations involving conflict was a constant part of the superintendent's job, and perhaps its essential feature. Some of the situations were trivial, and some were critically important to the life of the school district."[1] Conflicts seem to be a part of the superintendent's role. As the superintendent pursues the tasks of leadership—creating organizational movement or encouraging productivity, for example—he or she becomes the creator of conflicts.

Antagonists come from all parts of the community, including the school system itself. Conflicts erupt with principals, the school board, students, teachers, and factions of the community.

The conflicts and education problems that a superintendent and his or her staff may encounter is infinite. The role demands skills to compromise, to come as close as possible to a win–win result. For example, if financial problems occur in the district (as they often do) and the board decides that it must trim the teaching staff, the superintendent will face conflict from the teachers who are laid off or transferred; the principals who may want to participate in layoff decisions; the teacher's union, which may not accept the layoffs or transfers as viable solutions to the financial crisis; and the board members who proposed the solution.

Not all interactions are based on conflict, however, so the district must develop, maintain, and evaluate a system of communication that reaches as many people as possible, both inside and outside the district. The board, the superintendent, and other district staff members have a role in this effort. The ultimate goal is to raise the level of community awareness and influence the community opinion leaders so they will support the schools.

A successful communication system will include anyone and will be two-way and continuous.[2]

Since the board members, the superintendent, and his or her staff must work to develop and maintain a strong communications program, the board should adopt a policy that supports this goal. By taking this step, the board goes on record as supporting the philosophical position that the public has a right to know what is occurring in its schools and that the board is willing to listen to comments and recommendations from the public who attend board meetings.

The District Communications Specialist

Developing and maintaining a communications program can be time-consuming, and a superintendent has many other duties to perform. Many districts, particularly the large metropolitan ones, hire a full-time community relations person to aid the superintendent in carrying out this requirement.[3] This can ease the burden without diminishing the importance of the goal. Communication specialists are known by many different titles: "Some common titles are community-relations coordinators, communications director, school information services director, public relations director, coordinator of educational communications and administrative assistant."[4] Whatever the title, the person should be able to communicate easily with a variety of professionals and laypeople, be familiar with preparing media releases, and be knowledgeable about educational issues. For these and other reasons the person may have a background in either public relations or media.

Smaller districts may not have the funds or the desire to create a position of this kind and try to accomplish the same goal using part-time personnel. An existing district-level administrator, a district teacher (for example, a journalism teacher), or a part-time media specialist may be assigned to the job. A part-time person may be qualified but may not command the respect needed to carry out the job to its fullest. A part-timer will not be as well-known, cannot be available at all times, and may not find the time to meet all of the people who should be contacted both inside and outside the district.

The most important consideration, though, is finding the right person. The program will only be as good as the person selected to carry it out. That individual should be able to:

- Communicate clearly with all audiences, both in writing and speaking

- Get along with all of the people that he or she must deal with, including board members, administrators, district staff, newspeople, parents, and community leaders

- Use good judgment that contributes to sound decisions by school officials

- Converse with educators and be able to explain jargon to laypeople[5]

Working with the Board of Education

unique responsibility for a superintendent is his or her communication with the board of education. Boards derive their authority from the state and are authorized to operate a school district in terms of policies, curriculum, and budget. The superintendent is the board's executive officer and, as such, carries out the policies of that elected (or appointed) body.

Most superintendents seem to get along rather well with their board members. Why is this? Zeigler, Kahoe, and Reisman suggest one reason:

> It is possible that superintendents spend so little time in conflict because they always do what the board wants. Such a possibility is, of course, remote since superintendents have greater access to information and staff resources than do part-time board members, giving them an advantage in the policy-making arena. In addition, superintendents have the advantage of setting the school board agenda.[6]

A less cynical viewpoint is that board members usually respect the opinions and recommendations of appointed professional leaders. Board members are often businesspeople or are themselves educators and support the concept that the recognized educational expert (that is, the superintendent) should exercise his or her expertise on substantive matters that come to the board.

It is the superintendent's duty to influence the board by disseminating information to its members. This should probably begin when new representatives are elected to the board. The districts that provide in-service programs establish a positive relationship with these new members right away. In-service sessions provide background information that can help board members function knowledgeably from the first meeting. On this issue, Danzberger et al. comment: "Board members generally agreed that they lack preparation for board service. . . . One study revealed that far too little attention is given to the development of working relationships among board members or to the development of boards as corporate governing bodies."[7] There are many ways to keep the board informed. Here are some examples:

- *Provide background information for an upcoming meeting prior to the meeting.* Background information might address topics planned for the meeting, problems with some history, and so on. Each member should get a set of information. This is a recognized, established method of encouraging board members to do the background reading necessary to keep board meetings flowing smoothly.

- *Provide notebooks during a meeting.* These notebooks would be distributed or placed at each board member's assigned seat and would include information that the board might be expected to know. They might contain a brief outline of the budget, board policies, and previous minutes.

- *Encourage school visits.* New members might be given a tour of the district schools, but all members should be encouraged to visit the schools they represent. Some districts hold information-only board meetings at the schools on a rotating basis and conduct no actual business at these times.

- *Provide additional reading material.* In addition to the background information, other district-produced materials can be sent to board members to present an overview of the district and its schools: annual reports, copies of the district bulletin, student-produced school newspapers, and so on. Many districts also give board members a subscription to the *American School Board Journal* or other professional publication dealing with "good boardmanship."

- *Attend board conventions.* State and national board conventions are held yearly. They deal with common education issues and trends across the United States and give district representatives an opportunity to share problems and successes.

- *Conduct personal conferences.* Generally, a superintendent holds personal conferences to inform members about the conditions and needs of schools. The law prohibits the "holding of secret board meetings." So personal conferences provide an alternative and allow a free flow of information. However, superintendents must be careful to treat all board members the same and not to fragment the board.

- *Send a weekly letter to board members.* This should be a kind of specialized weekly bulletin that keeps board members apprised of what has happened since the last official meeting. If personal conferences are held with members of the board, this form of communication might not be needed.

All of these efforts to provide information to board members will produce favorable results: (1) The board members will be better informed at the board meetings and less time will be lost explaining the nature of the agenda items; (2) the members will get the impression that, as the policy-making body, they are entitled to all of the information possible; and (3) a trust will form between the superintendent and the board members.

Influencing a board is not an easy task because each elected member is unique and may be forced to take a specific stance related to his or her particular constituency. Many superintendents do not think of the board as a group but as individuals who collectively form the board. The efforts listed above cannot be used to influence the board itself, but they can help inform individual members who will be called upon to vote a particular issue. The Blumbergs explain:

> Both the superintendent's professional reputation and his personal welfare depend greatly on his ability to influence its decisions. Further, it is primarily through the one-to-one linkage between superintendent and the school board member that attempts to influence take place.[8]

BOARD MEETINGS

A superintendent can establish and maintain positive feelings about a school district simply by observing the businesslike atmosphere of board meetings. A strong superintendent will impress his or her board members, employees, visitors, and the media with a well-planned, rapidly moving series of meetings.

He or she should generate an agenda in plenty of time to be delivered to the board members prior to the meeting. Ample copies should be on hand for visitors. Well-focused meetings will help avoid negative reactions from the public.

Barring unforeseen circumstances, board meetings should start on time. If the board has a history of starting meetings late, participants and visitors become careless about arriving on time, which can aggravate on-time visitors.

Many boardrooms have limited seating capacity for visitors. If a larger crowd is anticipated—for example, if a controversial topic is on the agenda—then plans should be made to move the board meeting to another location (a school auditorium, for example). The communication specialist (or other staff) should announce the change of location as soon as it is known. Board members and school officials who occupy positions at the board table should be identified by nameplates that can be read at the rear of the boardroom. Places for media regulars should also be provided, because the stories of these reporters can engender positive or negative feelings among readers who do not attend these meetings.

Executive sessions, which are limited to designated topics by the legal framework of the states, are best held at either the beginning or the ending of the public forum. Although details of the executive session cannot be divulged, it is best to announce the purpose of the closed meeting (personnel matters, for example) so as to avoid sowing seeds of mistrust.

Because boards of education represent the public-at-large community, people have the right to speak out about issues on the agenda. The board should have established policies about the topics that may be covered, the length of the time for each speaker, and the amount of time reserved for public input.

Finally, board meetings often schedule time for presentations about aspects of the district's education programs. Presentations may include site-level administrators, classroom teachers, students, or representatives of some other phase of the district's operation. Some districts even alternate meetings with presentations, at which no actual board business is conducted. Of course, these are clearly public relations activities intended to generate positive feelings among the participants, the parents of the students involved, and the board members.

As part of the total district communication program, the board has a vital role to play. All board meetings are open to the public and, although only a small percentage attend, those that do carry the message back to others. Those who are part of the district family—certificated, classified, and administrative staff—almost always have representatives at these meetings who duly note the board's actions and reactions.

A major strategy for the successful superintendent of schools is to encourage the board of education to develop and adopt policies that reflect its collective feelings about the goals of the district. New superintendents may discover these already in place. But, even if policies are established, they should be carefully reviewed to see if they still reflect the needs of the community and the schools. After all, times change, boards change, and communities change.

As mentioned previously, many superintendents indicate that conflict is a normal part of their positions. Potential disagreements can be professionally handled better if there are carefully thought out policies in place before the issues are raised. Policies place objectives in perspective, enable a more consistent handling of similar situations, and assign responsibility for carrying out directives. In general, well-designed policies cause less negative reaction from the public than spur-of-the-moment reactions to an issue. Parents, other community residents, and employees are more apt to accept a decision based on a previously developed board policy. General understanding of where a district stands on issues often increases the confidence that the district has direction.

A district cannot create policies for every conceivable situation, however, and many unique problems need to be handled at the school-site level. As Clemmer writes:

> Policies should be established to enable consistent treatment of common problems. When principals or teachers regularly encounter certain issues having to do with attendance, discipline, grading, homework, textbook selection, instruction on controversial issues, athletic eligibility, graduation requirements, and many others of similar magnitude, no time should be lost in debate about what the district's standards are.[9]

Some board policies cover issues directly related to school–community relations. Policies may address how the public communicates with the board, how the public participates at the school, and how the public uses the facility when school is not in session. All board policies have an impact on school–community relations. Boards set policies, but it is up to the superintendent and staff to implement them.

■ COMMUNICATING WITH THE PUBLIC

A school board may well develop a statement of philosophy that supports the idea of the educational program reflecting the needs of the local community as well as society in general. The policy may also show a commitment toward providing public information in a timely and understandable fashion.

The board may set guidelines for school newsletters and other publications, including responsibilities for editing and distributing. Some districts adopt policy statements regarding advertising in school-sponsored publications.

Chapter 10 discusses how to work with the media. The board is in a unique position in this regard, because board meetings by law are public meetings. Boards generally designate the superintendent as the press liaison, but in larger districts specialized personnel act in this capacity.

Complaints concerning school personnel, instructional materials, and special kinds of programs are common. Board policies usually encourage the public to voice such complaints at regular meetings. They may even state specific procedures for such presentations. Some boards' policies are so specific that they spell out the procedures to be followed if the verbal complaints are initially made to an individual board member rather than the board itself as a whole. Students and their parents have legal rights to due process and hearing procedures. These rights should be indicated in the board policies, along with procedures for adhering to them. Any parent or student who wants a copy of board policies should be furnished one. Some districts also include as policy the steps that someone must follow in challenging a district decision. This may involve the county office of education, the State Board of Education, or, in the case of federally funded programs, the U.S. Secretary of Education.

■ THE PUBLIC'S PARTICIPATION AT SCHOOL

Governing boards have in recent years recognized the value of advisory committees and usually support their consideration of school problems, needs, and issues. It is wise to state as policy, however, that the committee's advisory function precludes it from becoming a policy-making body. Policies also may state rules and regulations concerning membership, length of time for serving on the committee, district resources available, as well as any legal requirements and limitations.

The district school board often authorizes other site organizations, such as athletic booster clubs and scholarship foundations. As with advisory committees, the board may hold decision-making power but welcome the organization's advisory capacity. District requirements also may spell out legal restrictions (as to the handling of funds, for example) and limitations as to the organization's operation.

Volunteers are always welcome at schools and often are authorized by board policies that specify any legal restrictions (replacing regular school personnel, for example, may be prohibited) and any insurance limitations on tasks they can perform. Districts sometimes adopt policies as to the volunteer's eligibility as well. Most states have statutes that prohibit visitors from disrupting normal school operations. Boards may include these restrictions as part of a policy, along with other reasonable requirements (for example, limiting the length of time for visits or requiring that visitors report to the office first).

■ THE SCHOOL, THE STAFF, AND PUBLIC ACTIVITIES

The right of school employees to engage in political activities on their own time is guaranteed by law. However, school employees cannot use school time, materials, or facilities for campaign purposes. Boards may adopt policies that spell out details of what employees can and cannot do in this regard.

Most board policies carefully delineate the use of school facilities. The use of public schools by residents and organizations at times when the schools are not in session is generally supported by state laws. Districts can adopt policies that indicate the process for obtaining approval, the fee schedule, conditions for use, eligibility for use, and the types of activities that are prohibited.

The openness of board meetings and the resulting input by individuals or groups does not always reflect the feelings of the district personnel. Many people who attend board meetings do so for a single purpose— for example, to protest the adoption of a particular textbook. Their appeal to the board may be emotional or inarticulate, and board members may react to the presentation rather than the issue. To avoid this problem, the board may appoint advisory committees to study specific school problems. Ad hoc groups may discuss school closures, the problems and merits of year-round school, district building needs, budgets, curriculum needs, and other significant issues. Some districts have ongoing committees whose members serve for a number of years and deal with numbers of district-wide topics. In forming advisory committees, it is wise to include some opinion leaders within the district. The important thing is that the committee represent the entire district.

Using advisory committees to study selected issues does not lessen the importance of the board of education. Rather, it increases the feeling that public schools belong to the community. And it develops a cadre of support for issues that may have been misunderstood by the public. As Bagin, Grazian, and Harrison remark: "Research indicates that when citizens are involved in studying school needs they support those needs much more than when they aren't involved."[10]

In studying an issue, the committee needs to be furnished with as much information about the topic as possible and, of course, must have access to district personnel who serve as consultants. Care must be taken that professional assistants avoid becoming the committee themselves. They are to provide needed information to the working committee and answer questions; they should not dominate or influence committee members, who should use their own judgment.

Generally, committees form a set of recommendations to the board of education. Although the board is under no obligation to agree with the recommendations, it should share them with the entire district. If recommendations are turned down, or are accepted in part, the board has an obligation to give reasons. Regardless of whether the committee's recommendations are accepted, the board should publicly thank each committee member for his or her efforts.

Bond Issues

hy is it that some districts cannot seem to obtain the necessary community support for a bond issue and others seem to gain support every time? There are many answers to this question. One answer is the organization of the campaign itself.

In campaigning for bond issues, the district should notify residents of the needs long before voting day—even years, in some cases. That way, the influx of new students or the replacing of old and obsolete buildings does not come as a surprise to the electorate. Another strategy is to specify where the money will be spent; voters are reluctant to approve a blank check but are more willing to vote funds for two science labs at school A, new kindergarten rooms at school B, and a new school C in a designated location. The district can demonstrate the need for additional classroom space by means of demographic data on community growth and student population and with photographs of existing structures.

The district should form a committee to plan and carry out the campaign. The committee should draw up a timetable and assign responsibilities for members of the district and school staffs. Many approaches can be used to inform the public about bond issues. News articles in various publications, endorsements, and panel discussions are three methods. Face-to-face contact is best, because it gives people the opportunity to ask questions and provide input if they have strong feelings about the bond issue.

The committee can form a speakers' bureau and assign informed orators to attend planned meetings. Some districts develop flipcharts, slides, or videotapes to graphically present the story of the district needs. Service clubs and other organizations may give time slots at their regular meetings to present the program. PTAs and other school support groups should be willing to sponsor meetings. Some individuals who feel strongly about the bond issue may also be willing to host small meetings in their homes. Here are some salient suggestions for campaigns:

- Obtain the support of the municipal government; its members are often influential and have a sizable following.

- Target the parents; they are likely to be supporters.

- Consider the possibility of absentee ballots, particularly for young voters; their age group contains the highest percentage of supporters.

- Try to pinpoint declared opposition and take steps to minimize its input. Be sure *your* representatives attend public meetings at which opposition groups will be present.

- If there is controversy about where the money will be used, include rationale for the decisions.

- Develop rapport with the parents of non–public-school students; they often vote *no* on public school bond issues.

- Develop a history of publicly supporting programs for seniors; because seniors have fixed incomes, they have reason to vote against these kinds of propositions.

There are, of course, many other important concerns regarding bond issues (fundraising, for example). But all other concerns hinge on having a strong district-level communication program. If the community perceives that the district board members and superintendent are concerned about the kinds of schools and programs the public wants, then bond issues have a good chance of being successful. Communication efforts of the superintendent are not limited to working with the board or members of the community. As the appointed leader of the district, he or she must come in contact with all of the individuals employed by the district. The superintendent can therefore communicate both plans and problems to these employees.

The larger the district, the more these contacts are delegated to others. Other district administrators who are subordinate to the superintendent may have greater opportunities and responsibilities to communicate directly with support personnel, both at the district office and at the school sites. Nevertheless, the superintendent should still find ways to interact personally with various groups that make up the district's work force, especially the principals. In part, it is through such interactions that a superintendent supplies the three basic commodities that principals need: information, resources, and support.[11]

It may take creative planning to find ways to meet regularly with other district employees. Some superintendents schedule times on a weekly or monthly basis to visit district schools on a rotating basis, meeting with the site administrator and the teaching staff. Some schedule annual meetings by responsibility (maintenance, food services, bus drivers, and so on).

The purpose of these regular interactions is to carry information to employees as well as to solicit impressions and ideas from those who participate in the organization's operation. Often, employees view both the board and the superintendent as being inaccessible. Even with these suggested efforts, not all personnel will be persuaded to think otherwise.

District Publications

t would be impractical for a superintendent to meet personally with everyone in the district. Print materials can instead be used to inform district staff and residents—to communicate policies, procedures, and goals. Districts publish many kinds of documents. All are designed to deliver messages about what is occurring within the district's schools. Some publications are targeted at people who work for the district. Others are aimed at external audiences—parents, residents, district voters, and anyone interested in the district's education programs. Each publication should be designed and written to convey a particular message and should be as attractive and accurate as possible.

DOCUMENTS FOR DISTRICT STAFF

- The staff development handbook is designed for both teachers and administrators. It describes teaching methods and district standards and can be used for in-service meetings for beginning or experienced teachers. This handbook may be written as a follow-up for previous in-service sessions and may include suggestions for the site-level administrator on teacher conferencing, analyzing lessons, and writing evaluations.

- A curriculum notebook contains the state framework and district guidelines for either elementary or secondary levels. The elementary notebook lists requirements by grade level; the secondary notebook lists requirements by department and by individual course. Sample lessons, teaching ideas, and the suggested sequence of the material are often included.

- The procedure handbook is a how-to guide for teachers. It might include purchasing procedures, parent–teacher conferencing guidelines, field trip procedures, and work order procedures. Some districts publish each of these as separate documents.

- A resource center publication lists the curricular materials and equipment available on campus or from the district office by request. This publication may be updated every year. A list of audiovisual equipment may be included, along with an explanation of how to request and return each piece of equipment.

- A substitute handbook is a useful tool for substitute teachers. Small and even medium-sized districts include maps and directions for locating each of the district's schools; larger districts may not be able to include such detailed information, though. All include procedures to follow when arriving and leaving the school site as well as some general guidelines on what is expected from a substitute teacher.

- A board action brief is a summary of the major issues acted on by the board of education. Most briefs run one to two pages. They are issued to employees of the district the day after the board meeting.

DOCUMENTS FOR EXTERNAL GROUPS

- An abbreviated version of the district philosophy and goals summarizes the main objectives of the district. It can include a listing of the programs offered at various schools, facts and figures about the district (numbers of schools, teachers, costs, and so on), as well as budgetary information.

- Curriculum guides, published primarily for parents, summarize the skills taught in each grade at the elementary level, as well as performance expectations for each grade level. Curricular guides for middle school and high school give a short description of each class. Graduation requirements are included for high school seniors.

- Many districts publish and distribute a parent handbook to all parents at the beginning of the school year. A calendar for the year is included, along with district policies that apply directly to students. Information about bus schedules, lunch costs, and optional student insurance programs are also included. Some districts suggest appropriate study conditions for the home.

- Program booklets summarize the district's various educational programs. Districts often offer magnet programs that may be located away from the neighborhood school. Booklets explain how to apply to the school. At the high school, each of these programs may have its own publication describing the entire four-year sequence of studies.

- Recruitment brochures are aimed at new teachers who may be interested in working in the district. These brochures outline the advantages of accepting a contract at the district. A description of the community is a must, along with the availability of universities, colleges, and cultural activities. Although it may be considered a sales pitch for the district, the brochure needs to be completely honest.

- A welcome leaflet often is of great help to new families. This small document briefly describes the district program, the school locations, telephone numbers, dates for the school year, and special services (such as busing) available to new residents. These can be delivered to new housing developments or given to realtors and the chamber of commerce for distribution.

Positive school–community relations requires commitment at all levels and includes a multitude of tasks at both the district and site levels. But as Zuelke and Willerman point out:

> The superintendent establishes the climate of relations with the principals. If the superintendent enjoys the responsibility, possesses concern for others, works cooperatively with other personnel and has an "open door" communication policy, successful district-wide administration is possible. [12]

Such philosophical commitment by district leaders helps build close working relationships with site-level administrators and allows for continuous communication. If a school principal is to develop and oversee strong school–community relationships, then the district and school approaches should be interrelated as well as interdependent.

SUMMARY

1. Superintendents and other district level administrators must also concentrate on communication with people inside and outside the school district. The superintendent must interpret the schools to the public and has the responsibility of shouldering criticism of what goes wrong —or what is thought to go wrong—within the entire school district.

2. A successful communication program must be two-way, for all people, and continuous. The tasks of such a program are often carried out by specialists in public relations or the media field.

3. One of the superintendent's unique responsibilities is communicating with the board of education. Generally, the relationships between boards and superintendents are harmonious.

4. The board meetings should convey a positive, businesslike impression. This means having well-planned, organized, rapidly moving meetings and enough space to accommodate foreseen audiences.

5. One way to communicate the impression of a well-organized district is for the board to adopt policies on major issues. Although policies cannot be written for every conceivable situation, there should be policies for common problems such as attendance, grading, controversial issues, and graduation requirements.

6. The operation of the district may call for policies about communication with the public. These may indicate a commitment toward providing public information in a timely and understandable manner.

7. Advisory committees often extend community participation beyond the board. The board should commit itself to consider the recommendations

of advisory committees, although it is under no obligation to adopt the suggestions.

8. Bond issues need to be carefully planned and organized if they are to be successful at the polls. Needs of the district should be presented to the community in a variety of publications, media releases, and face-to-face contacts.

9. Communication efforts by the district superintendent must go beyond the public and the board. Communication with district employees at all levels of the district's functioning is essential so that they can be informed and their feelings and ideas considered.

10. A variety of district publications may be available for district staff and an external audience. These may include handbooks, guides, program booklets, and newsletters.

DISCUSSION QUESTIONS

1. What kind of working relationship exists between your board of education and the superintendent of schools? Why do you think their relationship is as it is?

2. Who handles the communications program in your district? Do you think the program is as good as it could be? Share the major reasons you think so.

3. What contacts do board members have with your school? Do they ever visit the site? How often? What do they do when they get there? How do teachers react to these visits?

4. How does your board regulate public speaking at board meetings? Has this ever been a problem in your district? Why?

5. In what ways does the superintendent attempt to communicate with the staff at your school site? Do your fellow teachers think these efforts are sufficient? Explain.

1. From your own experience, or by asking your site administrator(s), list the kinds of conflicts that have developed between the board and the members of the community. Explain how these conflicts were handled, and share with other members of your class.

2. Attend one or more board meetings. Note the organization of the meeting in terms of its strengths and weaknesses. Is the board meeting run by the board members or the superintendent, or do they share leadership? Compare your observations with those of other students.

SUPPORTING A TOWER OF BABEL

The new assistant superintendent, Ruth Brookhart, was employed by Anytown School District after a nationwide search. She came from the Midwest, was educated at prestigious universities, and recently earned her doctorate. When Bill Johnson, principal of Elm School, first met her during the three-day administrative retreat in August, he was impressed with her people skills and her warmth. He thought she was sure to add some new ideas and needed strengths to the district office staff.

Johnson's predictions proved to be accurate; the site-level in-service programs conducted for teachers were both original and helpful, and the participants were generally impressed by Dr. Brookhart's enthusiasm and the array of materials she shared with those in attendance. If there were any misgivings, it was that on occasion she could be somewhat authoritarian and opinionated in her educational views. Personally, Johnson didn't note these characteristics during the workshop. A few teachers commented, but sometimes teachers could be challenging and obstinate; they didn't always bring out the best in others. Some people rationalized these negative characteristics of Dr. Brookhart by suggesting, "She is from the Midwest." This comment seemed to satisfy the critics for some mysterious reason.

Johnson had supported the in-service sessions she had

3. Determine the role of the school board in your district; speak with district administrators and make your own observation. Complete the form on page 255. Compare with class members from other districts and develop some generalizations about local school boards.

4. Obtain a list of ad hoc committees that currently exist or have existed in the past in your district. Compare these groups with those of other districts, according to their purpose.

5. Bring to class three district publications developed for internal groups and three developed for external groups. In small groups, discuss these publications in terms of purpose, quality, and effectiveness.

developed for the faculty and had dismissed her occasional rigidity by way of her youth and new degree. It was, therefore, with anticipation that he planned to involve her with the school's bilingual program. Elm School had the largest population of Spanish-speaking students in the entire district, and hardly a week went by that there were not additional students to enroll, most of whom possessed only limited English abilities with their parents speaking only Spanish.

Johnson contacted Dr. Brookhart to ask her to work directly with his group of bilingual teachers. She readily agreed to do so, but during the planning negotiations he was startled to hear her state, "It's probably only fair to tell you I don't believe in bilingual education." Johnson also was surprised that she would make this verbal admission. But then he recalled a few state requirements and programs that he didn't believe in either. Besides, her well-organized presentation would more than offset her personal opinions. He simply said "Oh" and didn't pursue the matter.

His faith in Dr. Brookhart proved to be valid. She had obviously done her homework and had dealt with the laws of the state, the recommended curriculum, and the fundamental processes for the acquisition of language. A few times she said, "Personally I do not agree with that." But her opinions did not overshadow the ways in which her ideas about the learning process were presented. Even her major generalization that "Everyone in America should speak English" did not dampen the enthusiasm of the participants. The teachers and Johnson left the session feeling it was an afternoon well spent.

Subsequent meetings by the bilingual teachers at Elm School brought forth new ideas about the curriculum and about some methods of communicating with the parents of their students. A newsletter in both English and Spanish had traditionally been sent to the parents, but the teachers felt strongly that the school bulletins on homework

REFERENCES

1. Arthur Blumberg with Phyllis Blumberg, *The School Superintendent Living with Conflict* (New York: Teachers College Press, 1985), p. xi.

2. Don Bagin, Frank Grazian, and Charles H. Harrison, *School Communications: Ideas That Work* (Woodstorm, N.J.: Communicaid, 1972), p. 2.

3. Ibid., pp. 4–5.

and discipline would also receive greater attention if they were translated into Spanish.

Abbreviated versions of both policies were written in English and sent to the district office to be translated by the district translator. When the school used the translator's services in the past, the district would also duplicate the document and send sufficient copies for the school to distribute.

Johnson was reviewing his schedule of teacher evaluations a week later, when one of the bilingual teachers entered the office. "They've forgotten to send our Spanish bulletins," the teacher said. "And we're supposed to send them home with the students this afternoon."

"It's probably an oversight, or they've sent them to the wrong school," Johnson replied. "I'll call downtown."

Johnson dialed the district duplicating facility and asked what happened. After talking with the person in charge, he hung up, slowly turned in his chair, and said to the teacher, "The order for the bilingual materials was canceled. Dr. Brookhart has stated that communications will no longer be sent home unless they are in English."

DISCUSSION ISSUES

Past

1. What different communication approaches was Dr. Brookhart using at the administrative retreat that were not used at the school in-service?

2. What communications should have taken place between Johnson and Dr. Brookhart before he involved her in the bilingual program? What clues might have indicated this need?

3. What attitude is Dr. Brookhart expressing when she states that "Everyone in America should speak English"?

4. If Johnson had heard the decree before the last minute, what tactics could he have used to change the decision? What possible additional conflicts could have developed?

5. What are the best communication tactics to use when

4. Ibid., p. 6.

5. Ibid., pp. 4–5.

6. Harmon Zeigler, Ellen Kahoe, and Jane Reisman, *City Managers and School Superintendents* (New York: Praeger, 1985), p. 74.

7. Danzberger, Jacqueline, "Governing the Nation's Schools: The Case for Restructuring Local School Boards," *Phi Delta Kappan* 75, no. 5, p. 369.

8. Blumberg, p. 76.

there are differences of opinion over the curricula or school programs? Who should bring the opposing parties together? How does one avoid a win–lose scenario?

Present

1. What communication tactics should Johnson use in discussing the missing translated materials with the bilingual teachers?
2. Diverse opinions exist in the United States concerning bilingual education. Whose opinion should prevail about the translated materials, the teachers' or the assistant superintendent's? Why?
3. If you were the superintendent of schools in Anytown, what would you communicate to Dr. Brookhart? What skills would you use?
4. Assuming the district backed Dr. Brookhart in her stand on the Spanish-language materials, what should Johnson suggest to his bilingual staff as an alternative?
5. Even though the decision affected only the bilingual teachers at Elm School, the word will soon spread. How will this affect her relationships with other teachers in the district?

9. Elvin F. Clemmer, *The School Policy Handbook: A Primer for Administrators and School Board Members* (Boston: Allyn & Bacon, 1991), p. 15.

10. Bagin, Grazian, and Harrison, p. 24.

11. R. M. Kanter, *The Change Makers* (New York: Simon and Schuster, 1983), p. 159.

12. Dennis C. Zuelke and Marvin Willerman, *Conflict and Decision Making in Elementary Schools* (Dubuque, Iowa: Wm. C. Brown, 1992), p. 129.

THE ROLE OF THE SCHOOL BOARD (Activity 3)*

1. Identify functions that school boards are currently not performing that they should perform.

_____

_____

_____

_____

2. Identify functions that school boards are currently performing that they should *not* perform.

_____

_____

_____

_____

3. Identify appropriate relationships between school board members and

the superintendent _____

_____

_____

assistant or associate superintendents _____

_____

_____

principals _____

_____

_____

vice-principals _____

_____

_____

teachers _____

_____

_____

WORKING WITH THE MEDIA

Forming Positive Relationships

nless major problems occur at a school, a site-level administrator is not apt to be deluged with contacts from the media. However, there are times in every principal's career when he or she works with a newspaper reporter or a representative from a local radio or television station.

It's best to understand that all media groups are interested in anything that is newsworthy—good or bad. As administrators, we tend to remember news stories that are unfavorable toward schools. That's because negative publicity often causes a greater reaction from the public.

Schools usually operate routinely and are generally successful. News crews do not report on the students who walk to school safely every day, but they will report on a child who is killed en route to school. Likewise, they will not report on the thousands of teachers who teach their grades or subjects with appropriate relationships with their students, but, should a teacher interact inappropriately with a child, the story will be either published or aired. Why? Because it's news!

Site-level administrators must have a positive philosophy about working with representatives of the media. The National School Public Relations Association publishes guidelines that help educators and administrators with media relations.[1] Other agencies, including some district offices, also produce guidelines. As Black and English state in their education text, "Learning how to deal with the press is a survival skill."[2]

Reporters are highly professional people doing their jobs as best they can. However, as Martinson writes, "Some of their brethren have been known to resort to using questionable means to gather what they believed to be important information relating to the coverage of a particular news story."[3] Administrators who run into such circumstances won't want to revert to the same practice; no professional leader can ever justify unethical behavior. It may be necessary to involve the district superintendent in the interaction. The important thing for the administrator to remember is to respond in the same way as with any interested party that he wishes to communicate with. This is when a positive philosophy toward media personnel will pay off. For example, suppose that a news reporter wrongly attributes remarks to a school principal. Such action would be unethical, unless, of course, it's done mistakenly. The principal might be tempted to furnish the reporter a biased statement to counteract the initial statement, but this would also be unethical. Falsifying information to tone down news stories, no matter how vitriolic, is unjustified.

From a school's point of view, media attention isn't always undesirable. Frequently, it is worth seeking. Again, a positive philosophy is an asset. Principals often need to take initiative to call the media or send news releases.

News is perishable and needs to be given to the media as soon as it occurs. The school can plan for many potential stories, as it would plan for parent conferences, open houses, or other methods of communication. Some administrators who consider operating as the school's press agent have developed a news and program calendar for each week of the school year. This technique simply means looking at a schedule of the major events happening at the school, usually a month ahead of time, and notifying the press. Just prior to an event, the principal can remind the media of the time and type of event to increase the chance of coverage. Following the event, the principal can release a story that recounts what happened.

Working with Reporters

Several public relations publications list the do's and don'ts of working with representatives of the media. All of these reinforce the central idea that one should be positive about any contact with the media, regardless of the particular situation. The following twelve administrative considerations are usually covered in these publications:

1. *Don't ever tell a lie.* People will remember statements that are found to be untrue. Credibility can be damaged permanently, and the media may never ask to discuss a story again. It is better to present the facts honestly, even if they tell a negative story, than to compromise the truth. If you don't know the answer to a question, say so.

2. *Be open to answering questions.* Reporters don't ask questions of site administrators very often. There simply are not many school stories that require a reporter's presence. An administrator can help the press by being available and contributing information that will help the writer. Reporters cannot possibly expect school people to contact them with stories that are unfavorable to the school, but they have every right to expect staff members to furnish them with the facts when they seek them.

3. *Don't talk off the record.* This strategy may work in movie or TV dramas, but it is impractical in real life. For an enterprising reporter, nothing is ever considered "off the record." School personnel should state only what they would be comfortable seeing in the next day's newspaper or hearing on the nightly news broadcast.

4. *Take time to furnish details.* Some ideas or programs take longer in explaining. It's better to take the extra time to explain something thoroughly than to have it written or stated based on garbled information. If the reporter is willing to visit the school site to see the program in action, that's even better.

5. *Avoid using education jargon.* Every profession has its own language, perfectly understood by those within the profession but not by

outsiders. In particular, a speaker should define all acronyms, and the education profession supports hundreds of them.

6. *Know what is public property and what is not.* Materials that have been presented to the board of education and paid for by tax dollars are public property. Reports and surveys often fall into this category and should be made available to the media if requested. The privacy of students and staff are protected by various laws, of course, and the release of student names is prohibited, except in some situations. Some reporters may not understand these limitations, so administrators must therefore educate them about school law or district policy.

7. *Return calls.* If a media representative phones an administrator, he or she should return the call. Failure to do so may be interpreted as uncooperative. Furthermore, it is important to return the calls promptly; news people have deadlines to meet.

8. *Stay calm regarding errors.* If the facts of a published story are incorrect, the school staff has the right to call the reporter about the mistake. However, it's generally unwise to make an issue of a minor infraction. Everyone makes mistakes on occasion. Calling it to the reporter's attention will often depend on how much difference the error makes in the functioning of the school itself. For example, if a school program is scheduled for Thursday night and the paper runs it as Wednesday night, then a retraction may be necessary.

9. *Don't ask to see a story before it is printed or aired.* Often, reporters will call to check facts. If the story contains data that could be confusing, the school staff could ask the reporter to check those details later. However, reporters are professionals, and they are generally reliable and interested in accuracy. Asking to approve a story may be interpreted as wanting to suppress unfavorable news.

10. *Don't be overly concerned about detail accuracy.* When relating statistical information, such as student body population or enrollment in a particular program, extreme accuracy isn't necessary. Rounded numbers will be acceptable, both for the impact of the story and for the media representative.

11. *Feel free to compliment a reporter.* If someone in the media has done an

excellent job of covering a story about some aspect of a school, let him or her know. A letter, with a copy to the editor, is one way to generate future positive media coverage.

12. *For substantive inquiries, contact the superintendent.* If a journalist is investigating a controversial issue and is interviewing school-site personnel about the issue, they should inform the district office about the interviews. For example, suppose a reporter is seeking information about drugs in the schools. He or she may go to the district office or to a board meeting next, so it's a good idea to have someone alert the superintendent beforehand.

District Media Policies

ll school districts strive to work cooperatively with the news media. It is certainly to the advantage of the districts to do so. Such a positive philosophy avoids the many clashes that otherwise might occur between members of the media and superintendents and board members. These school officials are accustomed to working with the media. But other school employees frequently have poor press relations, either because they lack experience in dealing with the media or because they feel as if members of the media are trespassing on their private territory. Indeed, news people have been known to interfere with the daily operation of schools. For this reason, districts have adopted policies to minimize possible conflicts.

The following excerpt outlines the media-relations policies of the San Bernardino Unified School District in California. The policies were written by the late Al Bruton, who served as the Assistant to the Superintendent, in charge of communications. The entire document was adopted by both the elementary and secondary principals of the district.

Class I: *The school system will cooperate with the coverage of school-sponsored activities, both curricular and extracurricular. Coverage may include both reporting and photography.*

1. *Reporters and photographers from legitimate news media may come on the campus of the San Bernardino City Unified*

School District through established procedures (see procedure section) and report on or photograph any class, activity, or program.

2. *In cases where the subject of the news inquiry may reflect on students to indicate reduced learning capacity, a discipline or social adjustment problem, a physical handicap, or an achievement level below fellow students, the school district reserves the right to require written parental approval for the publication of names or identifiable pictures of students involved.*

3. *While the school district encourages cooperation with news media, adult employees may make their own decision on whether to answer questions in an interview or pose for a picture. On the other hand, it is accepted that they may be photographed as they work in the normal course of their employment.*

4. *Questions about the school operations or a school-sponsored activity which a member of the news media feels are proper, but which an employee at the school campus has not answered to the newsman's satisfaction, may be submitted to the Central Administration (addressed to the Communications Office) as an official inquiry.*

Class II: *Employees of the San Bernardino City Unified School District recognize the right of a news media to cover such incidents as may be classified as "breaking news" involving the public safety.*

1. *In the case of a major fire on a school campus, reporters have the right to cover the incident within the regulations that the Fire Department normally impose.*

2. *In the event of a major campus disturbance, the school district recognizes the right of the news media to cover the event. Normal police press regulations would be in effect. Major disturbances may be characterized by one or more of the following:*

   a. *Those cases where demonstrations are taking place in public view, such as in view of the street.*

   b. *Those cases where police are called to restore peace. This* classification does not apply to those cases where police have been called as a precautionary measure. In such cases, normal school conditions and news gathering procedures are in effect.

    c. Floods, earthquakes, other natural disasters, or major accidents on school grounds are also covered in this section.

Class III: In cases where the school, because of its role as custodian of large numbers of children and youth, is contacted for cooperation by the press for various feature story purposes, it must be recognized that these stories are in a different category than Class I and Class II. In Class III are such stories as general opinions of youth, youth customs and mores, and so forth. While a school campus is a convenient place to collect such data, it must be noted that permission for such contacts with students would not normally be considered as implied by a parent sending a child to school.

    1. Photographs and interviews with children and youth on routine and non-controversial matters may be handled as items in Class I. (Examples: pictures and stories illustrating holidays, seasons, good citizenship, etc.)

    2. Subject matter which may provide embarrassment to a student and/or their parents should:

        a. Include an arrangement for parental consent, or

        b. Should take place off the school campus.

News Media Procedures

    1. Any newsman, reporter, or photographer coming on a school campus must first stop by the office of the principal to announce his presence and purpose.

        a. When a principal will not be on campus or available to clear the presence on campus of a reporter or photographer on a previously arranged assignment, he shall notify office personnel of clearance and designate a member of his staff to accompany the member of the press if the principal deems the necessity for a campus guide.

        b. The principal shall delegate a staff member to act for him in matters of press relations when the principal is away from the campus.

2. *It is reasonable to assume that a principal may be contacted at home by telephone after working hours for matters of urgency. This includes work on breaking news stories that occur after the close of the business day or when the principal was not available during the business day.*

3. *It is also reasonable that in-depth, feature, or stories being prepared for other than immediate publication can best be handled by school personnel when the school personnel are contacted at the place of assignment.*

4. *The most complete information might be available if the following procedure is followed for feature assignments:*

   a. *Appointments:*

      i. *Feature and in-depth assignments can best be handled by making an appointment with the interview subject, setting time and place of mutual convenience.*

      ii. *Appointments can be made directly with the person to be interviewed or through the Communications Office.*

      iii. *School personnel should be cooperative in setting appointments in observance of publication time schedules.*

   b. *If a principal questions the appropriateness of a request by news media, he may confer with the district Communications Office.*

   c. *If a principal determines that the reporter's subject involves district-wide policies or procedures except as it applies to their own work or school, he may:*

      i. *Refer the matter to that member of the central staff as may be appropriate.*

      ii. *Refer the matter to the Communications Office, which may put the newsman in contact with the appropriate news source.*

      iii. *Delay or reschedule the interview until conferring with an appropriate person in the Central Administration on the district-wide considerations involved in the interview.*

      iv. *Suggest that the matter be continued at an interview/*

*press conference at which a member of Central Admin-
istration appears jointly to facilitate accurate information
concerning district-wide conditions and policies.*

5. *Disagreements on proper interpretations of the procedure by
either school personnel or newsmen should be referred to the
Communications Office.*

6. *Charges of inappropriate actions on the part of a newsman or
lack of cooperation by school employees should be made to the
Communications Office, which will attempt to work out differences to be mutually acceptable. If the matter cannot be solved in
this manner, the Assistant to the Superintendent, Communications will refer the matter to the Superintendent or whomever
the Superintendent should designate for action.*

Special Areas

1. *No employee of the district other than the Superintendent or
Assistant Superintendent may discuss the professional quali-
fications of another district employee. Questions involving
certificated personnel should be directed to the Assistant Superintendent, Personnel Services. The Assistant Superintendent,
Personnel Services, or another appropriate Assistant Superintendent heading a division might be contacted concerning
classified employees.*

2. *The identification of a student singled out for disciplinary
action will not normally be available for publication, nor will
names of students who are suspected of action that may result
in disciplinary action be revealed. If the offense in question leads
to legal action, the naming of the student by the police will be
subject to police agency policies. Decision on exceptions to this
policy can come from the Superintendent or his designee.*

3. *In event of an injury, the name of the victim may be withheld
pending notification of parent or guardian.*

4. *Information about an individual student including address,
parents' name, grades, etc., are, by law, not public information
and cannot be given out in many cases. Specifically not
precluded is the identification of such a student when he or she*

is the recipient of some honor or award. Questions on this mat-
ter should be addressed to the Superintendent or his designee.

5. *It should be noted that the Superintendent, as the chief execu-*
tive officer of the school district, may appropriately comment on
any subject mentioned previously. In cases where law or policy
of the Board of Education preclude the release of information,
of course, the Superintendent is also bound by the regulations.

6. *The preceding rules do not preclude the Communications*
Office from issuing statements on any of the above subjects.
It will be the responsibility of the Communications Office to
obtain clearance from the appropriate level before such state-
ments are issued.[4]

Getting Media Coverage

dministrators who wait for the media to come to their school may wait
a long time. They can give story ideas to the media on a regular and
systematic basis. The most common medium for school news stories is a
local newspaper. Unless a district supports a local radio or TV station,
the chances of obtaining such coverage are minimal. The network
stations focus on the major events of our state, nation, or the world and
rarely include local school items.

The degree of coverage also depends on the size of the community
and the focus of the publications in your area. Larger cities, for example,
have major newspapers with widespread circulations as well as several
editions and may not include local news to any great extent. On the
other hand, some major newspapers have regional editions, which
include sections on community news events. Large metropolitan dailies,
such as the *Los Angeles Times, Chicago Tribune,* and *New York Times,* address
a wide range of readers. Therefore, they seek stories that will appeal to a
mass audience with differing values.

A new principal needs to investigate how the district wishes to
operate with the press. He or she may be restricted by district policies
concerning the release of information. Some districts require that all

press releases be screened, and sometimes written, by personnel employed as part of the public information office within the district. Others leave news coverage to the site administrator and his or her staff. Even then, the principal's role will vary; sometimes he or she will write news releases, but other times he or she will meet with reporters who will recast stories in their own words.

If the site-level administrator *does* have a hand in the process, then he or she needs to know the local papers. There are both daily and weekly newspapers in most communities. Some of these have wide circulation, whereas others appeal to only a particular ethnic group, for example. The best way to understand the needs of the publications is to visit the offices of each one and meet with the editors. It's a good idea to keep a file of these contacts, with a list of names, telephone numbers, deadlines, and other information that may be of value in the future. Obviously, this file should be reviewed regularly and updated.

A short chat with the local editor will help the principal learn about the newspaper's style, what kind of stories the editors like, whether a staff member can be contacted, and when articles are due. A high school principal may be able to turn this information over to the school's journalism teacher, who may enlist the students' help in planning and writing articles. The principal may instead call on another faculty member or parent volunteer or may do the writing him or herself. Whomever is assigned the task should recognize that writing for newspapers requires a special style.

What people want to know about their schools varies from community to community and from time to time. Parents, for example, are generally interested in pupil progress and achievement. The media are not as interested in this aspect of education, except in the broad sense. Extracurricular activities (sports, in particular) and articles about teachers and school officials get the greatest coverage in newspapers.[5]

PREPARING NEWS RELEASES

Many newspapers have style sheets, which give directions as to how copy should be prepared. These handouts cover spacing, margins, and other pertinent information. Some guidelines, however, are standard.

These include the following:

1. Type the manuscript, double-spaced, leaving two inches of space at the top of the page and adequate margins along the sides and bottom of the page.

2. Stories should be factual; avoid editorializing.

3. Organize facts with the five *W*s (*who, what, where, why,* and *when*) in the first paragraph; the least important information should be in the last paragraph.

4. Be accurate with facts, and check spelling.

5. Use personal titles *Mr., Mrs., Miss,* or *Ms.* with last names alone; do not use them with full names.

6. Spell out numbers from one to nine; use numerals from 10 and above.

7. Limit paragraphs to about five lines each.

8. Avoid wordiness.

9. Avoid jargon.

10. Check for the correct use of abbreviations.

Simplicity, brevity, and clarity are the major requirements for good news writing. These are generally the qualities that news editors look for.

All articles written for newspapers should be edited for grammar, spelling, and punctuation. Special attention should be given to the accurate spelling of names, because the newspaper editors themselves probably will not check. All student-written articles should be carefully checked by the teacher before they are submitted.

The principal can share the burden of interacting with media personnel and getting coverage for events. Teachers, volunteers, and others may be willing to share in these responsibilities. However, some things remain the principal's sole responsibility. He or she must:

- Develop the staff's appreciation of the importance of good school–community relations

- Create the understanding that a positive school image can be fostered or maintained through regular news coverage

■ Explain to each teacher that he or she may have access to topics or programs that can be developed into articles for possible publication

NEWS-WRITING TECHNIQUES

There are many ways to obtain press coverage. A few tried and tested methods may increase the chances of publication. Seven techniques are described here.

■ TIMING NEWS RELEASES

Sometimes the time of year will bring about opportunities for publication. For example, at Thanksgiving, efforts by students to visit shut-ins or to collect money for the homeless might develop into a worthwhile story. Other holidays lend themselves to stories about students, teachers, and the curricula of any elementary, middle, or high school.

■ LINKING EVENTS TO TOPICAL ISSUES

To obtain positive publicity about ongoing school programs, the program can be linked to a current issue in the news. Discussions of political issues, science experiments that parallel state and national investigations, or student reactions to new laws can all draw media coverage. As Fox and Levin explain:

> Most op-eds must have some "hook" (also known as news "peg," "slant," or "angle") that is a strong connection to an important event in the news. This requires quick thinking and writing before interest in the issue wanes. As Tom Peeting of the Palm Beach Post remarked, "If you're commenting on something that happened more than 4 days ago, save it for a magazine."[6]

During the Gulf War, the students of Sycamore Elementary School in Upland, California, wrote to some of the people serving overseas. After the war, they held an assembly to honor these service personnel following their return. The school invited local media representatives to attend. Both the local newspaper and the local TV station covered the event and provided pictures to accompany the story.

■ LOOKING FOR ANGLES

Newspapers thrive on the unusual, and schools need to be prepared to furnish such material to the press. Many years ago, when I was a high school principal, I decided to remove the desk from my office to devote more time to visiting classrooms and chatting with students. (My theory was that if I didn't have a desk, I wouldn't have much reason to remain in the office shuffling papers.) The local newspaper published the story, and it was later picked up by the wire services. The story was retold across the United States.

Thousands of stories are unusual enough to get the attention of the press: identical twins who both graduated from high school at the top of their class with identical grade point averages; a family of five children, each of whom was at some time elected as student body president; a special grandparents' day celebration at an elementary level; and so on. The human interest aspect of any story is potentially newsworthy. Students or teachers who overcome physical or emotional difficulties are prime topics for news stories. With young people, of course, permission must be obtained from a parent before information can be released.

■ UPDATING STORIES

People are interested in human interest stories and often are desirous of knowing how something worked out. For example, a family of refugees who enrolled in a school and was written up by a newspaper might be the making of another story three years later. Exchange students are often interviewed by newspaper when they first come to the community and then again just before they return to their own countries.

■ DISTRIBUTING FACT SHEETS AND ADVANCES

Athletic directors routinely distribute fact sheets to the media about their teams, including schedules for the year, win-loss records, and game statistics for individual athletes. The same process can be used for other activities at the school, such as the colleges represented by new teachers or the costs, goals, and past achievements of a particular school program.

Advances notify the media of upcoming school events. They can be sent out to all media representatives on a monthly or yearly basis. Newspapers or TV stations may want to cover an event. Radio stations may use the items as fillers for a "community bulletin board."

■ INVITING LOCAL NEWSPEOPLE TO EVENTS

Although it won't guarantee attendance, a personal invitation to the local newsperson who covers educational news may encourage that person to attend a special event. Efforts to obtain coverage may reap rewards if the event is uplifting—for example, if the school is honoring students for a special reason, or is holding a scholarship assembly or is celebrating an anniversary. An even stronger relationship may be developed if the local contact person happens to be a graduate of the school.

The key is to contact the media representative well in advance of the event. If the invitation is not rejected outright, then it may be appropriate to call and remind the person one or two days before the event. This technique may help secure the coverage desired.

■ KEEPING A STOREHOUSE OF STORIES

Many school stories are newsworthy but may not require immediate release. Keeping a backlog of these stories may be helpful, particularly for smaller newspapers, which often seek items for their publications. One midwestern high school claims that it generates 15 to 20 stories a week concerning a broad spectrum of the academic curricula. The stories are there if an editor needs them. Many of them get published during the school year.

CHECKING NEWS RELEASES

At times, the principal may begin to think that everything that goes on at the school site is newsworthy. Unfortunately, the newspaper editors will probably not agree. One way to see if a story is worth developing is to ask the following ten yes-or-no questions about the story. A higher percentage of *yes* responses means that the story may interest the press.

1. Does the story concern something other than the day-to-day operation of the school?

2. Is the story about students, and is it uplifting?

3. Is the story unusual?

4. Would other people besides parents be interested in the story?

5. Does the story have a human interest touch?

6. Might the story appeal to a minority group that has a local newspaper with a large circulation?

7. Does the story pertain to a topic that frequently appears on page 1 of the news?

8. Does the story cover events that are easily understood by the general public?

9. Is the story written in a newspaper style?

10. Are photographs (black and white) available if needed?

SUMMARY

1. On occasion, school principals will have to deal with the media. Representatives of the media are interested in anything that is newsworthy—good or bad.

2. The ability to deal with the press is a survival skill. It helps to have a positive philosophy about working with representatives of the media.

3. Administrators working with the media should always tell the truth, should not talk off the record, and should avoid educational jargon. When in doubt about an issue, the administrator should contact the district superintendent.

4. District media policies may help school-site administrators handle situations that draw media attention, especially if the administrator is working directly with reporters.

5. If media coverage is desired, it is often up to the school to make contact with reporters. The amount of coverage that can be obtained is often directly related to the size of the community and the importance of local news to the media.

6. Developing a steady acceptance of news releases to the media requires planning. All staff members can be a part of this total school effort.

7. If the principal has a role in the securing of news coverage, he or she must be familiar with the local newspapers and other media. Up-to-date files of contact persons, deadlines, and kinds of news desired can help this process.

MEDIA CRISIS FOR SCHOOL PRINCIPAL

The school was deserted at this hour of the day, but Bill Johnson was still in his office. He was leaning back in his chair thinking of his ten years as principal of Elm School. He was particularly concentrating on his relations with Philip Downey, the editor of the local newspaper, the *Anytown Arrow.*

Johnson first met Downey the year he came to Elm School. Downey wanted his sophomore son to be on the school newspaper staff. But there was a policy that only juniors and seniors could assume staff positions, so Johnson turned down the request. At the time, Johnson wondered about that decision. Later, the boy proved to be an outstanding editor of the school paper and graduated with honors from Columbia's School of Journalism.

Johnson and Downey never really got to know each other well. They had no social organizations in common and Downey had only one child. The *Anytown Arrow* regularly supported the school district in various elections, but Johnson felt that news releases about Elm had been few and far between.

Johnson was so concerned about the publicity surrounding Elm School that he publicly commented about the situation when members of his PTA, booster club, and other groups asked about the limited press

8. Most newspapers have style sheets for preparing copy. It's important to follow the guidelines in these handouts. Otherwise, the news release may not be accepted.

9. Topical issues, human interest items, and unusual situations can make a school-related story newsworthy. Timing news releases carefully can also help obtain press coverage.

10. All stories released to the media should be of interest to others. The media is more likely to cover items that have broad appeal.

coverage. Other parents also inquired, and he was honest with them as well.

Recently, Elm School was mentioned in the *Arrow* more than in the previous five years combined, but it was not the kind of publicity Johnson desired. It all started with a letter to the editor from one of the school's parents:

Editor:

Recently, my daughter tried out to be one of the cheerleaders at Elm School. Although she may not have been the very best candidate, she was certainly one of the eight finest and should have been one of those chosen. As a parent,

I resent the undemocratic way in which the selection process is carried out. I strongly feel that there is a political motive that guides the teachers and administrators in their decisions rather than basing it on the students' talents and abilities.

Mrs. Dudley Blake
Anytown

After the letter appeared in the *Arrow*, Johnson received several comments from members of the student council and faculty. The coordinator of the team spirit groups was nearly in tears when she came to the office, but Johnson assured her

that he was behind her handling of the cheerleader situation. The comments had moved Johnson to reply to the local newspaper:

Editor:

As principal of Elm School, I want to assure the citizens of Anytown that democratic principles are always followed at Elm. The process for the selection of the cheerleading squad is done by committee vote; the members of the committee include graduating seniors who have been on the squad in the past, three teachers selected by the student council, and the coordinator of the team

1. In thinking through your school's educational activities for the past year or two, which ones would have been significant enough to invite a media person to attend? Why?

2. Could you ever justify telling a lie to the media? Explain.

3. What rights do media people have in working with school employees? What limitations seem logical for a school or district to impose?

---

spirit groups. The same makeup of the committee has been used for the past ten years. It's unfortunate that everyone who tries out for the cheerleading squads is not able to make it, because all of the students at Elm should have the opportunity to represent our fine school.

Bill Johnson, Principal
Elm School

Following Johnson's reply to the newspaper, a series of letters appeared in the *Arrow*—some about the selection system for cheerleaders, some about other school issues. Most of them had been positive, but there were enough of them that contained negative comments that both faculty and community members began to ask questions.

Even with these comments, Johnson may have been able to overlook the situation. But it was election year for the school board. One of the past members was not seeking re-election, and an unusually high number of candidates filed for the vacant position.

One of the candidates, Dudley Blake, filed at the last minute and was placing ads in the *Arrow* and other newspapers with the slogan: "Let's return democracy to our schools." The *Arrow* endorsed Blake and carried substantial quotes from Blake's speeches in the coverage of the board election campaign. Blake had been very candid in these talks and had specifically mentioned Elm School and the cheerleading incident.

Finally, yesterday the *Arrow* proposed in one of its editorials that the superintendent and Johnson publicly debate the candidates about the meaning of democracy in public education. Johnson planned to meet the next day with the superintendent to go over the issues and decide on an appropriate strategy.

4. Does your school or district have positive relations with the media? What makes you think so?

5. What are the strengths and weaknesses of the San Bernardino Unified School District media policies?

DISCUSSION ISSUES

Past

1. What communication skills could principal Johnson have used with Downey about the request for his son? What could have been done about the limited coverage for Elm School in the *Anytown Arrow*?

2. What communication efforts should have been used by Johnson rather than replying to the letter to the editor?

3. Was Johnson's letter to the editor entirely accurate? What might have been included that would have eased the situation?

4. What errors in communication skills did Johnson make in responding candidly to the various school groups that were concerned about the limited newspaper coverage for Elm? How could this have been handled to the school's advantage?

5. How should Principal Johnson have handled the comments he heard from faculty and parents after the deluge of letters to the newspaper?

Present

1. What decision should be made by Johnson and the superintendent regarding the proposed debate with the school board candidates? Why?

2. If the district decides to attend the debate, what approach should the participants take? What reactions can the district expect if it decides not to attend the debate?

3. Is there any justification for reviewing the selection procedure for cheerleaders at Elm? Why?

4. What communication procedures can be used to improve relations between Elm School and Phil Downey?

5. What long-term implications will this episode have for school–community relations in Anytown?

1. Visit the local newspaper(s) in your district and ask them for style sheets for writing news releases. Compare those obtained by your fellow students for likenesses and differences.

2. Read your local newspaper(s) thoroughly for one week. Clip out all stories pertaining to education. Measure the number of column inches that are generally positive and those that are generally negative. Share the results with the class.

3. Talk with your school-site administrator and decide on a current newsworthy activity. Write the story, submit it to your local newspaper(s), and bring copies to critique with your fellow students.

4. Develop a list of jargon used at your own school or district. Compile a class list and discuss how these terms could be explained or substituted in a press release.

5. Check with your district to see if there are any written policies in regard to working with the media. Bring the policies to class and compare them with those brought in by other students.

REFERENCES

1. The National School Public Relations Association, National Association of Secondary School Principals, New York.

2. John A. Black and Fenwick W. English, *What They Don't Tell You in Schools of Education About School Administration* (Lancaster, Penn.: Technomic, 1986), p. 92.

3. David L. Martinson, "How Should the PR Practitioners Respond When Confronted with Unethical Journalistic Behavior?" *Public Relations Quarterly* (Summer 1991), p. 18.

4. *Your Public Relations,* San Bernardino (California) Unified School District, 1987.

5. James J. Jones et al., *Secondary School Administration* (New York: McGraw-Hill, 1969), p. 399.

6. James Alan Fox and Jack Levin, *How to Work with the Media* (Newbury Park, Calif.: Sage, 1993), p. 71.

EVALUATING THE SCHOOL–COMMUNITY PROGRAM

The Value of Evaluation

valuation is a key word in any administrator's vocabulary. A successful principal is constantly observing, communicating with various groups, and listening to opinion leaders about aspects of the school program. The term *evaluation* should become a byword for all members of the school faculty; *self-evaluation is the most important method of improving school programs.* If everyone at a school looks critically and realistically at what goes on in their school programs, they will be able to make appropriate changes.

Evaluation has long been accepted as a critical element of education, particularly in the areas of curriculum and learning. There have been major disagreements, however, over the methods used to evaluate programs and over the interpretation of data gathered in studies. There are some basic beliefs about how to structure policies from evaluation. They include the following:

- Research is more authoritative and trustworthy than commonsense judgment.

- Policies consist of discrete decisions.

- Better knowledge results in better decisions.

- Evaluations affect policy by influencing defined choices among competing options.[1]

School–community relations, like all components of a school's operation, need to be scrutinized systematically and regularly to see what progress is being made. It's probably inevitable that this self-evaluation will reflect on school personalities and the shortage of funds, but the focus should be the goals, objectives, and activities of the communication program itself. As people realize the value of discussing weaknesses and subsequent improvements, they will voice fewer comments about what can't be changed.

As in most school activities, the site-level administrator must be prepared to provide the leadership. A major role for the administrator is managing the evaluation process. Many distinct tasks make up this process, including formulating credible evaluation questions, constructing an evaluation design, planning for data collection, analyzing the obtained data, and reporting the results.[2] The administrator must assign tasks along with a time line.

The word *evaluation* is a danger signal to many teachers. It reminds them of tenure, promotion, and hierarchy. The principal's role is to alleviate these fears and show teachers how an ongoing evaluation program can bring about school improvement. Whether faculty members understand it or not, the school's programs are being evaluated every day by others—students, parents, and the community at large.

Some facets of the communication program will be easier to evaluate than others. For example, suppose one goal was to increase attendance at school events during the school year. This number can easily be tabulated and compared with the total attendance figure for the previous year. However, measuring the quality of an administrator's communication with faculty or students is not as easy to accomplish.

Even in an area like school–community relations, some evaluation data will directly relate to teaching in the classroom, to observed attitudes of the clerical personnel, or to the quality of contributions by volunteers. Not all of the feedback will be positive. The principal must emphasize the advantage of accepting the criticism and build on it. As a friend of mine says, *"In order to grow you need to hear what you don't want to hear."*

If the faculty recognizes the importance of developing a program of evaluation, the next step is to develop the procedures for collecting data. Information can be collected in many different ways, and a school principal cannot do it alone; other people will have to be involved. Although the school's administrative team will play a major role, it may be necessary to form an evaluation committee that represents the school community. The committee may also foster a cooperative attitude about evaluation and its place in monitoring school programs.

The committee, designated individuals, or the principal will collect and analyze data in an orderly and careful manner. Although the self-study does not pretend to follow a thorough, scientific research procedure, it should be done carefully.

Because the self-study will be limited by practicality, the committee should take care not to become careless in their procedures, which might lead to false assumptions about the results. Not all instruments or methods used in a self-study will be scientific, but the data should be carefully analyzed to avoid making important decisions based on misleading information.

For example, suppose a school wants to find out about parents' attitudes about the school. A committee collects data from many parents, representing a cross-section of the school population. However, it takes only a single sampling, right after report cards are issued. The timing of the study most likely would skew the results. Parents' feelings and attitudes may be affected by a recent incident that occurred on campus (a shooting, for example), a recent decision made by the board of education (such as the adoption of a controversial sex education program), a recent award from the state to the school, or other events. A more accurate study would include several samplings at various times during the year. As Berry and Lewis-Beck explain: "This dilemma suggests the real strength of investigations based on time-series data, repeated measures on the same units of analysis [in this case, the parents] across time."[3]

A Sample Evaluation Program

ach aspect of a school–community relations program has its own goals, objectives, and activities. Consequently, the evaluation process needs to focus on these goals and activities. For example, as Chapter 7 mentions, the faculty can develop ways to increase parent participation at the school. They might plan a tutoring program for students, parenting classes, and a parent advisory committee, for example. Each plan should be carefully developed to achieve the goal. The administrative team, the teaching staff, and others involved in the program should evaluate each plan in relation to the general goal. The three lists that follow itemize the process that might form each of these plans.

TUTORING PROGRAM FOR STUDENTS

1. Hold teacher meetings to decide which academic levels need the most help.

2. Hold teacher meetings to decide which grade levels should be targeted.

3. Decide how to select students for tutoring.

4. Notify parents that their children have been selected.

5. Determine methods for selecting volunteer tutors.

6. Plan and conduct in-service training for volunteers.

7. Select the physical location for tutoring.

8. Select the materials to use for tutoring.

9. Develop a student questionnaire for program evaluation.

10. Conduct pre- and post-testing of students.

PARENTING CLASSES

1. Poll parents to determine needs.

2. Analyze information obtained.

3. Select dates and times for classes.

4. Select teachers to conduct the classes.

5. Advertise the planned classes.

6. Hold the first class.

7. Determine how to increase attendance if it is low.

8. Conduct an evaluation of the classes by parents.

9. Conduct an analysis of the classes by the instructors.

10. Poll the parents for interest in future classes.

A PARENT ADVISORY COMMITTEE

1. Select participants.

2. Establish convenient meeting times.

3. Identify the purposes of the group.

4. Notify other parents of who is on the committee.

5. Determine how to disseminate meeting minutes.

6. Analyze member attendance.

7. Analyze issues discussed.

8. Evaluate the meeting processes.

9. Evaluate how well the committee helps the faculty.

10. Determine how to make committee replacements.

Only a limited number of activities are listed for each of the three plans; dozens more could have been listed. Any activity demands an extensive number of planned events to carry it out and all of them need to be examined in some manner to determine if they should be continued, altered, or abandoned.

Foremost in the total process should be evaluating the plan itself—in this case, the tutoring program, the parenting classes, or the parent advisory committee. The evaluation should establish criteria to determine if the goal has been reached. For example, if 25% of the students with academic needs regularly attend tutoring and show improvement (determined by tests or teacher observation), the goal might be considered accomplished. If 75% of the council members regularly attend the meeting and 70% of those surveyed believe the council is of value, the goal of that plan might be deemed obtained. It's important to decide beforehand how to realistically judge how well a goal has been reached.

Two types of evaluation are commonly used in research. They are **formative evaluation** and **summative evaluation.** De Roache writes:

> *Formative evaluation refers to gathering and using information during the process of doing something. It is ongoing, requiring continual feedback for decision making and change along the way. . . . Summative evaluation refers to gathering and using information at the end of something.*[4]

Both types of evaluation are useful in the total evaluation process. Formative evaluation can be used on a daily, weekly, or monthly basis to measure progress. Summative evaluation also plays an important part. Pre- and post-testing of students, for example, can only be done in this manner. Information gathered over an extended period of time is valuable for the decisions that need to be made for the ensuing year. Such information is critical to evaluating the worth of an entire program. Limiting evaluation to the summative approach is gambling that the final results will show change or growth, though. This form of evaluation does not allow for changing direction or emphasis while the program or focus is underway. Neither approach guarantees success, but both are critical to the evaluation process.

Evaluation Methods

he methods used to evaluate programs for either formative or summative approaches can be either formal or informal. The danger in relying on informal methods is that they can be highly subjective. By contrast, formal methods tend to be more objective.

No one method or technique of evaluation will work all the time. The choice of method should depend on the objective to be measured. Evaluators should learn what techniques are available and how each one can be used appropriately. Each method has its strengths and weaknesses. Consider the following example. One middle school had a goal of increasing attendance at PTA meetings. Plans were made to inform parents about these meetings in a variety of new and innovative ways. The third meeting of the school year featured a nationally syndicated newspaper columnist as the speaker. Attendance at the meeting was standing room only. Everyone was jubilant about the increased attendance and the new notification system, until the following monthly meeting; that's when attendance returned to the normal low. It seemed that the speaker, not the new method of communication, was responsible for the increased turnout. Any method of evaluation—whether formal or informal—might have revealed the problems with the plans. The faculty needed to focus on measuring the objective of the plan itself—that is, the new system of notification—rather than the general goal of attendance.

INFORMAL METHODS

Observation is the most common informal method of evaluating. Careful planning, with distinct identified objectives, can make observations more accurate. Repeated observations of a given situation will give more reliable results, too. Observing is the only way to provide firsthand information about a program. It is also an economical way to evaluate programs.

There are some pitfalls with this method. First, it is not always easy to plan what to observe. For example, suppose someone wants to observe the relationship between the principal and the members of the parent advisory committee. The person might need to plan which values to observe, the times and situations in which the observations will be made, and so on, beforehand. Second, subjects often change their behavior—intentionally or unintentionally—because they are being observed. Third is the danger that the observer's own interests affect his or her observations. In spite of these pitfalls, observation can yield data that are useful in evaluating school–community programs.

Other informal methods, besides visual observation, include attention to:

1. Verbal comments made by teachers, parents, or students

2. Letters received by the school district from parents or other community members

3. Remarks made by laypeople at public meetings

4. Amount of space and the slant of news stories in the local media

5. Public support of school programs and other activities

6. Membership in the PTA or other school organizations

7. The number and type of complaints voiced by students, teachers, or parents

8. The kinds of issues brought forth at meetings of the advisory committee

In addition, brief questionnaires sent out to the public may be considered informal, because the respondents may not be representative of the total population.

FORMAL METHODS

Formal methods of evaluation generally are more scientific and systematic than informal methods. Some formal methods of gathering and analyzing data include questionnaires, opinion polls, rating scales, checklists, and focused interviews.

Nationally developed instruments for measuring student, parent, and community attitudes about schools are advantageous but costly. Unfortunately, they do not always center on the specific areas that need to be evaluated. Developing localized measuring instruments requires time. Sometimes previously developed instruments can be used. Generally, however, the principal and the evaluation committee develop their own documents to focus on particular aspects of their own program. All formal methods require extended time to prepare the instruments and procedures for obtaining the data and to display the results. Despite the time involved, these techniques can help obtain needed information for decision making by school personnel.

■ QUESTIONNAIRES

A questionnaire is a self-administered survey consisting of a series of questions. Respondents may give short answers (the free-response method) or choose from a list of multiple-choice answers (the forced-choice method). Questionnaires are frequently used to obtain participants' attitudes or opinions. A major weakness in this method of collecting information is that the evaluator cannot be sure that the respondents answer questions truthfully. (See page 302 for a sample questionnaire.)

A questionnaire should be carefully designed to cover a specific issue. It should be sent out to a carefully selected but stratified random sample of the total population. By distributing the instrument to a representative population of the total group, the results are assumed to be similar to that of the total population. The use of questionnaires is important in the evaluation of a program, and their development is a skill in itself. Here is a list of steps that are usually required:

1. Be sure the program objectives determine the information sought in the instrument. Other information may be of value, but the major objective is to measure how well the stated objectives have been obtained.

2. Write the questions in a format that can be read and scored easily. If a question can be interpreted differently, this will affect the results of the survey.

3. Limit the number of questions to be scored. Generally, people will not complete a questionnaire that exceeds a single page, although both sides can be used.

4. Include a scale with the questions, if appropriate. Most scales run from 1 to 3 or 1 to 5. Some researchers suggest a 1-to-4 scale because it forces respondents off the middle position.

5. Include instructions for completing the questionnaire. Directions should be clear and simple with a cover letter that explains the purpose of the questionnaire itself.

6. Try out the questionnaire on a similar group. Testing it allows you to make changes if the directions are not clear, if there are different interpretations of questions, or if other problems occur. Revise the questions if necessary. Feedback from the trial group will determine if any changes should be made.

7. Distribute the questionnaire and determine follow-up procedures to maximize the return. If the instrument is mailed to the respondent's

home, it should include a stamped, addressed reply envelope. Follow-up telephone calls will maximize the return.

8. Tally the returned questionnaires. If the questionnaire has been carefully devised, then the tallying should be simple.

Administrators should seek outside help if the development of such instruments is not one of their own strengths. Parents or others may have expertise in developing questionnaires and may be willing to help develop evaluation questionnaires. Another resource might be college professors or graduate students seeking research opportunities. They may donate their time and expertise in exchange for the use of the data as part of a larger study.

■ OPINION POLLS

Opinion polls are similar to questionnaires but usually are collected in person or by phone. One of the strengths of this method is that the respondents are able to make in-depth inquiries to clarify a question and may expand the answer beyond a scaled response. The main weakness of opinion polls is that people are often reluctant to share their feelings or give personal information to strangers, especially over the telephone. This type of polling also requires a great deal of time for the discussion that takes place between the caller and respondent. Callers should be trained so they can consistently handle respondents' questions or divergent answers. Here are a few general steps to follow when conducting an opinion poll:

1. Develop the questions to be asked. They will be similar to those of a questionnaire but must be phrased so they are easily heard; long, complicated questions often must be repeated or may be misunderstood.

2. Select a scale to use with the questions. The scale should be described verbally to the respondent at the beginning.

3. Select the interviewers. The people chosen can be members of the staff, volunteers, or paid callers; those selected should have a neutral, accepting attitude.

4. Train the interviewers. A practice session should cover making an introduction, describing the process briefly to the respondent, politely limiting long-winded answers, and clarifying misunderstandings.

5. Try out the interview on a group that is similar to the target group. This step is the same as in the questionnaire approach. It provides an opportunity to discuss unexpected reactions from those called, and it allows the researcher to reword questions as necessary.

6. Select a random sample for the group to be called. One commonly used method is an ordered selection (every fifth name, for example) on an alphabetical list of names.

7. Set the days and times for calling. Usually, the caller sends a letter to the prospective respondents indicating the days or evenings and times the calls will be made.

8. Collect the data from all callers, tabulate the data together, and summarize the results.

■ RATING SCALES

A rating scale is used to measure the direction and intensity of people's attitudes about a total program or one of its segments. (See the sample rating scale on page 301.) Two different kinds of scales may be used. These are the **ordered scale** and the **agreement scale.** Researchers Henderson, Morris, and Fritz-Gibbons define these scales as follows:

> The ordered scale consists of a collection of statements that express a range about an attitude object. . . . The agreement scale achieves a wide range of scores by having respondents report the intensity of an attitude.[5]

The advantage of rating scales is that they force the respondent to make a choice that produces a numerical score. As in the other types of instruments, there are some general steps to follow. The researcher should:

1. Develop a number of positive and negative comments about what is being evaluated. A balance of comments encourages the responder to think about each comment and not give the same answer for all items.

2. Develop a scale that can be used with both positive and negative statements. The scale should measure the intensity of a feeling—from highly favorable to highly unfavorable, usually on a five-point scale.

3. Try out the scale on a similar group to test the understanding of the comments and the purpose of the total instrument.

4. Construct the final rating scale. Comments should appear in random order.

5. Administer the scale. Use the same procedures as for questionnaires.

6. Tabulate the ratings. Results will be two sets of scores: the highly unfavorable and the highly favorable.

■ CHECKLISTS

This technique is generally used to measure the presence, absence, or frequency of behaviors as they occur. (See the sample checklist on page 300.) Only a few selected behaviors can be tracked at once, though. The strength of this kind of evaluation approach is that it focuses on single behaviors (listening, for example). It also enables immediate feed-back and analysis. The major weakness of checklists is that they require the observer to be in the vicinity of those being observed, which can influence behavior. Another weakness is that this method requires training for consistency, especially if there are multiple observers. Here are some general steps to follow when applying this technique:

1. Select the behaviors to observe. Those selected will be based on the goals of the program and generally will be limited.

2. Develop the checklist for recording the observed data. This can include a numerical scale of high incidence to low incidence or a written nar-rative that can be scored by the evaluator.

3. Select the observers.

4. Train the observers to use the checklist. The training may include two or more observers looking at a trial situation and comparing the obtained observations for reliability.

5. Set the times for the observations.

6. Collect the data from the observers. These data can be evaluated in different ways, depending on the original goal and the checklist.

■ FOCUSED INTERVIEWS

A focused interview is a technique whereby an interviewer talks with a respondent, probing for in-depth reactions to a program or whatever. This method often involves the use of outside consultants or persons who are not a part of the school organization. Focused interviews can be either unstructured, in which the conversation takes its own course, or structured, as if the interviewer and the respondent were completing a questionnaire together.

The advantages of this method of data collection are (1) it allows a respondent to discuss *why* he or she likes or dislikes a program or its component parts, rather than giving a single response on a continuum, and (2) it allows the interviewer to clarify the questions. Focused interviews also permit the interviewer to probe sensitive topics, attitudes, and values. Two disadvantages are: (1) data collection is time-consuming, and (2) respondents may be unduly influenced by the interviewer. In addition, with unstructured interviews the responses are open-ended and therefore difficult to summarize. Here is a list of steps to follow in conducting a focused interview:

1. Write a list of questions to ask. The style of the questions will depend on whether the interview is structured or unstructured. For example, an unstructured interview might have completely open-ended questions, such as, "How do you feel about this year's program?"

2. Select the individuals to be interviewed. This might mean interviewing everyone involved in a program (for example, all faculty members) or a random sample (for example, of students).

3. Select the interviewer(s) carefully so undue influence will not jeopardize the results. For example, the teacher of a particular class would not be a good choice if you were seeking information about how students liked that class.

4. Set the times for the interviews. These may be made during the day for students and teachers but may have to be scheduled in the evening for parents.

5. Collect the data from the interviewer. Summarize the results in a written report.

THE REPORTING OF DATA

A written report is the primary means of communicating research findings. The basic purpose of the report is to communicate factual information and interpretations of data to the recipients of the report. Sometimes reports are customized for different audiences. Parents, for example, might receive a report that highlights significant results in lay terms, whereas those with scientific knowledge might receive a report that contains more details about the statistical analysis of the data.

People who take part in evaluations by completing questionnaires or by granting interviews often want to see the results of the survey. A report that summarizes the data should be available to those who are interested. For example, if a monthly poll is taken in the school news-letter, the results might be included in the next issue of that publication. An annual report might include a summary of year-end questionnaires. Even if the results are somewhat negative, it's better to share these with the patrons of the school than to be accused of withholding information.

An annual report in any form is the official document of what went on during the school year. It should be truthful, believable, and easily understood. By contrast, technical reports to the board of education, for example, would contain greater detail than annual reports, which should give an overview of the evaluation just detailed enough to be usable. Annual reports are widely read and circulated, so they should be carefully prepared and edited before being released. Graphics can be included to present clear and meaningful ideas in a visual form. As Schmid and Schmid claim, "An effectively designed chart is tantamount to a visual statement, not infrequently equivalent to many paragraphs or even many pages of written words."[6]

If a questionnaire or poll taken annually is included in the report, a bar graph can be used to compare the results from one year to the next.

Attendance at school functions (such as PTA meetings), for example, might be presented on a line graph to show growth from month to month. A pie chart can be used to show the percentage of parent volunteers involved in each aspect of the school program.

Accuracy is important in annual reports. Sometimes people report information they believe to be factual, but that is not necessarily true. All claims should be verified as fact. Likewise, evaluators should be careful about making generalizations based on a limited research study or on limited data. If possible, computers should be used to figure statistical data to reduce mechanical errors. Even so, scores should be double-checked.

The evaluators—or at least the individuals drafting the data report, should have an understanding of statistics. The wrong statistical treatment may lead to invalid conclusions. The use of invalid assumptions, the use of group data to predict individual behavior, and the misuse of deduction are just a few of the errors that can be made in data reporting. Unless data are interpreted correctly and reasonably, researchers can enact the wrong decisions for the future.

Researchers need to be objective. This is difficult to achieve if the people are part of the school. In this case, they must be careful not to dismiss evidence that is contrary to the hypothesis or to overemphasize favorable data. A knowledge of research techniques helps evaluators see possible relationships so they can develop generalizations within the rules of sound research.

Reporting the evaluation results in some format brings even greater visibility to the school. The accomplishments that have been realized through an extensive school–community relations program gives additional feedback to the people who receive the annual report. Even if none of the efforts were as successful as desired, everyone will know that these efforts were made. This knowledge will foster a positive feeling about the schools.

A final report also signifies closure. To the administrative team, the faculty, the volunteers, the officers of the school support organizations, and to many others, the report signifies that their work resulted in change. A principal might send a copy of the report, along with a personally written note of thanks, to each of the key people who are part of the school–community relations program.

1. Self-evaluation is the most important method of improving school programs, but it should be done systematically and regularly. The results of an evaluation program can lead to improved policy decisions.

2. Some aspects of programs are easier to evaluate than others. Some require the tabulation and comparison of numbers, whereas others require careful observation by trained evaluators.

3. The faculty, as well as others, need to understand the importance of the evaluation processes. The leadership for the program must come from the school principal.

4. Evaluation can use both formative and summative approaches. The former allows for changes during the entire school year whereas the latter is used at the end of a school semester or year.

5. Both formal and informal methods of evaluation are appropriate and useful in evaluating a school–community program. Informal methods can be highly subjective if not properly planned, however.

6. A variety of instruments are available for formal methods of evaluation, including questionnaires, opinion polls, rating scales, checklists, and focused interviews. These can be purchased or developed by the school or district.

7. All instruments need to be carefully selected or developed, administered, and scored. Each type has a particular purpose based on the knowledge required to appropriately evaluate a goal or activity.

8. Developing evaluation tools can be expensive and time-consuming, especially for training observers or poll takers.

9. Reports to members of the district, the school board, or the public are part of the evaluation process. This type of reporting highlights accomplishments and brings visibility to the school.

10. Consideration should be given to the audience receiving the report. Those who are sophisticated in statistics might receive a different version than parents, for example. Both would communicate the same findings, however.

1. What parts of the school–community relations efforts at your school are regularly evaluated? Why do you think they are singled out?

2. What concerns do you think would be expressed by the other teachers at your school about program evaluation? Do they support the self-study concept? Why or why not?

3. What are the major practical reasons for selecting formative over summative evaluations?

4. Do you have a self-study committee at your school? If so, what tasks do they perform in the evaluation process?

5. How important do you think student, parent, and faculty opinions or attitudes are to the operation of your school? Defend your position.

ACTIVITIES

1. Talk with your principal to find out what aspect of your school's program needs to be evaluated by the faculty. Construct a short questionnaire, administer it at a faculty meeting, summarize the results, and discuss it with your principal and fellow students.

2. This chapter lists three sample plans with accompanying activities. Select one of the plans and choose an evaluation method (either formal or informal) that best matches each of the activities. Discuss your selections with your fellow students.

3. Ask your school-site administrator if data have ever been misinterpreted as a result of faulty evaluative techniques. Share the incident(s) with your fellow students.

4. In your class, brainstorm all of the informal methods you can think of that might help evaluate various school programs. Discuss the list.

5. Collect any parent, student, or faculty questionnaires that are used at your school or by your school district. Bring them to class, and, as a group, analyze the strengths and weaknesses of the questionnaires.

With the media as well as the state clamoring for higher academic results, several of the teachers at Elm School got together to devise a new approach for the teaching of reading and mathematics. They spent a good part of the previous school year developing, writing, and submitting a grant proposal to focus on these two academic skills. The proposal team included many of the school's teachers, representatives from the district office, and several residents who had been part of a district ad hoc group called the "Committee to Improve Basic Education." Last spring, Principal Bill Johnson was elated when the grant proposal was approved, and money was allotted for new textbooks, computer materials, and in-service training needed to begin the program in the fall.

The year started well, with an excellent series of in-service sessions conducted by Dr. Ruth Brookhart from the district staff, two professors from the local university, and a representative from the company that had developed some of the materials. Feedback from some of the teachers indicated that the sessions were well received. Many of the teachers were highly complimentary about Dr. Brookhart. Informal contacts with both students and parents were positive; the students generally liked the new texts and the supporting materials. The parents with whom Johnson came in contact echoed the same positive feelings.

One part of the proposal that had not been funded was the position of a part-time program director, which originally was requested. In part, that person was to have been the designated evaluator of the program. The grant document had included a section on evaluation, and the committee had indicated a sizable number of goals, objectives, and activities to be evaluated. Unfortunately, without a director, there was no one to plan or conduct the evaluation, because the teachers who initially created the proposal were in their own classrooms teaching.

Johnson was busy with routine administrative tasks when one March day he received two phone messages about the project. The first was from the state, which indicated that in two months' time a representative of the grants committee would come to visit and would appreciate having all evaluative documents set aside for review at that time. The second call was from Mrs. Richard Learner, chairperson of the Committee to Improve Basic Education, wanting to know if a representative from the principal's office could give a slide presentation at the June or July meeting about the results of the wonderful new project at Elm School.

Johnson got up from his desk and closed the door to his office. He needed time to think, because no evaluation of the program had been undertaken and he needed to return both of these calls as soon as possible.

DISCUSSION ISSUES

Past

1. What should have been Johnson's role when it was known that the project was only partially funded? What alternatives could have been taken to evaluate the program adequately?
2. What techniques of communication were overlooked between Johnson and the project committee after the project was funded?
3. Did the district office have a role in the project in addition to being a part of the in-service program? What was that role?
4. Do you think that things would have been different with regard to the evaluation if the informal feedback had been negative? Why?
5. If you had been a part of the committee that created the project, what kinds of evaluation techniques would you have included?

Present

1. What should Johnson do before he answers either of the two phone calls? Should he communicate with anyone first? If so, who?
2. What, if anything, can be done in the remaining two months of the school year to conduct a reasonable evaluation?
3. What should the visiting grants committee representative be told when he or she arrives?
4. What should the Committee to Improve Basic Education be told if Johnson decides to speak to the group?
5. Assuming the program is funded again, what kinds of plans need to be made for evaluation? Who should be involved in developing those plans?

CHECKLIST*

XYZ School District   **Problems Checklist for Faculty**

We need to assess <u>your</u> feelings about our existing school climate. Please complete this checklist and return it to _____ by 3:00 P.M. Friday. <u>Do not write your name on this page</u>. We are seeking your honest opinion on each item. We will discuss the results and make appropriate plans at our next faculty meeting.

	Extent of Problems		
Problems	**Extreme**	**Moderate**	**Almost Nil**
1. Tardies			
2. Truancy			
3. Absences			
4. Thefts			
5. Vandalism			
6. Student discipline			
7. Students' attitudes about school			
8. Students' attitudes toward teachers			
9. Crowded classrooms			
10. Total school spirit (student)			
11. Total school spirit (faculty)			
12. Student behavior at assemblies			
13. Student behavior at athletic events			
14. Parent apathy			
15. Community support			
16. Local newspaper coverage of school			
17. Parent complaints about the school			
18. Teacher/staff cliques			
19. Teacher/staff communication			
20. Teacher participation in extracurricular activities			

Additional comments _____

_____

_____

Permission is granted to reproduce this page for classroom use.

RATING SCALE*

XYZ School District   **Teaching Skills Workshop**

	(Low) 1	2	3	4	(High) 5
1. The objective of today's workshop was clear.					
2. The objective was accomplished.					
3. I can use or adapt what I learned in my own classroom.					
4. The presenters communicated the concepts and examples clearly.					
5. There was adequate individual and/or group participation in the workshop.					
6. Materials were made available.					
7. Overall appraisal of this presentation.					

Permission is granted to reproduce this page for classroom use.

QUESTIONNAIRE*

XYZ School District   Multicultural Pupil Survey

General Information to Students:
We are trying to find out what students think about a number of important topics. In order to do so, we need your help and would like you to complete these questions. There are no right answers. <u>The best answer is your personal opinion.</u> For each question, put a checkmark in the appropriate box at the right.

	Yes	No	Not Sure
1. Have you learned a lot about people who are different from you?			
2. Would you like to learn more about people who are different from you?			
3. Do you think that the color of a person's skin makes a lot of difference in whether he or she is a good person to know?			
4. Do you think most people are treated fairly in your school, no matter what is their skin color?			
5. Do you think people of other races have different values?			
6. Do you think all Americans should speak the same language?			
7. Do you have friends who speak a different language than your own?			
8. Would you like to be able to speak more than one language if you don't already?			
9. Do you think it's OK to celebrate holidays of other cultures?			
10. Do you think all Americans should have the same general way of life?			

Permission is granted to reproduce this page for classroom use.

REFERENCES

1. Nigel Norris, *Understanding Educational Evaluation* (New York: St. Martin's Press, 1990), p. 50.

2. Arlene Fink and Jacqueline Kosecoff, *An Evaluation Primer* (Beverly Hills, Calif.: Sage, 1978).

3. William D. Berry and Michael S. Lewis-Beck, *New Tools for Social Scientists* (Beverly Hills, Calif.: Sage, 1986).

4. Edward F. De Roache, *An Administrator's Guide for Evaluating Programs and Personnel* (Boston: Allyn and Bacon, 1981).

5. Marlene E. Henderson, Lynn Lyons Morris, and Carol Taylor Fritz-Gibbons, *How to Measure Attitudes* (Newbury Park, Calif.: Sage, 1987).

6. Calvin F. Schmid and Stanton E. Schmid, *Handbook of Graphic Presentations* (New York: John Wiley and Sons, 1979).

APPENDIX A:
SAMPLE WRITTEN
COMMUNICATIONS

he preferred form of communication is a one-on-one interchange of ideas and feelings. A listener can watch for reactions, including body language, and restate a position or clarify an idea instantly. This isn't possible with written communication, unless the recipient responds in some manner.

Written communications are necessary in any organization, though, and they serve a special purpose when addressing large groups of people. Putting words to paper automatically makes a message more formal and official. Although one cannot predict the effect of written communication on an individual or a group of people (such as teachers, parents, or students), the written word generally has a more lasting impact than oral statements, which often are soon forgotten or recalled differently.

Form letters are appropriate for many school purposes, including student tardiness, faculty reminders, and parent conferences. But personalized letters generally create a stronger impression on the receiver. Obviously, they take additional time to compose, but the positive reactions far outweigh the time required.

This appendix contains sample letters for seventeen different situations. An introductory paragraph explains the main purpose of the letter and suggests items that should be included as part of the message.

This letter gives the principal an opportunity to establish a positive working relationship with a member of the community. Use the letter to comment on what the person has contributed in the past. Be specific. The letter may also point out organizational plans for the future and may set a time for working together.

Phyllis Brown
111 First St.
Anytown, State 00001

Dear Ms. Brown:

Congratulations on your recent election as chairperson of the Elm School PTA. The years you have devoted to the organization in the past and the leadership you displayed last year as vice-president make you an ideal person to head this important group. I was particularly impressed with all of the ideas you contributed to the brainstorming session held last spring when we were attempting to develop goals for Elm. Although we were not able to get all of them under way this past year, perhaps additional ones can be initiated under your guidance.

As you know, we still have two projects that were not completed last year—the fundraising for the new choral robes and the scholarship program for our graduating students. We should include these among the goals we set for this year.

Our first board meeting is scheduled for the first Monday of October. If you would like to get together with me prior to that time to discuss agenda items, please give me a call at school. My secretary, Irma Collins, knows my schedule and will be pleased to make an appointment convenient to both of us.

Again, congratulations on your recent accomplishment and best wishes for another successful year.

Sincerely yours,

This is one of the first opportunities for the principal to establish rapport with a new teacher. The letter may offer services to the teacher as well as highlight the strengths of the school. Referring to something mentioned in the interview (if the principal was a part of that process) can make the letter much more personal. New teachers are particularly interested in their teaching assignments, so they should be mentioned; however, it is best to refer to any plans as tentative.

Joanne Quackenbush
777 S. Walnut
Anytown, State 00001

Dear Ms. Quackenbush:

Congratulations on your recent appointment to Anytown School District. All of us at Elm School are anticipating your joining our staff. We believe that your strong background in music and your expressed interest in helping sponsor a choral group will add immeasurably to our school program.

As we indicated during your interview, Elm is a relatively new school, having opened just three years ago. The teaching staff is a balanced group that includes several veteran teachers, a few teachers who began their careers when Elm first opened, and three new faces, including yours, who will join us in the fall.

Tentatively, you are scheduled for a fourth-grade class with an enrollment of thirty-two. Darlene Jones, another of our fourth-grade teachers , has volunteered to be your "buddy" and has suggested that I give you her home phone number, in case you arrive in town before orientation. It is (222) 555-2222.

School begins on September 10. We will meet at 9:00 A.M. in the high school auditorium for the start of our three-day orientation. Later, more details (and a map) will be sent to you by the district. I will be on duty from 9:30 to 4:30 each day after August 25. Feel free to drop in to obtain your room keys, textbooks, and curriculum guides during those times.

We hope this finds you enjoying the remainder of the summer. We are looking forward to working with you this school year.

Sincerely yours,

Some principals write a letter to each member of the faculty at the end of the school year rather than on birthdays. The key is not to miss anyone, even if a birthday falls during the traditional summer vacation. The tone should be positive and should be specific about praiseworthy items; standard phrases carry little meaning and may not be worth the effort.

Dear John,

Congratulations and best wishes on another milestone in your life. It doesn't seem like another year has slipped by since I was last able to wish you the very best on "your day."

It goes without saying that as the principal of the school I appreciate the professionalism you continue to give to your work. Your relationship to the students, parents, and fellow teachers does much to make Elm School a positive place to work.

It's also the little things that you are willing to volunteer for that also add immeasurably to the team concept that everyone mentions when discussing our school. Your volunteering to replace Darlene Jones as faculty coordinator when she became ill was most appreciated by the entire staff, and your waiting an extra hour for Mr. and Mrs. Doug Green's parent conference when their car broke down was also appreciated by them.

We've been working together now for ten years, and I hope that it will become ten more! Again, best wishes for your birthday and thanks for all you contribute to Elm School.

Sincerely yours,

Most parents are apprehensive about moving into a new area, particularly about the schools their children will attend. A positive communication from the school principal may help alleviate these concerns. The letter might suggest an informal meeting. Although most parents will not take up the offer, some will. The important thing is the effort shown by contacting the parents and offering to listen to their concerns.

Mr. and Mrs. Charles Smith
333 W. 3rd St.
Anytown, State 00001

Dear Mr. and Mrs. Smith:

Welcome to our community. Your son Jeff and daughter Mary have been attending Elm School for the past three weeks, but we have not yet had an opportunity to chat with you.

You may already have received the list of our scheduled parent events for the school year. The faculty and I would like to have a chance to discuss the school and our programs with new parents before the first activity in October.

We have set up a series of times for informal get-togethers—some in the early morning, some late afternoon, and others in the evening—to meet with you to discuss how your children are adjusting to their new school. At these meetings we will be able to answer questions about our academic program, our homework policies, the after-school recreational events, as well as others. These meetings will last approximately one hour.

Enclosed is a listing of the available times. We would appreciate your calling the school and indicating the best time for your family. We are limiting each parent group to twelve, so the sooner you respond the more likely you will obtain your first choice of meeting time.

We hope your entire family is becoming better acquainted with our city and that your children are enjoying the new school year. We believe that Elm School is doing an excellent job and are glad your children are part of our school family.

Sincerely yours,

A letter of this type should emphasize the wrongdoing (in this case, frequent absences) but also indicate the possibility of working together to improve the situation. It's best not to accuse the youngster of truancy or lying to the parents, because these two factors may not be known for sure.

Mr. and Mrs. Charles Smith
333 W. 3rd St.
Anytown, State 00001

Dear Mr. and Mrs. Smith:

Although attendance alone does not always measure how well a student is doing at school, frequent absences can seriously impede the progress of any student. This seems to be the case with your son Jeff. Although only three months of the school year have passed, he has already missed twenty days of school, which represents about a third of the time.

Some may well have been excused absences, but others have not been so noted. Perhaps you were unaware of the number of days Jeff has missed this year or of the effect it is having on his grades. Although Jeff had not achieved exceptionally high grades, he had been maintaining slightly better than a "B" average (3.14) until this semester. According to his current teachers, Jeff is failing three classes and is barely passing in the other three.

It is important that school staff and parents work together in the education process. One of the ways you can help your son is to make sure that he attends school on a regular basis.

After you have talked with Jeff, please feel free to contact us. A member of the school staff may be of assistance. We appreciate your working together with us to solve this problem.

Sincerely yours,

Sometimes schools use form letters to thank businesses for contributions. Letters are more effective when they specify how the contribution helped the school. It's usually a good idea to include a statement about the future. This recognizes the organization's long-term commitment.

Mr. Charles Smith, President
AJAX Manufacturing Co.
Anytown, State 00001

Dear Mr. Smith:

Another school year is about to end, and we at Elm School want to thank you for the continued support your organization has given the students and the school programs. Without your efforts a number of our activities would not be as successful as they have been.

Specifically, the monies your employees donated to our renewed scholarship program, the prizes you donated for the school dance, and the contributions to our new choral uniform drive were appreciated by all of the students and faculty involved in those activities.

Perhaps your greatest contribution to life at Elm School has been the human resources you have provided us. The employees from your company who have come to speak to our consumer classes, donated time in their area of expertise, or assisted with our new computer lab have greatly enriched the academic programs at Elm.

It goes without saying that the community support you have given us adds to the lives of our students. We hope we can count on your continued efforts next year and for many years to come.

Sincerely yours,

Personalized invitations often attract more people to an event than the notice that goes to all parents. Emphasizing the importance of the event also reminds parents that this is the last opportunity of the year. Include the date and time of the event, even if it has been sent in an earlier form invitation.

Mr. and Mrs. Dudley Blake
444 S. Maple St.
Anytown, State 00001

Dear Mr. and Mrs. Blake:

Our students have been working for the past several months on a number of new songs for the annual Spring Choral Concert. The opportunity for the students to present the songs is just two weeks away, and we are hoping that you will be able to attend the production.

Students elect to take choral music because they have talent in the field and a desire to perform. We believe that the spring concert is the culminating event for all of our young singers.

To gain the most from the opportunities, our students need an audience. And no group could be better than their own parents! If your schedule permits, the students and those of us at the school would be most appreciative if you could attend the event.

Remember the date: Tuesday, April 10, at 7:00 P.M. We hope to see you there.

Sincerely yours,

This kind of letter is rarely sent but will be well received by both the parents and the student at any level. Too often, parental support is taken for granted; parents like to be told they have contributed to their child's efforts in learning.

Mr. and Mrs. Richard Learner
222 N. Rosewood St.
Anytown, State 00001

Dear Mr. and Mrs. Learner:

Last February you came to school for a conference about your son Daniel's behavior. At that meeting, we mutually agreed on a plan to help Daniel improve his classroom actions.

It is now June and we wanted to report that the plan worked! During the intervening months, Daniel was sent to the office only twice, and both of those instances (for tardiness and for an argument with another student) had nothing to do with the previous concerns expressed by his teachers.

We want to thank you for the help you gave us in February and for the support you're continuing to give. We need the full cooperation of our students' parents as you have so willingly given us.

The future looks good for Daniel. Not only has his classroom behavior improved, but his grades also have improved. We are proud of the effort he has made and hope this will continue during the remaining two years he will be attending Elm School.

Sincerely yours,

This kind of letter to parents should be specific about the student's behavior. It should also remind parents about what action has been taken, how many conferences have taken place, and how many weekly reports have been sent. When it is necessary to point out parent failings, it is best to do so without labeling that failure. Leaving the door open for future cooperation and further discussion keeps the letter positive.

Mr. and Mrs. Charles Smith
333 W. 3rd St.
Anytown, State 00001

Dear Mr. and Mrs. Smith:

As you are aware we have been dealing with a series of instances in which your son Jeff has been unwilling to remain in his seat during class sessions. We have held three parent conferences, which you attended. You agreed to support our efforts by withholding some privileges at home if this same behavior continued.

Since the last conference, we have sent home three weekly reports. None of these has been signed and returned as agreed. When we talked on the telephone, you indicated that you have not withheld any privileges.

Obviously, both you and the school want Jeff to improve his classroom behavior, which interferes with his academic work. As we discussed, frequent referrals to the office by his classroom teachers cause him to miss valuable classroom time.

It was our understanding during the last conference that we would both work cooperatively to modify Jeff's outbursts. We believe that we have followed through with the counseling program and the weekly reports. May we count on you to do what you had indicated you would do? As we are all aware, your son is the one who will gain from all of our efforts.

If you would like to discuss the situation with us again, please feel free to contact us for another appointment. Otherwise, we will expect to receive a signed copy of the last weekly report and subsequent ones, which will continue to be sent home.

Sincerely yours,

This kind of letter to a student recognizes a specific contribution that he or she has made to the school. The same kind of letter could be used for any achievement—athletics, music, academics, or working in the office. In most cases, it should be specific in nature.

Carole Smith
333 W. 3rd St.
Anytown, State 00001

Dear Ms. Smith:

During my ten years as principal at Elm School, I have seen many excellent students graduate from our school and go on to fine universities. With the academic record you have established at Elm, you have consistently shown yourself to be among that select group of graduates.

But this letter is not intended to summarize your school accomplishments. Rather, its purpose is to compliment you on the way you handled the senior graduation practice session when it got out of hand yesterday. Your awareness of the situation and the calm way in which you quelled the outbreak was admirable. Few faculty members could have obtained such immediate attention, and I believe the spontaneous standing ovation the students extended you shows their appreciation for your efforts.

You have accomplished many things while you have been a student here, Carole, and you will undoubtedly continue that tradition as you further your education. However, I believe yesterday can be considered one of your finest hours. We all thank you for your leadership.

Sincerely yours,

cc: parents of Carole Smith
board of education

In this kind of letter sent to parents, it's important to be specific in terms of the number of tardies. Point out the disruptions that occur when students arrive late. Indicate the next step in the process—a parent conference.

Mr. and Mrs. Charles Smith
333 W. 3rd St.
Anytown, State 00001

Dear Mr. and Mrs. Smith:

During the past few months you have received two other communications regarding your son Jeff's continued tardiness to school. Despite our combined efforts, this still remains a problem.

Since the beginning of the school year, Jeff has been tardy to school 36 times; this represents over 30% of the school year. Although we understand that extenuating circumstances cause unavoidable tardiness on occasion, there is no justification for frequent tardiness.

We are not concerned about this problem simply because of our school policy but because of what it does to Jeff and his classroom. When students arrive late to school, their entrance disrupts the class. Of even greater importance, tardiness causes Jeff to miss important instruction and announcements given at the beginning of class.

Because this is the third reminder about Jeff's tardiness, we are asking that you call the school for an appointment for a conference. We need to make his schooling as profitable as possible, which means having him here for the entire day. We will be looking forward to meeting with you.

Sincerely yours,

This letter, sent on behalf of a teacher, should be specific about the grade levels and the number of years taught, as well as other contributions the teacher has made to the school. The letter should mention areas of particular strengths and may mention observed weaknesses and attempts by the teacher to remediate these weaknesses. The letter also may mention the new position sought, along with the overall evaluation of the teacher's background.

To Whom It May Concern:

Joanne Quackenbush taught fourth and fifth grades at Elm School for six years while I was the principal there (from 1986 to 1992). In addition, she aided several of the other teachers with the music program and sponsored an after-school choral group all six years.

In the classroom, Ms. Quackenbush was strongest in mathematics, reading, art, and music. She developed a variety of stimulating approaches in each of these areas, which involved the use of manipulatives in math and group work in both reading and art. Her unique approach in art earned her a citation of merit by the County Art Institute on three different occasions.

Her major weakness was in the area of discipline. Because of her group approach to learning, there were times when some of the students were not on task and the room atmosphere was noisy. To her credit, however, Ms. Quackenbush continued to improve by taking classes in behavior modification, classroom control, and cooperative learning and was a much stronger disciplinarian her last two years.

She tells me that she is a candidate for the position of school-site coordinator of special programs and I believe that she is qualified for such a position. She works well with other people (as was evident by her leadership in our music program), has at her disposal a variety of teaching methods, and is always enthusiastic about education. I highly recommend her for this position without reservation.

Sincerely yours,

Most administrators neglect to send this kind of message as often as they might. A letter of appreciation can be sent to individuals who often go unrecognized for what they do on a routine basis. The letter should focus on a specific deed the person did.

Ms. Barbara Brown, Secretary
Director of Transportation
Anytown, State 00001

Dear Barbara:

For the past four years that I have been principal at Elm School, we have sent special field trip requests from our teachers to your office and, despite the fact that some of them were sent past the required one-week-in-advance deadline and two were submitted on the wrong form, all have been handled accurately and sympathetically.

Obviously, this kind of service is an extension of the person responsible for handling the requests. My staff and I want to thank you for your consistent efforts to help us run a good school. Often, people like yourself do not realize how important the handling of routine requests is to an organization. We at Elm School know and appreciate the service you give us.

In addition, I want to make a personal comment about your unwavering ability to be pleasant and positive under what must be, at times, trying circumstances. The smile in your voice does much to lift the spirits of all of us.

Thanks again from the entire staff of Elm School!

Sincerely yours,

cc: Assistant Superintendent of Business
    personnel file

This type of written communication has numerous purposes. It serves to explain new programs to parents whose children may be affected, and it solicits parents' input. If controversy surrounds the program, the letter may provide a buffer. The responses that follow may even warn the administrators not to proceed further.

Mr. and Mrs. Charles Smith
333 W. 3rd St.
Anytown, State 00001

Dear Mr. and Mrs. Smith:

We are currently considering a special summer school session for students who have displayed exceptional academic abilities or talents. Although our school and district staffs have some exciting and creative ideas for this session, nothing has yet been finalized.

We believe that your son Jeff and daughter Mary would both be eligible for this program, if it is adopted—Jeff, because of his strong interest in piano, and Mary, for her academic grade average. Before we go any further with this proposal, we would like to discuss the merits of the idea with you and the parents of other students who would be eligible. We believe that you, as parents, could augment the ideas of our professional staff and could comment on what should be included and perhaps what should be avoided in such a venture.

Therefore, we would like to hold our first parent meeting on April 2 at 7:30 P.M. in the school library to discuss the proposed program. We have invited approximately 50 families and hope you will be among those who will be able to attend.

Sincerely yours,

A letter of this kind needs to be as positive as possible. The principal should resist the temptation to react in the same manner as the parent. It's important to provide a thorough, detailed account of the problem, with an appropriate summary for the parent. An ongoing negative feeling on the parents' part may be reversed by such a letter.

Mr. and Mrs. Charles Smith
333 W. 3rd St.
Anytown, State 00001

Dear Mr. and Mrs. Smith:

Thank you for your recent letter expressing your concern about the school situation involving your son Jeff and the reaction of our physical education teacher. I've delayed sending an immediate reply so I could thoroughly investigate the matter.

If the situation had occurred as you were told, I, too, would have been enraged. However, that was not the case. I believe that Jeff presented his own involvement in a much better light.

After interviewing Janet Williams, the physical education teacher in question, two other teachers, and four students who were in the vicinity that day, I was able to obtain a version of the events that everyone agreed to.

Two students dared your son to enter the girl's shower facilities, which he then did. He was not "asked" by the teachers, as you had been told. Ms. Williams did grab him by the shoulder to hasten his departure. She did not push him with a baseball bat, as you were told.

Under the circumstances, I believe the teacher used unusual restraint. As for Jeff, I don't believe he meant any harm but was wrong to take the dare, which undoubtedly embarrassed several girls. I've talked with Jeff and he now admits that this version is true.

I'm sorry you were upset about the situation, but I can assure you the school does try to handle problems in a professional and logical manner. Let us hear from you if there are any other questions about this matter.

Sincerely yours,

These letters are always difficult to write but are important. A principal should send condolences to parents whose children die, even if the student has already graduated from the school, or to families of faculty or staff who die. Citing some aspect of the person's work or contributions makes the letter more personal.

Mr. and Mrs. John Douglas
444 E. 4th St.
Anytown, State 00001

Dear Mr. and Mrs. Douglas:

All of us at Elm School were deeply saddened to read about the death of your son, Jason, in the tragic automobile accident last week. As you are aware, Jason was highly thought of by our teaching staff and still has many friends here at school.

We share your loss of this truly outstanding young man. His scholastic record and dedication to athletics and music made a lasting contribution to our school as well as bringing honors to himself and his family.

Although nothing we can possibly say can lessen the deep sorrow you are experiencing, we know you must be proud of what he accomplished in his all-too-short life. The student council and faculty have contributed to a memorial scholarship fund in his name. We believe this is something Jason would have wanted.

Again, I extend our sympathies in your loss. Our thoughts and prayers are with you in this time of sorrow.

Sincerely yours,

Although dinners and banquets honor teachers who retire, a letter from the principal can mean a lot to the person who is leaving. If the teacher has proved to be outstanding, there will be many things to say about the person's contributions. Even an average teacher, though, contributes a great deal to a school and its students.

Dear Bill:

I was both delighted and saddened when you told me yesterday that you were going to retire at the end of the school year. I was delighted because it will now give you the opportunity to carry out the plans you have for your retirement years. And of course I was saddened to think that Elm School will no longer be enriched by your teaching and your commitment to students.

When I first came to Elm, some of the administrators here (including the former principal) told me which teachers they believed to be the strongest. Your name was on everyone's list! The intervening years have proved their accolades to be an understatement, as you have proved time and time again that you are one of the finest teachers in the entire district.

All of us—teachers, parents, and students—will miss you next fall when the school year begins. However, you have left a tradition that will remain at Elm for many years to come.

We all wish the very best for you and your wife in your retirement. It goes without saying that anytime you are in the area we hope you will drop in to see your many friends here.

Sincerely yours,

APPENDIX B: HANDBOOK TOPICS

his appendix provides lists of topics that might be covered in separate handbooks for teachers, parents, and students. These handbooks are often used for teacher orientations, PTA meetings, and student orientations.

Because this textbook will be used by both potential elementary and secondary principals, the listings cover both levels. Not all items are appropriate for both levels.

Consider the following topics to include in a handbook for students:

- Assemblies
- Attendance requirements and procedures
- Awards/special recognition
- Bicycle facilities
- Calendar for the school year
- Course offerings
- Counseling services
- Daily time schedules
- Discipline policies
- Dress code
- Eligibility requirements (high school)
- Extracurricular activities
- Grade reports
- Graduation requirements (high school)

- Homework
- Honor societies
- Immunization requirements
- Independent study (grades 7–12)
- Late buses
- Lost and found
- Parking (high school)
- Proficiency tests
- Scholarships (high school)
- Student government
- Student organizations
- Tardiness policies
- Transportation
- Work permits (high school)

Consider the following topics to include in a handbook for parents:

- Absences
- Alternative schools
- Attendance boundaries
- Bus transportation
- Child abuse reporting
- Discipline policies
- District programs (ROP, magnet schools, pregnant minors, and so on)
- Drug use
- Eligibility requirements
- Family life, sex education
- Gifted programs
- Grading procedures
- Graduation requirements
- Guidance services
- Home teachers
- Homework policies
- Immunization requirements
- Intradistrict transfers
- Newsletters
- Parent complaint procedures
- Parent organizations (PTA, booster club, and so on)
- Parent volunteers
- Parent classes
- Parking
- Proficiency tests
- Special education programs
- Student records
- Tardiness
- Truancy
- Use of school facilities

Consider the following topics to include in a handbook for teachers:

- Absences (reporting procedures)
- Assemblies
- Audiovisual equipment (types of, procedures for use)
- Bulletins
- Calendar
- Child abuse reporting
- Classroom aides
- Clubs (sponsorship possibilities)
- Counseling referrals
- Curriculum
- Discipline referrals
- Duty schedule
- Facilities, use of
- Faculty meetings
- Faculty parking
- Faculty teaching assignments
- Fire drills
- Grading policies
- Graduation
- Homerooms
- Homework policies
- Keys
- Library use
- Map of school
- Office machines, use of
- Opening/closing procedures
- Parent conferences
- Parent volunteers
- Recognition programs
- Report cards
- Room environment
- Schedule, yearly
- Special schedules (rainy day, assembly, parent conferences, and so on)
- Student attendance procedures
- Student tardiness regulations
- Substitutes
- Supplementary program schedules (art, music, and so on)
- Supplies
- Support groups (PTA, booster club, and so on)
- Telephone use
- Textbooks, availability and procedures for ordering

Index